The Frugal

BOOKS BY ROBERT ACKART

The Frugal Fish

A Celebration of Soups

Soufflés, Mousses, Jellies, and Creams

The Cheese Cookbook

A Celebration of Vegetables

The One-Dish Cookbook

Fruits in Cooking

Cooking in a Casserole

The Hundred Menu Chicken Cookbook

The Frugal Fish

COOKBOOK

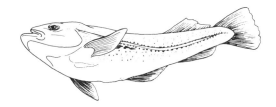

BY

ROBERT ACKART

LITTLE, BROWN AND COMPANY   BOSTON-TORONTO

A

LIBRARY OF CONGRESS CATALOGING IN PUBLICATION DATA

Ackart, Robert C.
The Frugal fish.

Includes index.
1. Cookery (Fish)   I. Title.
TX747.A27   1982   641.6'92   82-13985
ISBN 0-316-00645-9 (pbk.)

Designed by Janis Capone

*Published simultaneously in Canada
by Little, Brown & Company (Canada) Limited*

PRINTED IN THE UNITED STATES OF AMERICA

To the memory of my mother

Contents

Introduction

I remember, when I was a child, Mother's overturning onto the floor of the screened porch a pail of some two dozen angry blue crabs which I had caught in the river; any crab that did not at once scamper off sideways was considered insufficiently fresh to steam. Fortunately, there were no losers — if that is the proper word — and that evening for supper we had crab salad, filled out, I admit, with rather a lot of chopped celery. I also recall Mother's near-horrified shock when Father once brought home a *boned* shad, given him by the manager of the local hotel — such extravagance! We often had shad, but always with the bones *in,* which I hated.

We ate fish frequently because, as Mother knew, it was nourishing and inexpensive, and therefore a help to her in keeping to a rigorously planned food budget. (For the same reason, we also ate a good deal of calf's liver and sweetbread!) Well, times have changed. Fish and seafood have become nearly unaffordable luxuries on the dining table of greater America. Nearly, but not entirely.

That fact is one reason for the existence of this book. Less expensive fish are still on the market. I will not say "cheap" fish — nothing, it seems, is cheap anymore — but comparatively inexpensive fish do exist and are capable of producing dishes at once nourishing and delectable and, not infrequently, elegant. The second reason for my writing the book comes from a desire to share with you the pleasure and ease of preparing and the delights of eating fish, one of our most nutritive and least fattening foods.

Fish, indeed, scores high as health-giving nourishment. As a source of protein, it is without rival; the six-ounce serving of fresh fish per person suggested in the recipes yields well over fifty percent of our daily requirement. Even the much-touted beefsteak runs second to fish in this consideration, but well *ahead* of its finny competitor in calorie count. Moreover, there is usually much less waste with fish than with red meats or poultry, and no waste at all if you prepare filleted fish, fresh or frozen.

Fish is rich in minerals and vitamins. Both salt- and freshwater fish contain phosphorus, iron, and potassium; in addition, saltwater fish offers iodine, helpful in prevention of glandular disorders. Both lean- and fat-fleshed fish contain the B vitamins; fat-fleshed fish supply vitamin D, while fish-liver oils have the fat-soluble vitamins A *and* D. (Fat-fleshed fish, by the way, are those with five percent fat per weight unit — which is *not* very fatty.) Sodium is not found in appreciable quantity in any fish, a boon to people on low-sodium diets. Because fish has little connective tissue, it is welcome on low-bulk diets. Fish supplies polyunsaturated fatty acids which contribute to the reduction of blood cholesterol. Fish, it seems, is food for everybody — for the growing youngster, the active adult, the senior citizen, and for the recuperating — for it is very easily digested.

While I am always glad to know that what I eat is good for me, such a checklist of nutritional virtues does not necessarily endear the food in question. Let us leave dietetics, therefore, and turn to the pleasures that cooking, serving, and eating reasonably priced fish will afford you, your family, and friends, for such is the purpose of the book.

Although there are well over two hundred and forty species of edible fish swimming about over the globe, we are not concerned with those that will require you, in order to pay for them, to go hungry for a week or to attempt to rob the local bank. Hence, we regretfully but firmly say farewell to shellfish — crab, lobster, scallops, shrimp, and their cousins — with the exception of clams and mussels, still affordable, to which a section of the book is assigned. We also bid adieu to shad, sole, swordfish, tuna, and other piscatorial aristocrats.

We admittedly concentrate on lean-fleshed fish available in the United States and Canada — cod, flounder, haddock, hake, halibut, scrod — for they are to be had at your fishmonger's virtually year-round. Fat-fleshed fish are not spurned, but the fact is that there are simply fewer of them than of lean-fleshed fish. As a general rule, lean- and fat-fleshed fish are interchangeable in the recipes, although I allow myself the privilege of pointing out in specific sections of the book where one or the other might be somewhat more successfully prepared. Reasonably priced freshwater fish are included so that people living away from a ready supply of East Coast and West Coast saltwater fish may also enjoy preparing and eating fish dishes.

The book is written for the urban cook who procures prepared fish from either fishmonger or supermarket. For this reason, a few notes, but no lengthy disquisitions, are given on the buying and storing of fish; directions for scaling and dressing them are omitted. What is emphasized, in addition to specific recipes, are the basic techniques of fish cookery: baking, barbecuing, broiling, deep frying, poaching, sautéing, and steaming.

These methods are made applicable to all fish in the Lexicon of fish, chapter one, so that, if you multiply the number of fish (about 40) by the number of cooking methods (7) by the varieties of sauce with which you may dress them (about 30), you will find that you can eat fish for something over twenty years without repeating yourself. Add to this nonsensical calculation the particular recipes for hors d'oeuvre and first courses, soups and stews, main dishes, and salads and chilled dishes for fresh and frozen fish, canned fish, clams and mussels, and salt and smoked fish and — well, what have you? You have what in my native Delaware was called "a mess of fish"!

Not that this is "the complete book of less-expensive fish cookery." There is no complete cookbook on any subject — which is as it should be: the innovation of the cook, *your* creativity in using this or any cookbook, will at once increase its scope and value. To this end, I urge you to experiment with these recipes. If you care to use them as guidelines, fine — but be creative on your own, too. Cooking fish is easy, it can be inventive, and it is fun. For your greater pleasure in using the book, allow it to be all three.

The book deals with fresh and frozen fish (used for the most part as fillets and steaks prepared by the fishmonger), with canned fish, with smoked and salt fish, and finally with clams and mussels (both fresh and canned). If this organization is somewhat arbitrary, it does allow inclusion of less expensive fish and shellfish in a reasonably logical order, making easy your selection of the kind of fish you want to prepare and, second, of the possible part that the fish, once cooked, will play in your menu: as hors d'oeuvre or first course, as the main dish of the meal, or as a salad or chilled dish. I had in mind two purposes with this organization: an easy workability of the book and an immediate clarity for the convenience of the cook.

If a recipe has a particularly national flavor, I identify its country of origin. Occasionally, an anecdote about a given recipe is given. For the convenience of the cook, the yield of the recipe is indicated, as are the times required to prepare and cook it. Oven readings, when used, are stated at the outset of the recipe. Ingredients are listed in order of their use, and for cooks who (like me) store their herbs and spices from A to Z, seasonings — save sugar, salt, and pepper — are called for in alphabetical order. Last, when it is feasible to prepare part of a recipe in order to return to it sometime later, directions to this effect are given. (Please read the section "How to Cook Fish: Useful Terms," page 16; doing so will increase your pleasure and ease in using the book.) The book concludes with a few selected recipes for foods that are complementary accompaniments to fish.

I have had special enjoyment in creating from less expensive fish these dishes which, I believe, are appealing to the eye and pleasing to the taste. For you, I hope the book will lead to many satisfying, readily affordable meals based upon the frugal fish.

ROBERT ACKART

Katonah, New York

The Frugal Fish

ONE

What Fish to Buy: A Lexicon of Frugal Fish

The fish described in this abbreviated lexicon are purposely restricted to those applicable to the purposes of this book — less expensive fish readily available fresh, frozen, or canned, which you will find easy to work with in the preparation of these recipes and which will be tasty and satisfying at table. I make no pretense at being scientific — an ichthyologist I am not — but rather give a few facts about each variety that may interest you. Whether the fish in question is lean- or fat-fleshed is stated at the outset because this fact may have a bearing on how you wish to cook it.

Blowfish (*lean-fleshed*): so called because of its habit of inflating itself to twice its size as a threat to enemies, the sea squab — euphemistic handle — is ugly to look at and rather spiny. Sometimes known as puffer, rabbitfish, or swellfish, its sole edible portion is the tail, which I think tastes like frog's legs. The internal organs can be toxic; for this reason, you should carefully rinse and dry the tail, which resembles the third joint of a chicken wing. An inhabitant of the Atlantic Ocean, blowfish is often marketed as "chicken of the sea," and is delicious sautéed or broiled. You should allow at least six tails per serving, for there are only a few bites per tail.

Bluefish (*fat-fleshed*): blue above and silvery below, the bluefish is an important food fish plentiful along the Atlantic and Gulf coasts. While it may attain ten pounds, it is generally marketed at between three and six pounds. Its delicate flavor is enhanced by baking, broiling, or sautéing.

Bluegill (*lean-fleshed*). See *Sunfish*.

Butterfish (*fat-fleshed*): sometimes called dollarfish, this flat-bodied, silver-blue fish is available from Cape Cod to Brazil; a related species is found on the Pacific Coast from British Columbia to Mexico. Varying in weight from one-half to one pound, butterfish has a fine texture and delicate flavor.

Calamari (*lean-fleshed*). See *Squid.*

Catfish (*fat-fleshed*): this freshwater denizen derives its name from the barbels or feelers at the sides of its mouth which resemble a cat's whiskers. Catfish live in streams, and are especially plentiful in the Mississippi Valley. The so-called channel catfish is considered the best flavored; the mature specimen ranges from five to ten pounds. The smaller bullhead catfish, weighing about one pound, is more common. Usually marketed whole or sometimes filleted, catfish is traditionally deep- or pan-fried, but its nutty full flavor is also enhanced by baking or broiling.

Chub (*fat-fleshed*). See *Whitefish.*

Clam (*lean-fleshed shellfish*): rich in protein and minerals and low in calories (about one calorie per average-sized clam), this bivalve mollusk comes clothed in either a hard or a soft shell. Clams are found along both the Atlantic and Pacific coasts in a number of varieties, each with its own flavor. Used for food and the shells for wampum by the American Indians, who called them *quahogs,* clams were important to the colonists; in 1616, Captain John Smith wrote, "You shall scarce find any bay or cove of sand where you may not take any clampes . . . at your pleasure." Undisciplined harvesting diminished their supply, especially with the invention in the 1950's of the hydraulic dredge, which enabled a vast and indiscriminate taking of them; with recent legislation, their supply is once again increasing.

Cod (*lean-fleshed*): a white-fleshed fish of the North Atlantic with relatives in the North Pacific and colder regions of the Southern Hemisphere (neither of the latter being of commerical value), cod is said to have been discovered by Basque fishermen seeking whale along the Grand Banks of Newfoundland. It has been and is of great economic importance to New England (a codfish was on the seal of colonial Massachusetts Bay Colony), Iceland, Newfoundland, and Norway. Averaging ten pounds in weight and three feet in length, it may attain one hundred pounds and five feet. It is usually olive-green on top with dark spots and white on the underside. Its natural lair is near the ocean bottom, where it preys on virtually every fish except the shark. Much cod is split and dried or salted on the vessel catching it. In the market, it is available flaked, pickled, smoked, and salted; fresh when near the source of its supply; and frozen, nearly everywhere. Unusually accommodating, cod may be used in virtually every recipe calling for lean fish.

Crappie (*lean-fleshed*): small members of the group of freshwater sunfish, crappies are usually about one foot long and weigh one pound. For the most part found in the Great Lakes and Mississippi regions, they are a sporting fish, protected by the states in which they thrive. They are excellent sautéed.

Croaker (*lean-fleshed*): the name is generic for a number of different fish — the Atlantic croaker, the freshwater drum, the queenfish and the white sea bass, to name but four — which produce grunting noises by releasing air from a kind of bladder. Croakers are found on both Atlantic and Pacific coasts, and their taste is mild and sweet flavored.

Cusk (*lean-fleshed*): a large saltwater fish with a continuous dorsal fin from the back of its head to the base of the tail, the cusk is related to the cod. Fished in the North Atlantic for its firm white meat, cusk may be prepared in any manner suitable for cod.

Eel (*fat-fleshed*): not a very attractive fellow, being rather snakelike and without scales, but with an exceedingly slimy skin. There are several varieties, all of which spawn at sea but migrate to live in fresh water. If the eel is innocent of great personal charm, his flesh is entirely praiseworthy, being tender, delicate, and rich. Fresh eel is especially available in the fall of the year; smoked eel and canned eel — found in gourmet shops — are also procurable. Bake, broil, fry, or poach it.

Finnan Haddie (*lean-fleshed*): finnan haddie is, of course, haddock, but it has such a definite personality of its own that it deserves a separate entry here. Its name derives from the village of Finden in Aberdeen, Scotland, famed for its curing of haddock. The fish is split open, the spine is partially removed, and the head cut off; then it is lightly salted and smoked, originally over peat fires. Once imported to this country, finnan haddie is now a New England product.

Flounder (*lean-fleshed*): "flounder" is the name of a group of saltwater flatfish found in American waters from New England to the southern tip of Florida and off the Gulf Coast; a few varieties are found off the Pacific

Coast. The most common members of the family are dab, fluke, plaice, gray and lemon sole (which are not sole at all), and, from the English Channel, true sole (but still a member of the flounder family).

The flounder lies and swims on its side, although it swims upright when hatched. When the fish is between five and seven weeks old, one eye moves across the forehead so that both eyes are on the topside of the head. The mature fish grows dark on top as a camouflage to the ocean floor, where it lives, eating smaller fish, shrimp, and baby crab.

An excellent source of protein, a serving of plain baked flounder, unsauced, equals 200 calories. Sold whole or filleted, fresh or frozen, this lean, white-fleshed fish is one of the most useful to budget-minded cooks.

Grayling (*fat-fleshed*): sometimes called lake trout, the grayling is found in clear streams and lakes of the upper Missouri River basin. The one- to two-pound fish is, indeed, closely related to the trout and, like its cousin, may be cooked by any of the techniques described.

Grouper (*fat-fleshed*): living on or near the bottom in warm seawater, where it preys among the rocks, the grouper resembles the sea bass in taste. Its range is wide, from Virginia to Brazil, and it is an important food fish in Florida, the Gulf states, and the West Indies. (Some California rockfish are also called groupers.) To confuse its natural enemies, it takes on the coloring of its surroundings, like a chameleon. Grouper, marketed whole and as fillets and steaks, may be baked, broiled or sautéed.

Haddock (*lean-fleshed*): A relative of the cod (so many fish seem to be!), haddock boasts a very white, firm meat that may be prepared in countless ways. It lives in the deep waters of the Northeast Atlantic from Nova Scotia to Cape Hatteras. One of our most important food fishes, it averages about three and a half pounds in market, where it is available whole, filleted, fresh, and frozen. You may also purchase it flaked in cans, salted, and smoked (see *Finnan Haddie*).

Hake (*lean-fleshed*): a cousin of — that's right — the cod *and* haddock, hake is found in both the North Atlantic and Pacific oceans. The flesh of this one- to four-pound fish is soft and delicate, and is interchangeable in recipes calling for cod or haddock. Hake is marketed whole, filleted, fresh, and frozen; it is also available salted and smoked.

Halibut (*lean-fleshed*): this very important saltwater food fish with white, firm meat is the largest of the group known as flatfish; halibut looks like a gigantic flounder. Found in the cold waters of both the North Atlantic and

Pacific oceans, it varies in weight from five to one hundred pounds; the so-called chicken halibut, however, weighing about ten pounds, is considered best for cooking. Available year-round, it is especially good on the East Coast from March through September; on the West Coast, its prime season is the spring months. Halibut is suitable for any cooking method you wish to use.

Herring (*fat-fleshed*): a small saltwater fish related to the shad and sardine, the herring is an important source of food for human beings — and for other fish! The herring is rather chicly streamlined and has small iridescent scales. The mature fish, averaging ten inches in length, is migratory, living for the most part in deep offshore waters, but coming to beach areas to spawn. The enterprising female will lay between ten thousand and sixty thousand eggs at a spawning. Herring has always been fished commercially; Holland's great foreign trade during the fifteenth and sixteenth centuries was largely founded on herring fisheries. In Europe, fresh herring is enjoyed at table; preserved in various ways, it is also a food staple of the Netherlands and Scandinavia. In this country it is more generally available pickled, salted, smoked, or bottled with various sauces.

Kingfish (*fat-fleshed*): kingfish is the name applied to a number of saltwater food fish found along the Atlantic and Pacific coasts. Related to the Spanish mackerel, it may weigh as much as seventy-five pounds. The Florida kingfish is a notable game fish. Kingfish has a distinctive flavor — very good — and few bones; it may be prepared by all methods.

Lingcod (*lean-fleshed*): also ling cod, is a Pacific Coast fish, rather green with brown spots. It is *not* related to the cod, indeed does not even resemble it, but is cousin to the greenling. Its long, slender body has flesh with a greenish cast, which might be off-putting but should not be — it is an excellent eating fish. Averaging four to twelve pounds, it may attain forty pounds; these larger fish are available filleted and as steaks. Lingcod is popular in West Coast fish markets.

Mackerel (*fat-fleshed*): this long, slender saltwater fish inhabits the Atlantic Ocean from Labrador to North Carolina, from Norway to Spain. Running in schools, mackerel is caught in nets. Averaging one foot in length and one to two pounds in weight, mackerel has firm meat with a savory flavor. At one time, mackerel was chiefly available salted; today it is in the market nearly year-round.

Mako (*fat-fleshed*). See *Shark*.

Mullet (*lean-fleshed*): found in both fresh and salt water, mullet is one of the few vegetarian fish; it even has a gizzard. Although there are over one hundred species of mullet, the most plentiful is the striped or jumping mullet, averaging one and a half feet in length and found in Southern Atlantic and Pacific waters. The red mullet, another species, is a pond fish and, historically, was important in the cooking of ancient Rome. The tender yet firm flesh of mullet makes it suitable for cooking in any manner you prefer.

Muskie (Musky, Muskellunge) (*lean-fleshed*): a close relative of the pike, this North American freshwater game fish is known today by the name the Indians gave it. One of the largest of lake and river fish, it may weigh as much as seven pounds. The Great Lakes are the principal source for muskie, which, although not often marketed, has a very delicate flavor.

Mussel (*lean-fleshed shellfish*): a bluish-black hinge-shelled mollusk, the oblong mussel, two to four inches in length, offers yellow to reddish meat, firm in texture and of unusual sweetness. There are fresh- and saltwater mussels, but only the briny denizens are used for food. Marketed live, canned, or frozen, mussels bought fresh should be tightly closed (any that are not should be discarded); they should be refrigerated and used within two days of purchase. See page 232 for directions on preparation.

Ocean Perch (*fat-fleshed*): not so much a fish as a name that appears on various packages of frozen fish — rosefish, redfish, red perch, sea perch — "ocean perch" accounts for a goodly portion of the fish eaten in this country. The firm, coarse-grained flesh is delicate, excellent for soup-making, and adaptable to all varieties of cookery.

Perch (*fat-fleshed*): a carnivorous and voracious fish found in both fresh and salt waters. Freshwater varieties embrace some one hundred species, the most common of which is the yellow perch. Found in the quiet waters of the eastern United States, the Great Lakes area, and the waters of the upper Mississippi valley, the yellow perch has an olive-green back lightening to yellow on the sides, which are marked by dark vertical bands; the fins are orange and red. This colorful cousin of the pike yields firm, white, rather coarse-grained flesh of delicate flavor. The saltwater perch — the Atlantic and Pacific sea perch — lives in cold waters and varies its coloring from orange to bright red, or sometimes from gray to red-brown. Saltwater perch is often called ocean perch, above.

Pike (*lean-fleshed*): a family of voracious freshwater fish with long bodies, flattened backs, and small scales, the pike has a large mouth, many very sharp teeth, and a protruding lower jaw. This Hapsburg of the fish family is not an attractive fellow, especially when one remembers that he can grow to be four feet long. The species includes the common pike, muskellunge, and pickerel; they are found, preying with lightning speed on any poor fish who chances to get too close, in the lakes and rivers of North America and Europe. At the fishmonger's the pike is less fearsome, being sold whole at from three to four pounds or as fillets. His firm, white, flaky flesh is sweet flavored. I am all in favor of pike in the kitchen, where it responds handsomely to poaching and steaming.

Pollack (*lean-fleshed*): also pollock, Boston bluefish (although it bears no relation to bluefish), or coalfish. It is found in the North Atlantic from Norway to the Mediterranean; a cousin, the Alaska pollock, is plentiful in the Bering Sea and North Pacific waters. Weighing from three to fourteen pounds, the pollack is of greenish color, blending to yellowish or gray; its underside is silver-gray and a light lateral line runs along its body. Available year-round, and often used in place of haddock, pollack yields a firm, white, delicately flavored flesh.

Porgy (*lean-fleshed*): also called scup, the name applies to various food and game fish found along the Atlantic Coast from Cape Cod to South Carolina. Averaging twelve inches long and one and a half pounds, porgy is usually served whole. It is rarely marketed filleted, nor is it shipped inland. Cousins of the porgy are found in warm coastal waters throughout the world.

Salmon (*fat-fleshed*): native to both the Atlantic and Pacific oceans and to some freshwater lakes, the salmon was an important food to American Indians, especially those of the Pacific Northwest. On the opposite side of the continent, where it was eaten both fresh and smoked by Indian and colonist, the abundance of salmon was one reason for the early settlement of New England. The name derives from the Latin word for "leap," which is exactly what salmon do to go upstream to spawn in native waters. Present-day pollution on the East Coast has made scarcer the supply of salmon; the greater part come from Washington, Oregon, and Alaska. There are five major types of salmon: chinook, coho, sockeye, pink, and chum. Chinook bears an Indian name meaning "spring"; it is one of the largest, averaging over twenty pounds; its flesh is red and firm. Coho or silver salmon averages nine pounds. Sockeye, also called blueback or red salmon, varies between three and five pounds and is familiar to homemakers using canned salmon, for sockeye is one of the main sources of this commodity. Pink and chum salmon are also used for canning. Fresh salmon, of course, is available whole, or more frequently as steaks. It is very expensive, however.

Sardine (*fat-fleshed*): this saltwater, weak-boned food fish — a group including the pilchard, alewife, herring, and sprat — is named for the island of Sardinia, around which the fish run in large schools. Because of the size of their family, sardines in one guise or another are found off the coast of Maine, along the Pacific Coast, throughout the United Kingdom, in Scandinavian waters, near Portugal and Spain, and from South Africa to Iceland. Many sardines rise to the water's surface at night to feed, stirring up organisms that give an iridescent glow to the sea and so alerting the fishermen to bring their nets. The scales are removed as the fish are pumped aboard the fishing boats; salting takes place at once. At the fishery, they are washed and precooked, and their heads and tails are removed. They are then packed in cans, sauced or set down in oil, the cans are sealed, and the cooking is completed. Some sardines are sold fresh or salted or preserved in brine. The fresh are available especially in April and May and are cooked like any fat-fleshed fish.

Scrod (*lean-fleshed*): a term describing not a species but the market size of young cod or haddock. The tender, white, flaky meat is delicate; I find it one of the most useful of all fish for these recipes. Particularly popular on the East Coast of the United States (and in Europe), it is marketed year-round whole, filleted, and cut in steaks, fresh and frozen.

Scup (*lean-fleshed*). See *Porgy*.

Sea Bass (*lean-fleshed*): sometimes called rockfish or blackfish, this saltwater fish inhabits both East and West Coast waters. Averaging about two pounds, it is a popular game fish that is also caught commercially and sold whole, filleted, or cut in steaks. It may be cooked in any of the suggested ways.

Sea Squab (*lean-fleshed*). See *Blowfish*.

Sea Trout (*lean-fleshed*). See *Weakfish*.

Shark (*fat-fleshed*): the idea of eating shark was not very appetizing until I tried mako shark, often available in eastern fish markets. The fact that shark is a popular food fish in China perhaps spurred my daring. Mako, fished off Long Island, is somewhat similar in taste to swordfish, but considerably more moist; it is also boneless and cheaper. Sold as steaks, mako is admirable baked or broiled. It does not keep well and should be used within twenty-four hours of purchase.

Smelt (*fat-fleshed*): these slender, silvery, olive-green fish grow to about seven inches long and weigh about two ounces. Rich flavored, they are both salt- and freshwater fish, some few varieties of which are lean fleshed. The saltwater species are abundant along the Atlantic and Pacific coasts, and in times past were used by the Indians for food and trading. The Pacific Coast Indians dried a particularly oily type of smelt and burned it for light. In 1906, smelts were introduced to the Great Lakes as food for the salmon there: the salmon did not survive; the smelts did. Curiously, the smelt is related to the salmon, and like its cousin travels up rivers and streams to spawn. Easily netted, it is available fresh — dressed and whole — frozen, and canned.

Squid (*lean-fleshed shell-fish*): not a fish at all, but a mollusk, the most highly developed of that breed because of its having a central nervous system, and called a cephalopod because its feet grow out of its head (*kephale,* Greek for "head"). Once considered poor man's fare, squid and calamary (or *calamari,* the Italian spelling), now gaining popularity, are found on the menus of prestigious restaurants. Taken from the Atlantic Ocean from mid-summer until fall and from the Pacific year round, squid is sold live and frozen; occasionally canned squid or calamari appears in the supermarket. Frozen squid is already cleaned, save for removing the cuttlebone, which is sometimes left in. Ask your fishmonger to prepare the squid for you or, if you wish to do so yourself, lay it out flat and cut off the tentacles just below the eyes and reserve them to cook with the body; cut down the center of the body, pull out and discard the bone and attached viscera and the ink sac; rinse the squid well.

Sunfish (*lean-fleshed*): among the most abundant freshwater fish in North America, the sunfish belongs to a spiny-finned family that includes the bluegill, crappie, and rock bass, to name but three. Sometimes sunfish is called bream or brim because of its resemblance to the European bream — to which it bears no relation whatsoever. Marketed whole, sunfish is mild flavored and is particularly tasty sautéed.

Tuna (*fat-fleshed*): this saltwater game fish of the mackerel family is found in nearly all temperate and warm waters of Asia, Africa, and

America. It can grow to be enormous — as heavy as fifteen hundred pounds — although the tuna we meet in the market is in all probability very much smaller, averaging ten to fifteen pounds, and available to the cook whole or as fillets or steaks. The flavor of all tuna is robust, but that of albacore is the most delicate and white; the others — bonito, bluefin, and yellowfin — are not white but vary from an amberlike to reddish hue. For the purposes of this book, canned tuna is available packed in water (which I prefer for the most part) or oil, chunk-style, flaked, or solid pack.

Weakfish (*lean-fleshed*): inhabiting the Atlantic and Gulf coastal waters, the spotted weakfish is perhaps the most prevalent of the group of fish known commonly as sea trout. The California corbina is a Pacific Coast cousin. The flesh is very tender, hence the name weakfish. Because they tend to be small they are most often sold whole, although fillets are sometimes available.

Whitebait (*fat-fleshed*): this small saltwater fish is the fry of the common herring or sprat, prevalent in the Thames estuary and along the coast of the North Sea. Several other fish resembling whitebait, such as the smelts found along the California coast, various silversides, and some anchovies, are also called whitebait. Generally fried in deep fat, sautéed, or broiled, these little fish — rarely more than four inches long — are sold in eastern markets during the winter months. Because they do not keep well, they should be used as soon as possible after buying.

Whitefish (*fat-fleshed*): available year-round from the Great Lakes, other North American lakes and streams, and from Alaska, whitefish is one of the most important of our freshwater food fishes. Sold whole or filleted, ranging from two to six pounds, it is sometimes smoked and lends itself to any cooking method you prefer.

Whiting (*fat-fleshed*): a small, gray, saltwater fish that is sometimes called kingfish or silver hake, the whiting is found along the middle Atlantic Coast. Especially plentiful in spring and fall, the whiting yields a white, delicate-tasting flesh that may be prepared in any of the ways suggested.

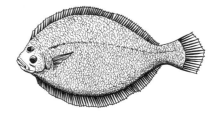

TWO

How to Buy and Store Fish

Fresh and frozen fish are available in various forms at your fishmonger's or supermarket: *whole or round* — that is, as the fish was caught, unscaled, undrawn, with head, tail, and fins intact; *drawn,* whole but eviscerated; *dressed or pan-ready,* scaled, eviscerated, and usually with head, tail, and fins removed (the term *pan-ready* generally applies to smaller fish, as larger ones are most frequently portioned into cuts). The cuts of larger fish are *steaks,* cross-sectional slices from dressed fish; *fillets,* nearly bone-free pieces cut lengthwise from the sides of the fish away from the backbone; and *chunks,* cross-sectional pieces considerably thicker than steak slices, which are usually cut to yield a single serving (the chunk cut is excellent for soups and stews, if you prefer it to the fillets suggested in the recipes).

Fish is also available *canned* in increasing variety, easily stored and ready to use; and *cured* — dried, salted, or smoked — which requires soaking the fish in several changes of fresh water before it can be cooked.

When *buying fresh whole or dressed fish,* ascertain that the eyes are bright and bulging (when stale they sink into the head and cloud); the scales should be shiny; the flesh should be elastic but firm.

When *buying fresh steaks, fillets, or chunks,* select fresh, firm-looking pieces; there should be no dried-out appearance at the edges; if the fish is prewrapped in the supermarket, it should be packaged in moistureproof and vaporproof material.

When *buying frozen fish,* make sure that the package is solidly frozen and that there is no indication of freezer burn or discoloration; there should be no odor and the package should be wrapped in moistureproof and vaporproof material.

When *storing fresh fish,* wash it under cold water, dry it with absorbent

13

paper, wrap it in moistureproof material or put it in an airtight container, and place it in the refrigerator for no longer than two days.

When *freezing fresh fish,* dip the dressed, rinsed fish in salted water, wrap, seal, and freeze it. Lean fish may be kept safely for six months, fat fish for three. Thaw the fish only when ready to use it.

When *storing fresh cooked fish,* wrap it in moistureproof material or put it in an airtight container and refrigerate it for only three or four days, or freeze it for up to three months. Refrigerating cooked fish does not enhance its texture or flavor (see page 16).

When *thawing frozen fish* (uncooked), transfer the wrapped package (usually one pound) from the freezer to the refrigerator for twenty-four hours; *or* remove the fish from the package and place it, sealed in a plastic bag, in cold water for one to two hours; *or* remove the fish from the package, arrange it in a flat pan or large bowl, and allow it to thaw at room temperature (this latter method is the one I use; when the fish is thoroughly thawed, I dry it with absorbent paper before proceeding with the recipe at hand). In each case, use the fish as soon as possible after thawing it. Frozen fish may be cooked unthawed. Merely double the cooking time, as suggested by the Canadian Cooking Theory on page 15.

Canned fish — anchovies, cod, haddock, herring, mackerel, sardines, and other fish, as well as salmon and tuna — may be safely stored for one year in a cool, dry place. The can sizes required are indicated in individual recipes. Salmon comes in several varieties: the darker the color, the higher the oil content — and the price; sockeye salmon is highest in oil. The pink, leaner kinds are suggested for these recipes. Tuna is available in vegetable oil or waterpack; most of these recipes call for waterpack tuna, but when oilpack is asked for it is because the oil is an ingredient of the recipe. There is also dietetic canned tuna, packed in distilled water without added salt. Canned tuna comes in solid pack, chunk-style, grated, and flaked; I recommend solid pack, which can be broken into chunks or flaked as the recipe directs and as you want the chunk size or the flaked texture.

How much fish to use? The following amounts are suggested for an average main-dish portion (this material is repeated for your convenience in the section "How to Cook Fish," page 16):

	WEIGHT OF INDIVIDUAL SERVING
Whole fish (undressed)	12 ounces
Whole fish (dressed)	8 ounces
Fillets, steaks, and chunks	6 ounces
Canned fish	3 ounces

THREE

How to Cook Fish: The Basic Techniques

Fish is tender before it is cooked; the purpose in cooking it, therefore, is to bring out its flavor and to coagulate its protein (as we do when we cook egg white). The cooking method used often depends upon whether the fish is lean or fat. I admit a prejudice for lean, white-fleshed fish, not only for its low calorie count, but also for its delicacy of flavor. Lean, white-fleshed fish may be cooked by any of the methods indicated here; fat-fleshed fish are especially suited to baking, broiling, grilling, and sautéing, for the fat content prevents the fish from drying out.

CANADIAN COOKING THEORY

The Canadian Department of Fisheries has made an important discovery about fish cookery — lean- or fat-fleshed, salt- or freshwater — that eliminates all guesswork from a process that, generally speaking, should be done as quickly as possible over high heat in order to preserve the full flavor and texture of the fish.

Briefly stated, the Canadian Cooking Theory directs that the fish be laid on a flat surface and then measured at its deepest point. For each inch of depth, allow 10 minutes of cooking. The method applies to whole fish, steaks, fillets; to baking, broiling, deep frying, poaching, sautéing, and steaming. It does *not* apply to fish cooked in soups and stews; 8 to 10 minutes is usually sufficient time to cook fish cut in bite-size pieces. Measure the depth of rolled fillets *after* you have rolled them.

The method also works for frozen fish direct from the freezer, although I prefer to thaw frozen fish and to dry it well with absorbent paper (frozen fish seems to acquire a great deal of water in the thawing). When cooking still-frozen fish, merely double the cooking time indicated by the depth of

15

the fish: if, for example, the depth is 1½ inches, the cooking time will be 30 minutes, as against the 15 minutes required for fresh fish of equal depth.

Any fish mentioned in this book (indeed, any fish I know of) may be cooked by the Canadian Cooking Theory. For your convenience, the method as it pertains to individual cooking techniques is described later on in this chapter, at the beginning of the sections on baking, broiling, deep frying, grilling (barbecuing), poaching, sautéing, and steaming.

For the convenience of the cook, a list of suggested serving portions:

	WEIGHT OF INDIVIDUAL SERVING
Whole fish (undressed)	12 ounces
Whole fish (dressed)	8 ounces
Fillets, steaks, and chunks	6 ounces
Canned fish	3 ounces

One final suggestion: cooked fish refrigerates safely but not very esthetically; it tends to break apart and lose its identity in a sauce, for example. Refrigerate these recipes only for re-serving in the privacy of family. Cooked fish does not freeze well under any circumstance; allow me to discourage you from trying it. The recipes for composed dishes may be doubled, if you desire; personally, however, I feel that they are never as satisfactory multiplied as they are when offered in the number of servings for which they were originally designed.

Useful Terms

In addition to the cooking techniques listed above and described later in this chapter, there are a few terms that recur throughout the book with which I feel the reader would be happier to have some acquaintance. Quite probably you know all or many of them already, but I feel you will enjoy using the book more and will find the preparation of these recipes easier for having read through these terms, arranged for your convenience in alphabetical order.

"At this point you may stop and continue later": a direction designed for the convenience and comfort of the cook. Once the recipe is *prepared*, it is often possible — not always, but frequently — for the cook to do something else before returning for the final cooking of the dish. If you do stop *in medias res,* cover the prepared ingredients — and the fish, if you

have been working with it — with plastic wrap in order to prevent sauces from skinning over, to preserve the moistness of the fish, and so forth. If you stop for longer than two hours, refrigerate the fish. Whenever possible, I suggest that you "stop and continue later" because, as we have seen at the beginning of this section, fish is at its best cooked quickly and served at once.

Béchamel (the basis of all white sauces): equal amounts of butter and flour cooked together for a few minutes, to which onion or some other simple ingredient may be added, and increased by the addition of milk, the mixture stirred constantly over medium heat until it is thickened and smooth. It is sometimes simpler to refer to "the *béchamel*" than to talk of "the flour mixture," and hence I take the liberty of using the French term. This sauce is named, incidentally, for its creator, Louis de Béchamel, a steward to Louis XIV — although the Greeks, who had a colony where present-day Marseilles stands, sometimes claim that they brought the sauce to France.

Beurre Manié (a thickening agent for sauces and soups): in a small mixing bowl combine equal amounts of soft butter and flour; using a fork, blend the mixture until it is smooth. Generally speaking, 1½ to 2 tablespoons each of butter and flour will thicken 1 cup of liquid. Add the *beurre manié* to the simmering liquid as directed and stir constantly until the whole is thickened and smooth.

Bouquet Garni: a selection of herbs and spices used to season soups and sauces; it is discarded upon completion of the cooking. To facilitate removal of a *bouquet garni,* tie fresh herbs together with string; dried herbs and whole spices such as cloves or peppercorns are easily discarded if tied in cheesecloth or put in a metal tea ball with screw-on top. I suggest three *bouquets garnis* useful in fish cookery (to flavor 8 cupfuls of liquid). One: 2 bay leaves, 2 whole cloves, 1 clove garlic (peeled and split), 8 sprigs parsley, 6 peppercorns, ½ teaspoon dried thyme. Two: 3 bay leaves, 4 celery leaves, 3 whole cloves, ½ teaspoon dried marjoram, 6 sprigs parsley, 8 peppercorns, ½ teaspoon summer savory, ½ teaspoon dried thyme. Three: 2 bay leaves, 3 celery leaves, ½ teaspoon dried marjoram, 4 sprigs parsley, 1 teaspoon rubbed sage, 1 teaspoon summer savory. To all of these may be added, if desired, a 4- or 5-inch piece of orange zest.

Cheese: several of the composed dishes in the book call for grated cheese. I urge you to grate a fresh cheese yourself; there is no comparison in the taste between the cheese you prepare and the product taken from a bottle or carton. Cheese may be grated in the containers of most blenders and all food processors (use the steel knife); the result is well worth the little extra trouble.

Cooking Time: as we have seen, the cooking time of most fish dishes is short. I often separate it from the preparation time of the recipe so that you may ready the ingredients, take leave of the kitchen for a while, if you desire, and return to complete the recipe so that it comes fresh to table.

Court Bouillon: a savory liquid prepared with wine or vinegar and seasonings and used for the poaching of fish and for the making of sauces. See page 90 and following for specific ways in which to make court bouillon.

Deglazing: to heat stock and/or wine, bringing it to the boil over high heat in a casserole or frying pan, so that the sediment in the utensil is released and becomes part of the liquid which, in turn, is used as an ingredient of a sauce or is poured over the cooked fish.

Preparation Time: The time suggested at the beginning of each recipe is only approximate, depending upon the expertise of the cook. The preparation covers the time you will be busy in the kitchen, cutting, peeling, assembling, precooking, and so forth, preparatory — usually — to adding the fish to the readied ingredients. The preparation time does not include preparing sauces or such accompaniments as Mixed Vegetable Salad. See *Cooking Time,* above.

Processors (and Blenders): we are pampered in today's kitchen, where we are able to achieve in virtually no time a smooth soup, sauce, or purée. I have two rules for the use of processors and blenders: 1) I never put more than 2 cups of a mixture into the container because the appliance operates more effectively on a smaller amount and because, in the case of blenders, there is less chance that the mixture will be thrown at the ceiling; 2) I do not use the processor or blender on ingredients taken directly from the stove. Allow the ingredients or the mixture in question to cool somewhat; to disregard this warning is to court the possibility of a small-size Mount St. Helens in your kitchen — which may indeed be very dangerous. When puréeing with a processor and when making such sauces as require cutting the ingredients as they are being mixed, use the steel knife.

Render: to cook bacon, salt pork, or other fatty meat until it is crisp and browned.

Roux: a term that, like *béchamel* and *beurre manié,* derives from French culinary practice, a *roux* is a combination of equal amounts of melted butter or other fat and flour cooked together over gentle heat for a few minutes to rid the flour of its pasty taste and texture. To the *roux* are then added seasonings and a liquid (milk, cream, *court bouillon*), and the mixture is then cooked over medium heat with constant stirring until it is thickened and smooth for use in the preparation of a soup or sauce. Incidentally, once the liquid has been added to the *roux* and the mixture cooked until thickened, it is called a *béchamel* (see above).

Scalding (milk and cream): I was once told — I think by my grandmother — that scalding milk and cream tends to prevent their curdling. Reason enough for doing so, as I sometimes suggest. Scalding requires that you heat the liquid only to the boiling point, not above it. When a film shimmers on the surface, the milk or cream has been sufficiently heated to deter its souring.

Seasoned Flour: flour to which has been added salt, pepper, and perhaps paprika or other spice, and in which pieces of fish are shaken before being baked, broiled, or fried. To ⅔ cup flour, add 1½ teaspoons salt and ½ teaspoon pepper; shake the mixture in a paper bag to blend it; add the fish a few pieces at a time, shaking the bag with each addition. It is important to flour fish only just before it is to be cooked, to prevent the coating from going doughy; in this regard, it is also advisable that you shake any excess flour from the prepared fish.

Shimmer: the bare movement, accompanied by small bubbles, of a cooking liquid heated to about 190° F.

Simmer: the slow cooking of fish in a stock or liquid of your choice. The water should be at about 197° F. and should barely move in a mildly agitated way (see "Shimmer," above). If you use a lid when simmering, make sure that it is a loose-fitting one, to prevent the fish from going soft. When poaching fish, use no lid.

Weights of Canned Goods: the weight of such canned foods as tomatoes is fairly well set: 8, 16, 28 ounces, for example. Sometimes canned goods come in 15-ounce sizes, but the difference between a 15- and 16-ounce can is negligible. For canned salmon and tuna, however, the problem is not so simple; on supermarket shelves I have found salmon and tuna in 6¾- and 7-ounce cans, in 13½- and 15-ounce cans, as well as in 16- ounce cans. Once again, the difference in content between a 6¾- and a 7-ounce can is negligible; to avoid confusion, therefore, recipes for salmon and tuna read "1 (about 7-ounce) can salmon . . ." If a recipe calls for a 16-ounce can and you cannot find it, use two 7-ounce cans; the recipe will taste just as good. Sometimes, too, sardines come in 4-ounce cans instead of the more common 3¾-ounce containers. In the case of all canned fish and canned clams, a near approximation of the suggested weight will work in the individual recipe.

Zest: the oily outer layer of lemon or orange rind, cut from the fruit with a fine vegetable peeler.

Baked Fish

Most recipes for baked fish are based on the Canadian Cooking Theory, page 15. Although I prefer to bake fish unsauced and then add sauce at the time of serving, if you wish the fish may be sauced before baking, add five minutes to the cooking time, as the sauce — particularly if it is thick — will insulate the fish against the oven heat. When you bake fish fillets or steaks with stuffing, spread the stuffing over the fish and measure the total depth, fish plus stuffing, to establish the cooking time; thin fillets such as flounder may be rolled around stuffing and arranged seam side down in the buttered baking dish, an attractive way to serve them.

Baking is a fine way to prepare whole fish. Ask your fishmonger to dress the fish, but to leave on the head and tail. The fish may be stuffed and the cavity skewered closed for cooking; or you may bake the fish unadorned. In either case, the cooking time will equal 10 minutes per inch of depth measured at the deepest point of the fish as it lies readied in the buttered baking pan. When baking whole lean-fleshed fish, cut three or four gashes on each side and insert a thin strip of bacon, a pleasant flavor accent and an assurance against drying — though with the Canadian Cooking Theory the fish simply has not time to dry.

Fat-fleshed fish take to the oven as they would, under other circumstances, to water. Baking releases some of the fat and the fish comes from the oven succulent and altogether delicious. For example, I cannot recommend too highly bluefish, whole or filleted, spread with Anchovy Butter, page 276, and baked; a sprinkling of chopped parsley and the addition of lemon wedges complete this simple but admirable dish.

To Bake: Preheat the oven to 450°. Cook the fish on the top shelf of the oven, allowing 10 minutes of cooking time per inch of depth for fresh fish; frozen fish will require twice the time. Measure stuffed fish at its deepest point. Fresh fish baked in foil should be allowed an extra 5 minutes; frozen fish baked in foil, an extra 10 minutes. Add 5 minutes to the cooking time if the fish is baked in sauce. If a recipe calls for flouring a fish, do so only at the last minute so that the moisture of the fish does not make the flour soggy.

Various sauces will be found in chapter eight. A selection of stuffings appears at the end of this section on baking.

Several examples of baked fish follow.

FISH BAKED IN A COVERED DISH

4 servings
PREPARATION: about 10 minutes
COOKING: 20 to 25 minutes in a 350° oven

1½ pounds fish in one thick piece
3 tablespoons soft butter
3 tablespoons dry white wine
Grating of nutmeg
Sprinkling of paprika
Fine-chopped parsley
Lemon slices

In a lightly buttered baking dish with cover, arrange the fish and spread it with the butter. Add the wine, nutmeg, and paprika. Bake the fish at 350° for 20 to 25 minutes, or until it flakes easily. Garnish with a sprinkling of parsley and lemon slices.

Aluminum foil may be substituted for a baking-dish cover.

Serve with new potatoes, page 290.

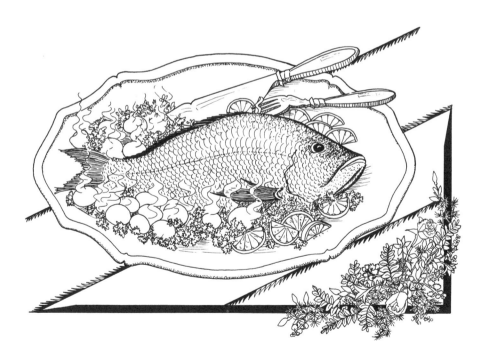

Baked Fish / 21

FISH BAKED IN FOIL

4 servings
PREPARATION: about 15 minutes
COOKING: 25 minutes in a 350° oven

1½ pounds thick-cut fish
2 scallions, trimmed and chopped fine
Thin-sliced lemon
Thin-sliced tomato
Sprinkling of celery seed
Salt
Grinding of pepper

On a sheet of lightly oiled heavy-duty aluminum foil large enough to fold over the fish and crimp together, arrange the fish. Over it, arrange in order the scallions and lemon and tomato slices. Add the seasonings. Bring the sides of the foil together and fold them to form a seal; bring the ends of the foil to meet the side pieces and crimp the two together. Bake the fish at 350° for 25 minutes.

If desired, the fish may be baked on a bed of vegetables: on the oiled foil, arrange a layer of 2 medium carrots, scraped and shredded, 1 small green pepper, seeded and cut in julienne strips, and 1 medium onion, peeled and sliced thin; over all, sprinkle the juice of 1 small lemon. Add the fish, season it, and bake as directed.

Serve with casserole-baked bread, page 288.

BAKED FISH, BOLIVIAN STYLE

4 servings
PREPARATION: about 20 minutes
COOKING: about 10 minutes in a 450° oven

2 tablespoons butter
2 tablespoons olive oil
2 medium onions, peeled and chopped
1 cup bread crumbs

In a saucepan, heat the butter and oil and sauté the onion until it is translucent. Add the bread crumbs and cook the mixture, stirring often, until the crumbs are golden.

> 2 *egg yolks*
> 3 *tablespoons heavy cream*
> ¼ *cup strained fresh lemon juice*
>   **Nutmeg**
>   **Salt**
>   **Grinding of white pepper**

In a small mixing bowl, beat together the egg yolks and cream; stir the mixture into the contents of the saucepan. Gradually add the lemon juice, stirring constantly. Season the mixture to taste with nutmeg, salt, and pepper.

> *1½ pounds fish fillet cut in serving pieces* or
> *4 large fillets of flounder*

Spread the bread crumb mixture on the fish; if you use flounder, you may roll each fillet. Arrange the fish in a buttered baking dish (rolled fillets should be placed seam side down).

> *At this point you may stop and continue later.*

> **Butter**
> **Lemon slices, cut paper-thin and**
> **seeded**

Dot the fish with butter and lay on top of each piece two or three lemon slices. Bake the fish at 450° according to the directions on page 20.

Serve with green peas, page 294.

BAKED FISH, GREEK STYLE

4 servings
PREPARATION: about 30 minutes
COOKING: about 10 minutes in a 450° oven

3 *tablespoons olive oil*
2 *cloves garlic, peeled and chopped fine*
1 *medium onion, peeled and chopped fine*

In a saucepan, heat the oil and in it cook the garlic and onion until translucent.

3 *large ripe tomatoes, peeled, seeded, and chopped* or
1 *1-pound can tomatoes, drained*
¼ *cup fine-chopped parsley*
½ *cup dry white wine*
½ *teaspoon thyme*
Salt
Grinding of pepper

To the contents of the saucepan, add the tomatoes, parsley, wine, and seasonings. Simmer the sauce, covered, for 15 minutes. Over the bottom of a buttered baking dish, spread half the sauce.

1½ *pounds fish fillet cut in serving pieces* or *steak*
Strained lemon juice

Over the sauce, arrange the fish in a single layer. Season it with a sprinkling of lemon juice. Spread the remaining sauce over the fish.
At this point you may stop and continue later.
Bake the fish at 450° according to the directions on page 20.
Serve with new potatoes, page 290.

For *Fish Baked with Currants* (Greek): soak 1 cup currants in 1 cup dry white wine for 1 hour; add them and their liquid to the sauce, omitting the ½ cup wine originally called for. Cook the sauce, uncovered, until it is slightly thickened and the currants are tender. Complete the recipe.

BAKED FISH, SPANISH STYLE

4 servings
PREPARATION: about 20 minutes
COOKING: about 10 minutes in a 450° oven

> **4 tablespoons olive oil**
> **1 clove garlic, put through a press**
> **1 medium onion, peeled and chopped
> fine**

In a small saucepan, combine these three ingredients, and over low heat cook the mixture for a few minutes to blend the flavors. Reserve the sauce.

> **Olive oil**
> **1 clove garlic, chopped fine**
> **1 medium onion, peeled and chopped
> fine**
> **1½ pounds fish fillet cut in serving
> pieces or steak**
> **Bread crumbs (optional)**

With the olive oil, generously grease a baking dish. Over the bottom sprinkle the garlic and onion. Arrange the fish in a single layer. Over it, spread the reserved sauce. Add a sprinkling of bread crumbs.

At this point you may stop and continue later.

> **⅓ cup dry white wine**
> **Fine-chopped parsley**
> **Lemon wedges**

To the contents of the baking dish, add the wine. Bake the fish at 450° according to the directions on page 20. Garnish it with parsley and lemon wedges.

Serve with casserole-baked bread, page 288.

BAKED FISH, HOME STYLE

4 servings
PREPARATION: about 20 minutes
COOKING: about 10 minutes in 450° oven

4 tablespoons butter, melted
Strained juice of 1 medium lemon
1 scallion, grated

In a small saucepan, combine these three ingredients, and over low heat cook the mixture for a few minutes to blend the flavors. Reserve the sauce.

1½ pounds fish fillet cut in serving
  pieces or steak
Salt
Grinding of white pepper

In a lightly buttered baking dish, arrange the fish in a single layer. Season it with salt and pepper. Over it, spread the reserved sauce.
At this point you may stop and continue later.

Fine-chopped parsley

Bake the fish at 450° according to the directions on page 20. Garnish it with parsley.

Serve with green beans, page 292.

Four tablespoons fine-chopped cashew nuts added to the sauce make a pleasant variation. *Or* ½ cup chopped pitted olives, green or ripe, depending upon your wish.

BAKED FISH, ITALIAN STYLE

4 servings
PREPARATION: about 20 minutes
COOKING: about 10 minutes in a 450° oven

1½ pounds fish fillet cut in serving
  pieces or steak
Salt
Grinding of pepper

In a well-buttered baking dish, arrange the fish in a single layer. Season it to taste with salt and pepper.

> **1 cup marinara sauce, page 280**
> **1 clove garlic, put through a press**
> **½ cup dry white wine**

In a mixing bowl, combine and blend these three ingredients. Pour the sauce over the fish.

At this point you may stop and continue later.

> **Grated Parmesan cheese**
> **1 cup shredded Mozzarella cheese**

Sprinkle the contents of the baking dish generously with grated Parmesan cheese; over all, sprinkle the Mozzarella. Bake the dish at 450° according to the directions on page 20.

Serve with casserole-baked bread, page 288.

FISH BAKED IN BEER
(*Netherlands*)

4 servings
PREPARATION: about 20 minutes
COOKING: 20 minutes in a 350° oven

> **4 scallions, trimmed and chopped fine, with as much green as is crisp**
> **1½ pounds fish fillet cut in serving pieces or steak**
> **¼ cup fine-chopped parsley**
> **Salt**
> **Grinding of white pepper**

Over the bottom of a greased baking dish, sprinkle the scallions. Over the scallions, arrange the fish. Sprinkle it with parsley and season it to taste with salt and pepper.

At this point you may stop and continue later.

> **1 12-ounce can stale beer, heated**

To the baking dish, add the beer. Bake the fish at 350° for 20 minutes, or until it flakes easily.

Serve with new potatoes, page 290.

FLOUNDER FILLETS BAKED WITH ALMONDS
(*France*)

4 servings
PREPARATION: about 30 minutes
COOKING: 25 minutes, starting in a 325° oven

The recipe may also be made with haddock or halibut fillets. Adapted from the classic *filet de sole amandine,* the recipe is delicate when made with flounder, a bit more robust with haddock or halibut.

> *1½ pounds flounder fillets*
> *Butter*
> *Curry powder*
> *Salt*

With absorbent paper, pat the fillets dry. Butter a shallow baking dish and in it arrange the fillets with as little overlapping as possible. (Flounder fillets may be rolled and arranged in the dish seam side down, a saving on space and an attractive way to serve them.) Sprinkle the fish lightly with curry powder and salt.

> *2 tablespoons butter*
> *1 teaspoon anchovy paste*

Cream together the butter and anchovy paste and spread the mixture evenly over the fish. Set aside the baking dish while you prepare the almonds.

> *¾ cup slivered almonds, toasted until*
> *golden brown in a 325° oven (about*
> *8 minutes)*
> *1 cup chicken broth*
> *1 tablespoon capers (optional)*

In a saucepan combine the almonds, chicken broth, and capers. Bring the liquid to the boil, reduce the heat, and simmer the almonds, covered, for 5 minutes.

> *1 tablespoon butter*
> *¼ cup bread crumbs*

In a small saucepan, heat the butter and into it stir the bread crumbs. Over medium heat, cook them, stirring, until they are golden brown. Reserve them.

At this point you may stop and continue later.

> *3 tablespoons melted butter*

Bake the fillets at 325° for 15 minutes, basting them twice with melted butter.

Reserved almond sauce
Reserved bread crumbs

Over the fillets, pour the almond sauce. Sprinkle with bread crumbs. Increase the heat to 350° and continue to bake for about 10 minutes, or until the fish flakes easily and the crumbs are slightly browned.

Serve with creamed spinach, page 295.

For *Flounder Fillets Baked with Olives:* complete step one; in place of steps two and three, make a sauce of 4 tablespoons soft butter, ½ cup ripe pitted olives, chopped, 1 small onion, peeled and grated, and 1 tablespoon cider vinegar; spread the sauce over the fish and cook the dish as directed, omitting the basting but using the bread crumbs, if desired. (This recipe may also be made with haddock or halibut fillet.)

FISH FILLETS BAKED WITH BANANAS

4 servings
PREPARATION: about 15 minutes
COOKING: about 15 minutes in a 450° oven

> **4 scallions, trimmed and sliced thin,**
> **with as much green as is crisp**
> **1½ pounds fish fillet cut in serving**
> **pieces**
> **Salt**
> **Grinding of pepper**
> **2 large very ripe bananas, peeled and**
> **sliced in lengthwise and crosswise**
> **halves**
> **Nutmeg**

Over the bottom of a greased baking dish, sprinkle the scallions. Over the scallions, arrange the fish. Season it to taste with salt and pepper. Top each piece of fish with two pieces of banana; add a sprinkling of nutmeg. (When measuring the depth, include the banana.)

At this point you may stop and continue later.

Parsley Butter, page 277
Lemon slices

Bake the fish at 450° according to the directions on page 20. Over it, pour a little parsley butter and garnish the dish with lemon slices.

Serve with Brussels sprouts, page 293.

FISH BAKED WITH CRANBERRIES

4 servings
PREPARATION: about 40 minutes
COOKING: about 15 minutes in a 450° oven

> *1½ cups cranberries, rinsed*
> *½ cup water*
> *3 tablespoons sugar*
> *Pinch of salt*

In a saucepan, combine these four ingredients. Bring the liquid to the boil and cook the cranberries, uncovered, until they have popped open and are tender.

> *2 tablespoons butter*
> *1 small onion, grated*
> *¼ cup chopped parsley*

In a small saucepan, heat the butter and in it cook the onion for a few minutes. Stir in the parsley and cook until it is wilted. Into the cranberries, stir the onion mixture.

> *1½ pounds fish fillet cut in serving*
> *pieces or steak*
> *Salt*
> *Grinding of pepper*

In a buttered baking dish, arrange the fish in a single layer. Season it to taste with salt and pepper. Over the fish, spoon the cranberry mixture. *At this point you may stop and continue later.*

> *⅔ cup white port wine*

To the contents of the baking dish, add the port wine. Bake the fish at 450° according to the directions on page 20.

Serve with curried rice, page 291.

FISH BAKED WITH PINEAPPLE

4 servings
PREPARATION: about 20 minutes
COOKING: about 15 minutes in a 450° oven

> *1 20-ounce can unsweetened pineap-*
> *ple chunks, drained (reserve the liq-*
> *uid)*
> *Strained fresh orange juice*
> *2½ tablespoons cornstarch*
> *½ teaspoon powdered cumin*
> *½ teaspoon salt*

To the reserved pineapple liquid, add orange juice to equal 2 cups. Mix together the cornstarch, cumin, and salt. Into a little of the pineapple liquid, stir the cornstarch mixture until it is smooth. In a saucepan, combine the remaining liquid and cornstarch mixture. Cook the sauce, stirring, until it is thickened and clear.

> *1½ pounds fish fillet cut in serving*
> *pieces or steak*
> *Salt*
> *Grinding of white pepper*
> *Reserved pineapple chunks*
> *Reserved sauce*

In a buttered baking dish, arrange the fish in a single layer. Season it to taste with salt and pepper. Over it, distribute the pineapple chunks. Over all, pour the sauce.

At this point you may stop and continue later.

> *Fine-chopped parsley*

Bake the fish at 450° according to the directions on page 20. Garnish the dish with parsley.

Serve with curried rice, page 291.

FISH BAKED IN CREAM

4 servings
PREPARATION: about 25 minutes
COOKING: 20 to 25 minutes in a 450° oven

Flour
1½ pounds fish fillet cut in serving portions or steaks
Butter

With the flour, dust the fish. Butter a flameproof baking dish that can be covered. In it, arrange a single layer of the fish.

4 large mushrooms, sliced thin
1 medium onion, peeled and chopped fine
½ cup dry white wine

Combine and reserve these three ingredients.
At this point you may stop and continue later.

Melted butter

Bake the fish in a 450° oven for 10 minutes, basting it once with melted butter.

Reserved mushroom mixture
1 bay leaf

Over the fish, spoon the mushroom mixture; add the bay leaf. Cover and cook the fish for 10 minutes longer. Discard the bay leaf. Remove the fish to a heated serving platter and keep it warm.

1 cup heavy cream, heated
Salt
Grinding of white pepper
Fine-chopped parsley

To the contents of the baking dish, add the cream. Over direct heat, cook the sauce until it thickens slightly. Season it to taste with salt and pepper. Serve the sauce separately, if desired. Garnish the platter with parsley.
Serve with curried rice, page 291.

FISH BAKED WITH LEEKS IN CREAM SAUCE

4 servings
PREPARATION: about 50 minutes
COOKING: about 10 minutes in a 450° oven

> **3 tablespoons butter**
> **1 bunch leeks (white part only) sliced in quarter-inch rounds, separated, rinsed, and spun dry**
> **2 tablespoons flour**
> **1 cup dry white wine**
> **½ cup heavy cream**

In a saucepan, heat the butter and in it cook the leek for 5 minutes, or until it is translucent. Stir in the flour, and over gentle heat cook the mixture for a few minutes. Gradually add the wine, stirring constantly until the mixture is thickened and smooth; stir in the cream. Over gentle heat, simmer the mixture, covered, for 30 minutes.

> **Strained juice of ½ medium lemon**
> **Nutmeg**
> **Salt**
> **Grinding of white pepper**

Season the sauce to taste with lemon juice, nutmeg, salt, and pepper. Over the bottom of a buttered baking dish, spread the sauce evenly.

> **1½ pounds fish fillet cut in serving pieces or steak**
> **2 tablespoons heavy cream**
> **Salt**
> **Grinding of white pepper**

Over the sauce, arrange the fish in a single layer. Over the fish, drizzle the cream. Season the fish to taste with salt and pepper.

At this point you may stop and continue later.

Grated Parmesan cheese (optional)

Sprinkle the fish with grated cheese. Bake the dish at 450° according to the directions on page 20.

Serve with rice, page 290.

FISH BAKED WITH CHEESE

4 servings
PREPARATION: about 25 minutes
COOKING: about 12 minutes in a 450° oven

The recipe takes on a Dutch or Greek character depending upon your choice of Edam or Feta cheese.

> *4 scallions, trimmed and sliced thin, with as much green as is crisp*
> *1½ pounds fish fillet cut in serving pieces or steak*
> *Salt*
> *Grinding of pepper*
> *½ cup dry white wine*
> *½ teaspoon powdered allspice*

In a buttered baking dish, arrange a layer of the scallions; top them with the fish and season it to taste with salt and pepper. Over the fish, pour the wine and sprinkle the allspice.

> *3 tablespoons bread crumbs*
> *4 tablespoons Edam or Feta cheese, grated*

Using a fork, blend the bread crumbs and cheese; reserve the mixture. *At this point you may stop and continue later.*

> *Reserved bread crumb mixture*
> *Butter*
> *Fine-chopped parsley*
> *Lemon wedges*

Over the fish, spread the bread crumb mixture; dot the top with butter. Bake the fish at 450° according to the directions on page 20. Garnish the dish with parsley; offer lemon wedges with each serving.

Serve with broccoli, page 292.

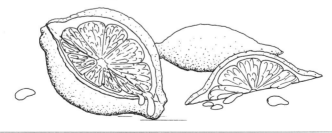

FISH BAKED WITH SPINACH
(*Baked Fish Florentine*)

4 servings
PREPARATION: about 35 minutes
COOKING: about 15 minutes in a 450° oven

> **2 10-ounce packages fresh spinach with the woody stems removed, rinsed, wilted for 20 seconds in lightly boiling salted water to cover, drained, and chopped, or 2 10-ounce packages frozen chopped spinach, fully thawed to room temperature**
> **3 tablespoons butter**
> **1 small clove garlic, put through a press**
> **½ teaspoon powdered cumin or nutmeg**

Prepare the spinach. In a skillet, heat the butter and to it add the spinach, garlic, and cumin. Over gentle heat, cook out most of the moisture.

> **¼ cup fine-chopped parsley**
> **Salt**
> **Grinding of pepper**

Stir in the parsley and season the mixture to taste with salt and pepper. Reserve it.

> **1½ pounds fish fillet cut in serving pieces or steak**

In a buttered baking dish, arrange an even layer of the spinach mixture. Over it, arrange the fish.

> **Mornay Sauce, page 281**
> **Grated Parmesan cheese**

Over the fish, spread the sauce. Add a sprinkling of grated cheese.
At this point you may stop and continue later.
Bake the fish at 450° according to the directions on page 20.
   Serve with curried or saffron rice, page 291.

FISH BAKED IN SAVORY SAUCE

4 servings
PREPARATION: about 20 minutes
COOKING: about 12 minutes in a 450° oven

1 *tablespoon cognac*
2 *tablespoons lemon juice*
4 *tablespoons Dijon mustard*
½ *cup dry white wine*
½ *teaspoon thyme*
½ *teaspoon salt*
   Grinding of pepper

In a jar with a tight-fitting lid, shake together these seven ingredients; allow them to "work" for one hour.

4 *scallions, trimmed and chopped, with as much green as is crisp*
½ *cup chopped parsley*
1½ *pounds fish fillet cut in serving pieces or steak*

Over the bottom of a buttered baking dish, distribute the scallions; over them, arrange the parsley. Over the parsley, arrange the fish in a single layer.

At this point you may stop and continue later.

Over the fish, pour the sauce. Bake the fish at 450° according to the directions on page 20.

Serve with new potatoes, page 290.

FISH BAKED WITH ZUCCHINI

4 servings
PREPARATION: about 25 minutes
COOKING: about 15 minutes in a 450° oven

2 *tablespoons Dijon mustard*
3 *tablespoons olive oil*
1 *small onion, peeled and grated*
⅔ *cup dry white wine*
½ *teaspoon powdered cumin*

Combine and blend these five ingredients. Reserve the sauce.

4 small zucchini, sliced very thin
1½ pounds fish fillet cut in serving
pieces **or steak**
Salt
Grinding of pepper

In a lightly oiled baking dish, arrange the zucchini; top them with the fish in a single layer. Season the fish to taste with salt and pepper. Over all, spoon the sauce. Cover the baking dish with aluminum foil.

At this point you may stop and continue later.

Fine-chopped parsley

Bake the fish at 450° according to the directions on page 20, having measured the depth from the top of the fish to the bottom of the zucchini layer. Garnish the dish with parsley.

Serve with bulgur salad, page 297.

FISH BAKED WITH SESAME SEED

4 servings
PREPARATION: about 30 minutes
COOKING: about 12 minutes in a 450° oven

¼ cup sesame seed, toasted until golden
in a 350° oven (about 5 minutes)
5 tablespoons butter
1 small onion, peeled and grated
¼ teaspoon powdered thyme
½ teaspoon salt

Prepare the sesame seed. In a small saucepan, heat the butter and in it, over gentle heat, cook the onion for a few minutes. Stir in the thyme and salt. Stir in the sesame seed. Reserve the mixture.

1½ pounds fish fillet cut in serving
pieces **or steak**
Salt
Grinding of pepper

In a lightly buttered baking dish, arrange the fish in a single layer. Season it to taste with salt and pepper. Over it, spread the sesame seed mixture.

At this point you may stop and continue later.

Bake the fish at 450° according to the directions on page 20.

Serve with muffins, page 289.

PORGIES BAKED IN TOMATO SAUCE

4 servings
PREPARATION: about 30 minutes
COOKING: about 15 minutes in a 450° oven

4 tablespoons olive oil
1 medium onion, peeled and chopped
4 large ripe tomatoes, peeled, seeded,
  and chopped
1 bay leaf
½ teaspoon basil
¾ teaspoon salt
  Grinding of pepper

In a saucepan, heat the oil and in it cook the onion until translucent. Add the remaining ingredients and simmer the mixture, covered, for 15 minutes.

3 to 4 pounds porgies, dressed
Salt
Grinding of pepper

In a buttered baking dish, arrange the porgies. Season them to taste with salt and pepper. Over them, pour the tomato sauce.

At this point you may stop and continue later.

Bake the fish at 450° according to the directions on page 20.

Serve with casserole-baked bread, page 288.

FISH BAKED WITH STUFFING

4 servings
PREPARATION: about 12 minutes
COOKING: about 15 minutes in a 450° oven

Hardly a bona fide recipe, but a convenient way of producing a fish dish from the freezer and larder, should the necessity arise.

> *½ 8-ounce package stuffing mix of your choice*
> *1½ pounds fish fillet cut in serving pieces or steak*
> *Powdered thyme*
> *Salt*
> *Grinding of pepper*
> *Butter*

Prepare the stuffing as directed on the package and with it line the bottom of a buttered baking dish. Over the stuffing, arrange the fish in a single layer. Season it to taste with a sprinkling of thyme, salt, and pepper; dot it with butter.

At this point you may stop and continue later.

Bake the fish at 450° according to the directions on page 20.

Serve with broccoli, page 292.

TUNA-STUFFED FLOUNDER

4 servings
PREPARATION: about 35 minutes
COOKING: about 15 minutes in a 450° oven

> **4 tablespoons butter**
> **1 medium onion, peeled and chopped fine**
> **4 large mushrooms, chopped fine**

In a skillet, heat the butter and in it cook the onion until translucent. Add the mushrooms and cook them until they are limp.

> **½ cup cracker crumbs**
> **1 7-ounce can waterpack tuna, drained and flaked**
> **¼ cup fine-chopped parsley**
> **½ teaspoon salt**
> **Grinding of pepper**

Stir in the cracker crumbs and then the tuna and parsley. Season the mixture to taste with salt and pepper. Over gentle heat, cook the mixture for a few minutes, stirring.

> **4 large or 8 small flounder fillets**
> **White wine sauce, page 287**
> **½ cup grated Swiss cheese (optional)**

Over each fillet, spread an equal amount of the tuna mixture. Roll the fillets and arrange them, seam side down, in a buttered baking dish. Over them, pour the sauce. Over all, sprinkle the grated cheese.

At this point you may stop and continue later.

Bake the fish at 450° according to the directions on page 20.

Serve with saffron rice, page 291.

For *Clam-stuffed Flounder,* use 2 7-ounce cans minced clams, thoroughly drained, in place of the tuna. Complete the recipe.

VEGETABLE-STUFFED FLOUNDER

4 servings
PREPARATION: about 40 minutes
COOKING: about 15 minutes in a 450° oven

4 tablespoons butter
**2 medium carrots, scraped and shred-
ded fine**
1½ cups bread crumbs
**2 scallions, trimmed and chopped
fine, with as much green as is crisp**
3 tablespoons fine-chopped parsley
**1 ripe tomato, peeled, seeded, and
chopped**
Pinch of thyme
Salt
Grinding of pepper

In a skillet, heat the butter and in it, over gentle heat, cook the carrot, covered, for 5 minutes. Stir in the bread crumbs, scallions, parsley, and tomato. Season the mixture to taste with thyme, salt, and pepper.

4 large or 8 small flounder fillets
Melted butter

Over each of the fillets, spread an equal amount of the vegetable mixture. Roll the fillets and arrange them, seam side down, in a buttered baking dish. Brush them with melted butter.

At this point you may stop and continue later.

Fine-chopped parsley
Lemon wedges

Bake the fish at 450° according to the directions on page 20. Garnish it with parsley and lemon wedges.

Serve with creamed spinach, page 295.

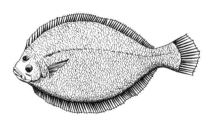

BACON-STUFFED FLOUNDER

4 servings
PREPARATION: about 30 minutes
COOKING: about 15 minutes in a 450° oven

8 slices bacon, diced

In a skillet, render the bacon until it is crisp and golden; remove it to absorbent paper and reserve it. Pour off half the fat.

*1 small onion, peeled and chopped
  fine*
1½ cups bread crumbs
*1 medium rib celery, trimmed and
  chopped fine*
*¼ cup fine-chopped parsley
  Reserved bacon dice*
1 egg, beaten

In the remaining fat, cook the onion until it is translucent. Stir in the bread crumbs, celery, parsley, and bacon dice. Allow the mixture to cool somewhat and then stir in the egg.

*4 large or 8 small flounder fillets
  Strained lemon juice
  Summer savory, crumbled
  Salt
  Grinding of pepper*

Season each fillet with lemon juice, summer savory, and salt and pepper. Place equal amounts of the bread crumb mixture on each fillet. Roll and arrange them, seam side down, in a buttered baking dish.

At this point you may stop and continue later.
Bake the fish at 450° according to the directions on page 20.
  Serve with bulgur, page 290.

Stuffings for Baked Fish

The following stuffings will dress a 4-pound whole fish. When the fish is stuffed, skewer the opening closed, arrange the fish in a greased baking dish, brush it with melted butter or other basting sauce, if desired, and bake it according to the directions on page 20.

The mixtures may also be spread on thin fillets, such as those of flounder, the fillet rolled and arranged seam side down in a greased baking dish. Brush the fillet with melted butter or other basting sauce, if desired, and bake it according to the directions on page 20.

BREAD CRUMB STUFFING

Particularly good for fat-fleshed fish.
PREPARATION: about 15 minutes

1 cup bread crumbs
2 tablespoons fine-chopped gherkins
2 tablespoons fine-chopped parsley
2 tablespoons fine-chopped scallions, with some of the green
½ teaspoon salt
½ teaspoon pepper
1 egg, beaten

In a mixing bowl, combine and blend the first six ingredients. Add the beaten egg, and with a fork, toss the mixture to blend it well.

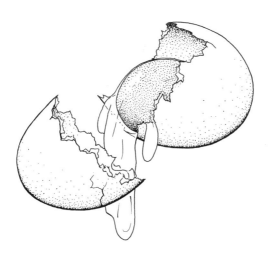

Stuffings for Baked Fish / 43

CARROT STUFFING

6 *tablespoons butter*
2 *large carrots, scraped and grated*
3 *scallions, chopped fine, with as much green as is crisp*

In a skillet, heat the butter and in it cook the carrot and scallions until the carrot is limp.

¼ *cup fine-chopped parsley*
1 *medium ripe tomato, peeled, seeded, and chopped*

Add the parsley and tomato, stirring to blend the mixture.

1 *cup packaged poultry dressing or croutons*
Water

In a mixing bowl, combine the poultry dressing with the tomato mixture, and with a fork, toss the stuffing to blend it well; if desired, a little water may be added for extra moistness.

CHEESE STUFFING

4 *tablespoons butter*
4 *scallions, chopped fine, with as much green as is crisp*
1¼ *cups bread crumbs*
½ *cup grated Cheddar cheese*
¼ *teaspoon ground thyme*
Salt
Pepper

In a saucepan, heat the butter and in it cook the scallions until they are wilted. Away from the heat, stir in the bread crumbs and then the grated cheese. Season the mixture to taste with the thyme, salt, and pepper.

1 *egg, beaten*
Water

To the contents of the saucepan, add the egg, and using a fork, blend the stuffing well; a little water may be added for extra moistness.

CLAM AND BLUE CHEESE STUFFING

For lean-fleshed fish.
PREPARATION: about 15 minutes.

1 *4-ounce package blue cheese, at room temperature*
1 *3-ounce package cream cheese, at room temperature*
1 *6½-ounce can minced clams, with their liquid*
2 *tablespoons fine-chopped parsley*
1 *scallion, chopped fine, with as much green as is crisp*
2 *teaspoons cognac*
2 *tablespoons strained lemon juice*
Drop or two of Tabasco sauce
½ *teaspoon Worcestershire sauce*
Salt

In a mixing bowl, combine the first nine ingredients. With a fork, blend the mixture well. Season it to taste with salt.

1 *cup bread crumbs*
1 *egg, beaten*

To the mixture, add the crumbs, stirring. Blend in the beaten egg.

If desired, you may drain the clams, making the cheese mixture as directed; omit the bread crumbs and egg; spread the mixture over thin fillets, roll them, and arrange them seam side down in a greased baking dish; or spread the mixture over thicker fillets to act as a basting sauce during the cooking.

CORN STUFFING

4 tablespoons butter
**1 medium onion, peeled and chopped
   fine**
¼ cup fine-chopped green pepper

In a saucepan, heat the butter and in it cook the onion and pepper until the onion is translucent.

1 cup bread crumbs
**1 10-ounce package frozen corn ker-
   nels, cooked according to package directions**
3 tablespoons fine-chopped parsley
Pinch of thyme
Salt
Pepper

Into the contents of the saucepan, stir the bread crumbs, corn kernels, parsley, and thyme; season the mixture to taste with salt and pepper.

1 egg, beaten
Water

Add the egg, and using a fork, blend the stuffing well; a little water may be added for extra moistness.

CORN BREAD STUFFING

4 tablespoons butter
1 small rib celery, diced
**1 small onion, peeled and chopped
   fine**
¼ cup fine-chopped parsley
**1¼ cups packaged corn bread poultry
   dressing**
Pinch of thyme
Salt
Pepper

In a saucepan, heat the butter and in it cook the celery and onion until the onion is translucent. Stir in the parsley and corn bread dressing. Season the mixture to taste with thyme, salt, and pepper.

> 1 egg, beaten
> Water

To the contents of the saucepan, add the egg, and using a fork, blend the stuffing well; a little water may be added for extra moistness.

HERB STUFFING

PREPARATION: about 20 minutes

> 4 tablespoons butter
> 2 medium onions, peeled and chopped
> 1 cup bread crumbs
> 3 or 4 fresh basil leaves, chopped fine (if available)
> 2 tablespoons celery leaves, chopped fine
> ¼ cup fine-chopped parsley
> ½ teaspoon thyme
> Salt
> Pepper

In a saucepan, heat the butter and in it cook the onion until translucent. Stir in the bread crumbs and herbs. Season the mixture to taste with salt and pepper.

> 1 egg, beaten
> Water

To the contents of the saucepan, add the egg, and using a fork, blend the stuffing well; a little water may be added for extra moistness.

LEMON STUFFING

4 tablespoons butter
2 medium ribs celery, chopped fine
1 medium onion, peeled and chopped fine
1¼ cups bread crumbs
Strained juice and grated rind of 1 medium lemon
¼ cup fine-chopped parsley
Salt
Pepper

In a saucepan, heat the butter and in it cook the celery and onion until the onion is translucent. Add the bread crumbs, lemon juice and rind, and parsley. Using a fork, toss the mixture to blend it well; season it to taste with salt and pepper.

1 egg, beaten
Water

To the contents of the saucepan, add the egg, and using a fork, blend the stuffing well; a little water may be added for extra moistness.

MUSHROOM STUFFING

4 tablespoons butter
3 scallions, chopped fine, with as much green as is crisp
½ pound mushrooms, chopped
¼ cup fine-chopped parsley
1 cup bread crumbs
Salt
Pepper

In a saucepan, heat the butter and in it cook the scallions until translucent. Add the mushrooms, stirring to coat them well with butter; over gentle heat, cook them until they are limp. Add the parsley and bread crumbs. Using a fork, toss the mixture to blend it well. Season it to taste with salt and pepper.

1 egg, beaten

To the contents of the saucepan, add the egg, and using a fork, blend the stuffing well.

SPINACH STUFFING

PREPARATION: about 25 minutes

3 tablespoons butter

1 medium rib celery, chopped fine

2 scallions, chopped fine, with as much green as is crisp

1 10-ounce package fresh spinach with the woody stems removed, rinsed, wilted for 20 seconds in lightly salted boiling water to cover, pressed dry in a colander, and chopped or 1 10-ounce package frozen chopped spinach, fully thawed to room temperature and pressed dry in a colander

In a saucepan, heat the butter and in it cook the celery and scallions until translucent. Add the spinach, tossing the mixture with a fork to blend it well; over gentle heat cook the spinach until it is quite dry.

1 3-ounce package cream cheese, at room temperature

¼ cup fine-chopped parsley

½ teaspoon mace

1½ teaspoons tarragon

½ cup bread crumbs

1 egg, beaten

To the spinach mixture, over gentle heat, add the cream cheese, stirring until it is melted. Stir in the seasonings and then the bread crumbs, tossing the stuffing with a fork to blend it well. Add the egg and continue to toss the stuffing until it is of homogenous texture.

Barbecued Fish

Fat-fleshed and full-flavored fish fare best on the barbecue grill; smoke enhances their flavor, and the loss of fat does not harm the quality of the cooked fish. Lean-fleshed fish are less successfully barbecued; being generally more delicately flavored, they may be overcome by smoke and may also become dry unless carefully wrapped in foil.

Fillets cut in serving pieces, steaks, and small whole dressed fish may be cooked directly on the greased barbecue grill; the fillet pieces and steaks should be cut thick, at least half an inch in depth. Place the fish over ash-coated coals and grill it, turning once, basting with melted butter or basting sauce, and allowing 10 minutes of cooking per one inch of depth, as suggested by the Canadian Cooking Theory, page 15.

Barbecue whole fish from five to seven pounds in a greased wire cage with hinged top, to allow for turning the fish; these utensils are available at cooking equipment stores. Season the fish cavity with salt, pepper, herbs, and thin lemon slices. Remove the fins; wrap the head and tail in waxed paper and then in heavy foil. Having measured the fish at its greatest depth, barbecue it over ash-covered coals at 10 minutes per one inch of thickness, basting it often with melted butter or basting sauce. When it is done, turn it onto a serving board, remove the foil and waxed paper and the top skin; serve.

Thick fillets of lean, white-fleshed fish may be barbecued by cutting them in serving pieces, marinating them in a nonmetal dish for 4 hours (I suggest the marinade under Barbecued Fish Steaks page 52), and skewering them (or you may put them in a greased wire cage). Grill the fish over ash-dusted coals, allowing 10 minutes of cooking time for each inch of thickness. Any remaining marinade may be heated and poured over the cooked fish.

4 servings
PREPARATION: about 25 minutes
COOKING: about 35 minutes

1 3-pound whole bluefish, dressed, washed, and dried with absorbent paper
Salt
Pepper

Season the fish to taste with salt and pepper, inside and out. Arrange the fish on a double thickness of heavy-duty foil, allowing sufficient extra foil to fold over and seal.

3 tablespoons butter, melted
⅓ cup dry white wine
1 large clove garlic, put through a press
2 scallions, chopped fine, with as much green as is crisp
1 teaspoon tarragon
½ teaspoon thyme

Combine and blend these six ingredients. Pour the sauce over the fish. Fold up and crimp together the edges of the foil to make a tight envelope around the fish. Grill the bluefish about 4 inches from the ash-dusted coals for 35 minutes.

Serve with green bean salad, page 297.

BARBECUED FISH STEAKS

4 servings
PREPARATION: about 20 minutes
MARINATING TIME: 4 hours
COOKING: about 10 minutes

The recipe may be also made with thick-cut fillet, whole or in serving pieces.

4 fish steaks, ¾ to 1 inch thick

Make sure that the steaks are free of scales; wipe them with a damp cloth. Arrange them in one layer in a shallow dish.

⅓ cup olive oil
½ cup dry vermouth
   Strained juice and grated rind of 1 small lemon
3 tablespoons fine-chopped parsley
¼ teaspoon thyme
½ teaspoon salt
   Grinding of pepper

Combine and blend these eight ingredients. Pour the marinade over the fish and refrigerate for 4 hours, turning occasionally. Remove the fish from the marinade, place it on a greased rack about 4 inches above ash-dusted coals and barbecue it, turning it once and allowing 10 minutes total cooking time per inch of depth. During the cooking, baste the fish with the remaining marinade. Offer the fish with lemon wedges.

Serve with casserole-baked bread, page 288.

Broiled Fish

All fish can be successfully broiled. Wipe it with a damp cloth or paper towel and arrange it on the greased rack of a broiling pan. Instructions for broiling fish are found below. Lean-fleshed fish broils better if brushed with melted butter beforehand or if basted during the process; fat-fleshed fish does not require this extra attention. Broiled fish is best seasoned after it is cooked.

I offer very few individual recipes for broiled fish — and for good reason: fish broiled plain, without the addition of a sauce or other embellishment, may be sauced after cooking without loss of flavor to either fish or sauce. I much prefer this simplest method of broiling fish, which respects the identity of both fish and accompaniment; it is easy and assures a dish that, although fully cooked, is tender and moist. Thus, in reality, this book contains as many broiled fish recipes as there are entries in the Lexicon of Frugal Fish, multiplied by the number of sauces for hot fish found in chapter eight. One of my principal aims in this book is to stimulate your interest in creative fish cookery: what numerous opportunities for you to experiment happily in your kitchen!

To Broil: Preheat the broiler for 10 minutes. Allow 10 minutes of cooking time per inch of depth for fresh fish; frozen fish will require 20 minutes per inch. Use the oiled rack of the broiling pan, cooking the fish 2 to 4 inches from the source of heat and basting it with melted butter or a sauce. Place frozen fish farther from the source of heat (about 6 inches) to prevent overcooking the surface before the inside is done. Turn thick cuts of fish once when the cooked side is browned; thin cuts may be broiled without turning.

BROILED FISH WITH
PESTO GENOVESE

4 servings
PREPARATION: about 15 minutes
COOKING: about 10 minutes in a preheated broiler

One of my favorite fish dishes because *pesto* is one of my favorite sauces; I urge anyone who has a garden plot to grow sweet basil in order to make this very special treat.

> *1½ pounds fish fillet cut in serving*
> *pieces or steaks*
> *Salt*
> *Grinding of pepper*
> **Pesto genovese,** *page 284, at room*
> *temperature*

On the greased rack of a broiling pan, arrange the fish. Season it to taste with salt and pepper. Broil the fish according to the directions on page 53. Garnish each serving with a tablespoonful of the sauce.

Serve with muffins, page 289.

BROILED FISH WITH
TOMATO SAUCE AND CHEESE

4 servings
PREPARATION: about 15 minutes
COOKING: about 10 minutes in a preheated broiler

> *1½ pounds fish fillet cut in serving*
> *pieces or steaks*
> *Salt*
> *Grinding of pepper*
> 1 *cup marinara sauce, page 280*
> *Butter*

On the greased rack of a broiling pan, arrange the fish. Season it to taste with salt and pepper. Over it, spread the marinara sauce and dot it with butter. Broil the fish according to the directions on page 53.

> *½ cup grated Swiss cheese*

Over the fish, sprinkle the cheese; return the pan to the broiler until the cheese is melted.

Serve with rice, page 290.

BROILED WHOLE BABY PIKE

4 servings
PREPARATION: about 25 minutes
COOKING: about 10 minutes in a preheated broiler

4 cups water
3 tablespoons vinegar
1 tablespoon salt
4 small pike (about 1 pound each), dressed and split in lengthwise halves

Combine the water, vinegar, and salt. Arrange the fish, split side up, in a shallow dish. Over them, pour the liquid and allow them to sit for 1 hour. Dry the fish with absorbent paper and arrange them in a buttered baking dish, skin side down.

At this point you may stop and continue later.

1 cup heavy cream
Salt
Grinding of white pepper

Over the fish, pour the cream. Broil the fish about 6 inches from the heat according to the directions on page 53. Season them to taste with salt and pepper.

Serve with green peas, page 294.

SAVORY MARINADE FOR BROILED FISH

YIELD: about 1¼ cups
PREPARATION: about 10 minutes

 1 *clove garlic, put through a press*
 ¼ *cup strained fresh lemon juice*
1½ *teaspoon Dijon mustard*
 ⅓ *cup olive oil*
 1 *small onion, peeled and grated*
 ½ *cup marinara sauce, page 280, or 1
    8-ounce can tomato sauce*
   Few drops of Tabasco sauce
 1 *teaspoon Worcestershire sauce*
1½ *teaspoons salt*

Combine and blend all of the ingredients. Pour the sauce over the fish and marinate it in a nonmetal dish for 1 hour at room temperature; turn the fish once. Remove the fish, cleaning it with a rubber spatula; reserve the sauce. Broil the fish in a single layer on the greased rack of a broiler pan; time it according to the Canadian Cooking Theory, page 15. With the reserved sauce, baste the fish twice during the cooking.

BASTING SAUCE FOR BROILED FISH

YIELD: about ⅓ cup
PREPARATION: about 10 minutes

 4 *tablespoons melted butter*
   Strained juice of 1 small lemon
 2 *teaspoons Dijon mustard*
 ¾ *teaspoon sweet paprika*
 ½ *teaspoon salt*
   Grinding of white pepper

Combine and blend all of the ingredients. Baste the fish with the sauce before and during broiling.

Deep-Fried Fish

Deep frying, in which the food to be cooked is completely immersed in hot fat, is one of our oldest culinary methods. It was practiced in ancient Rome, where olive oil was used as the medium; it has been known for centuries in the Far East, where *tempura* dishes, now universally popular, were and continue to be deep fried.

The fish should be allowed to come fully to room temperature. Because the fish is coated with egg and either bread crumbs, cornmeal, flour, or a batter, its moisture is sealed in and relatively little of the cooking fat is absorbed, save by the coating, which emerges pleasantly crisp while the succulence of the fish remains unchanged. Deep fry the fish according to the Canadian Cooking Theory, page 15, in fat at 375°.

It is important to cook only a few pieces at a time, so that the fat does not cool; it is equally important that the fat return to cooking temperature before other pieces of fish are added to it.

Although all fish listed in this book, suitably prepared, may be deep fried, I find lean-fleshed fish most satisfactory. (Fat-fleshed fish, as suggested in the sections on baking and broiling, are best cooked, I feel, by these oven methods.) Deep frying is the trickiest way of cooking fish: if the fat is too hot, the fish will overcook and become dry; if the fat is not hot enough, the coating will be pasty and the fish rubbery.

Granted the popularity of deep-fried fish (can one imagine England without its fish and chips?), I must admit prejudice against it: because it is a chancy method of preparing fish and because I do not care to consume more fat than is necessary, I generally shy from it and deep fry fish only upon particular occasions. One such is when I am able to purchase very fresh silver-gleaming whitebait, for which a simple but satisfying recipe follows.

To Deep Fry: preheat the fat to 375°. Prepare the fish for frying, using either egg and crumbs or a batter. Cook the fish a few pieces at a time, allowing the fat to return to 375° between batches. Drain the fish on absorbent paper.

DEEP-FRIED WHITEBAIT

4 servings
PREPARATION: about 10 minutes
COOKING: about 10 minutes in deep fat at 375°

1½ pounds whitebait, dried on absor-
bent paper
Seasoned flour, page 19

In a paper bag, combine some of the whitebait and a little of the flour; close the bag tightly and shake it to dust the fish. Repeat the process until all the fish are dusted. Fry the fish, a small handful at a time, in the basket of the deep frier in fat heated to 375° for about 1 minute, or until they are golden and crisp. Drain them on absorbent paper and keep them warm. Repeat the process until all the fish are fried.

Fine-chopped parsley
Lemon wedges

Offer the whitebait sprinkled with parsley and garnished with lemon wedges.

Serve with new potatoes, page 290.

BATTER FOR DEEP FRYING

4 to 6 servings
PREPARATION: about 10 minutes
RESTING TIME: 2 hours

1 cup flour
½ teaspoon salt
¼ teaspoon white pepper

In a mixing bowl, combine and blend the dry ingredients.

2 eggs, separated (reserve the whites)
⅔ cup milk
2 tablespoons melted butter

In a mixing bowl, combine the egg yolks and milk; with a rotary beater, blend them thoroughly. Add the butter. Into the flour, stir the egg mixture only until blended. Allow the batter to stand at room temperature for 2 hours.

Reserved egg whites

Beat the egg whites until they are stiff but not dry. Fold them into the batter. Dip the fish into the batter and fry as directed on page 57.

Poached Fish

Generally speaking, whole fish are poached with head and tail on, but dressed, of course, and scaled. Wrapping the fish in cheesecloth makes handling it easier; use pieces of cheesecloth long enough that the ends can serve as handles with which to lift the fish out of the liquid (large fillets may be treated in this same way). Smaller fillets or steaks may be removed from the poaching liquid with broad slotted turner or spatula.

Fish may be poached in water, milk, or a *court bouillon,* page 90 (which will unquestionably give it added flavor). Strain the poaching liquid and reserve it as a basis for an accompanying sauce or for soup-making.

Poached fish is appetizing served hot or chilled, dressed with a suitable sauce. If served hot with a sauce to be made from the poaching liquid, keep the fish warm on a serving platter, well covered to retain its moistness; prepare in advance all ingredients for the sauce so that it can be made quickly, thus assuring that the fish will be served when at its best. If the poached fish is to be served chilled, it should be well covered with plastic wrap to retain its moistness, allowed to cool, and then refrigerated for about 4 hours. Unless the recipe specifically directs to the contrary, do not allow the fish to cool in the poaching liquid, as it will continue to cook and be overdone.

Poaching is a very good way to cook lean fish; I feel that for the most part fat-fleshed fish are more successful baked or broiled than poached. Poached fish is excellent as an ingredient for recipes calling for cooked fish: 1 pound of uncooked fish yields 2 cupfuls of flaked fish.

To Poach: bring the poaching liquid to the boil and place the fish in it; the liquid should barely cover the fish. When the liquid returns nearly to the boil (it should shimmer at between 190° and 200°), begin to time the fish, allowing 10 minutes of cooking time per inch of depth measured at the deepest point.

The reader will note that some of the recipes in this section (Poached Fish, Chinese Style, for example) do not call for poaching so much as for braising (the fish is added to a sauce and cooked in it). The techniques are sufficiently similar that I hope you will forgive the inclusion of braised dishes in this section.

FISH POACHED WITH APPLES AND CIDER

4 servings
PREPARATION: about 25 minutes
COOKING: about 10 minutes

>   2 *tart apples*
>   *Strained juice of 1 medium lemon*

Peel, core, and dice the apples; toss them with the lemon juice to prevent their discoloring and reserve.

>   1½ *pounds fish fillets cut in serving pieces* **or** *steaks*
>   1 *small onion, peeled and chopped fine*
>   *Tarragon*
>   *Salt*
>   *Pepper*
>   *Reserved apple*
>   1 *ripe medium tomato, peeled, seeded, and chopped*

Over the fish, distribute the onion; add a sprinkling of tarragon, salt, and pepper. Add a layer of apple, reserving the lemon juice; top each piece with tomato.

>   *Reserved lemon juice*
>   2 *cups cider* **or** *1 cup cider and 1 cup dry white wine*
>   *Fine-chopped parsley*

In a poacher or other utensil large enough to accommodate the fish in a single layer, combine the liquids and bring them to the boil. Add the fish and poach it according to the directions on page 59. Garnish it with parsley.

Serve with curried rice, page 291.

FISH POACHED WITH CELERY ROOT

4 servings
PREPARATION: about 30 minutes
COOKING: about 10 minutes

1 pound celeriac (celery root), peeled and diced

In lightly salted boiling water to cover, cook the celeriac, covered, for 20 minutes, or until it is tender; do not overcook it. Drain it in a colander, reserving the water. Keep the celeriac warm.

1½ pounds fish fillets cut in serving pieces or steaks
Salt
Pepper
Reserved water

Season the fish to taste with salt and pepper. In a poacher or other utensil large enough to accommodate the fish in a single layer, bring the reserved water to the boil. Add the fish and poach it according to the directions on page 59.

Hollandaise Sauce, page 280

Remove the fish to a hot serving platter, surround it with the celeriac, and garnish it with Hollandaise sauce.

Serve with new potatoes, page 290.

POACHED FISH, CHINESE STYLE

4 servings
PREPARATION: about 25 minutes
COOKING: about 8 minutes

> 1 *10½-ounce can chicken broth, defat-*
>   *ted (refrigerate the can overnight and*
>   *then pour the chilled broth through a*
>   *sieve)*
> 3 *medium ribs celery, diced*
> ½ *medium green pepper, seeded and*
>   *diced*
> 6 *medium mushrooms, sliced*
> 4 *scallions, trimmed and cut in quar-*
>   *ter-inch rounds, with as much green*
>   *as is crisp*

In a wok or saucepan, heat the broth and in it cook the vegetables for 5 minutes, or until they are tender-crisp.

> 1 *tablespoon dry sherry*
> 1 *tablespoon soy sauce*
> 2 *tablespoons cornstarch*
> ¼ *teaspoon ginger*

Combine the sherry and soy sauce. Mix together the cornstarch and ginger. Into the liquid, stir the cornstarch. When the mixture is smooth, add it to the contents of the wok. Over medium-high heat, stir the vegetables until the sauce is thickened.

At this point you may stop and continue later.

> 1½ *pounds fish fillet cut in bite-size*
>   *pieces*

Bring the contents of the wok to the boil, add the fish, stirring gently. Cook the fish, uncovered, for about 8 minutes, or until it flakes easily; do not overcook.

Serve with rice, page 290.

FISH POACHED IN CURRY SAUCE

4 servings
PREPARATION: about 25 minutes
COOKING: about 10 minutes

4 tablespoons butter
1 clove garlic, peeled and chopped fine
2 medium onions, peeled, and chopped fine
1 small green pepper, seeded and diced

In a saucepan, heat the butter and in it cook the garlic, onion, and pepper until the onion is translucent.

1 tablespoon curry powder (or more, to taste)
½ teaspoon cinnamon
¼ teaspoon ground clove

Stir in the spices, and over gentle heat, cook the mixture for 5 minutes.

1 large tart apple, peeled, cored, and diced
1 13-ounce can evaporated milk
Salt
Pepper

To the contents of the saucepan, add the apple and evaporated milk. Bring the liquid to the boil, reduce the heat and simmer the sauce, covered, for 5 minutes. Season it to taste with salt and pepper.
At this point you may stop and continue later.

1½ pounds fish fillet cut in bite-size pieces or steak

Return the sauce to the boil, and if you use fillet, add the fish directly to the sauce, reduce the heat, and simmer it for about 8 to 10 minutes, or until it flakes easily. If you use steak, pour half of the sauce into a utensil large enough to accommodate the fish in a single layer; pour the remaining sauce over the fish and simmer it for about 8 to 10 minutes, or until it flakes easily.

Serve with rice, page 290.

FLOUNDER FILLETS WITH GRAPES

4 servings
PREPARATION: about 25 minutes
(have all ingredients readied)
COOKING: about 15 minutes

Adapted from the French culinary classic *filet de sole véronique,* the recipe may also be made with haddock or halibut fillet cut in serving pieces.

1½ pounds (4 large) flounder fillets
1½ cups dry white wine

Roll the fillets and arrange them, seam side down, in a poacher or other utensil large enough to accommodate the fish in a single layer. In a saucepan, bring the wine to the boil, add it to the poacher, and cook the fish, covered, according to the directions on page 59. Remove the fish to a heated serving platter and keep it warm. Over high heat, reduce the wine to ¾ cup; strain it into a saucepan.

1 tablespoon plus 1 teaspoon cornstarch
½ teaspoon salt
¾ cup light cream

Blend the cornstarch and salt; stir the mixture into ¼ cup of the cream. When it is smooth, add the mixture and the remaining cream to the wine, and over high heat cook the sauce, stirring constantly, until it is thickened and smooth.

1 cup seedless grapes, halved lengthwise
Fine-chopped parsley

To the sauce, add the grapes; bring it to serving temperature, spoon it over the prepared fish, and garnish the platter with parsley.

Serve with green peas, page 294.

POACHED FISH WITH LETTUCE

4 servings
PREPARATION: about 20 minutes
COOKING: about 10 minutes

> **2 tablespoons butter**
> **3 scallions, trimmed and chopped fine, with some of the green**
> **¼ cup dry white wine**
> **1 large head Boston lettuce, rinsed, spun dry, and chopped**
> **Salt**
> **Grinding of white pepper**

In a covered skillet large enough to hold the fish in a single layer, heat the butter and in it cook the scallions until limp. Add the wine and cook the mixture briefly. Add the lettuce in an even layer and season it lightly with salt and pepper.

> **1½ pounds fish fillet cut in serving pieces or steak**
> **Powdered thyme**
> **Salt**
> **Grinding of white pepper**
> **Fine-chopped parsley**
> **Lemon wedges**

Season the fish to taste with thyme, salt, and pepper. Over high heat, bring the contents of the skillet to the steaming point. Add the fish, reduce the heat somewhat, and cook it, covered, according to the directions on page 59. Arrange the fish and wilted lettuce on a heated serving platter and garnish the dish with parsley and lemon wedges.

Serve with muffins, page 289.

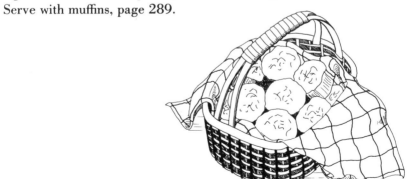

FLOUNDER FILLETS MARGUERY

4 servings
PREPARATION: about 1 hour
(time does not include readying the mussels, page 232)

A simplified version of the French *Filets de soles Marguery,* the recipe may also be made with cod, haddock, halibut, or scrod fillet cut in serving pieces.

1½ pounds (4 large) flounder fillets
1½ cups dry white wine

Roll the fillets and arrange them, seam side down, in a poacher or other utensil large enough to accommodate them in a single layer. In a saucepan, bring the wine to the boil, add it to the poacher, and cook the fish, covered, according to the directions on page 59. Remove the fish to a heated serving platter and keep it warm. Strain the wine into a saucepan and reserve it.

36 mussels, steamed and shelled

Keep the mussels warm in a covered bowl; strain the liquid into the poaching wine, and over high heat, reduce the contents of the saucepan to 1 cup.

3 tablespoons butter
3 tablespoons flour
Reduced broth
1 cup light cream
Nutmeg
Salt
Grinding of white pepper

In a saucepan, heat the butter and in it, over gentle heat, cook the flour for a few minutes. Gradually add the reserved broth and then the cream, stirring constantly until the mixture is thickened and smooth. Season it to taste with nutmeg, salt, and pepper.

2 egg yolks, beaten
2 tablespoons dry sherry
Fine-chopped parsley

At serving time, whip the egg yolk and sherry into the sauce. Arrange the mussels around the fish, pour the sauce over all, and garnish the platter with a sprinkling of parsley.

Serve with boiled new potatoes, page 290.

If you have kept the poached fish warm in an ovenproof serving platter, you may run the completed dish under a preheated broiler for about 3 minutes to glaze the sauce; in this case, omit the parsley.

FISH POACHED WITH NEW POTATOES

4 servings
PREPARATION: about 10 minutes
COOKING: about 30 minutes

Great Lakes fish "boil" is a traditional dish in that area of our country; the recipe may be made with any lean fillet, although whitefish steaks are preferred by Great Lakes gastronomes.

12 new potatoes, unpeeled
Boiling salted water

In a large covered kettle, cook the potatoes for 15 to 20 minutes, depending upon their size, until they are just tender. Reduce the heat, and over the simmering water, spread a layer of cheesecloth to facilitate the removal of the fish when cooked.

1½ pounds whitefish steaks (4) or fillet
cut in serving pieces

Add the fish and poach it according to the directions on page 59.

Parsley butter
Lemon wedges

Remove the fish to a heated serving platter; arrange the potatoes around it, pour a generous portion of parsley butter over all and garnish with lemon wedges.

Serve with mixed green salad, page 295.

POACHED FISH WITH SPINACH

4 servings
PREPARATION: about 35 minutes
COOKING: about 10 minutes

> *3 tablespoons butter*
> *1 clove garlic, peeled and chopped fine*
> *1 small onion, peeled and chopped fine*
> *1 10-ounce package fresh spinach with the woody stems removed, rinsed, wilted for 20 seconds in lightly salted boiling water to cover, pressed dry in a colander, and chopped or 1 10-ounce package frozen chopped spinach, fully thawed to room temperature and pressed dry in a colander*
> *¼ cup grated Parmesan cheese*
> *Salt*
> *Grinding of pepper*

In a skillet, heat the butter and in it cook the garlic and onion until translucent. Add the spinach, stirring to blend the mixture well. Off heat, stir in the grated cheese. Season the mixture to taste with salt and pepper. Reserve the spinach.

> *1½ pounds fish fillet cut in serving pieces or steak*
> *1 cup dry white wine*

Poach the fish in the wine according to the directions on page 59, until it just flakes. Remove it to an ovenproof serving platter. Strain and reduce the wine to ¼ cup.

> *½ cup sour cream*

Combine and blend the reduced liquid with the sour cream. Stir it into the spinach mixture. Over the fish, spread the spinach in an even layer.
At this point you may stop and continue later.

Pesto genovese, *page 284*

Heat the dish in a 400° oven for 10 minutes. Top each portion of fish with a tablespoon of *pesto*.

Serve with rice, page 290.

POACHED FISH IN SWEET-AND-PUNGENT SAUCE

4 servings
PREPARATION: about 30 minutes
COOKING: about 10 minutes

> ¼ *cup cider vinegar*
> ¾ *cup water*
> *Liquid from a 15¼-ounce can pine-
> apple chunks (reserve the fruit)*
> 1 *clove garlic, peeled and put through
> a press*
> 1½ *tablespoons cornstarch, mixed until
> smooth in 2 tablespoons soy sauce*

In a wok or saucepan, combine these six ingredients. Bring the mixture to
the boil, stirring until the sauce is thickened and smooth.

> 1 *8-ounce can bamboo shoots, drained*
> 1 *medium green pepper, seeded and cut
> in half-inch squares*
> *Reserved pineapple*
> 1 *ripe medium tomato, peeled, seeded,
> and chopped*

Into the sauce, stir these four ingredients.

> *At this point you may stop and continue later.*

> 1½ *pounds fish fillet cut in serving por-
> tions* or *steak*

Return the sauce to the boil and add the fish. When the sauce begins once
again to shimmer, start timing the fish according to the directions on page
59.

Serve with rice, page 290.

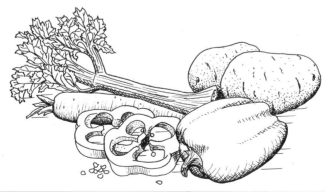

Poached Fish / 69

FISH POACHED WITH TOMATOES
(*Poached Fish Provençal*)

4 servings
PREPARATION: about 40 minutes
COOKING: about 10 minutes

3 tablespoons butter
1 large clove garlic, peeled and chopped fine
1 medium onion, peeled and chopped
6 large mushrooms, chopped
4 large ripe tomatoes, peeled, seeded, and chopped
¾ cup dry white wine
½ teaspoon thyme
Salt
Grinding of pepper

In a saucepan, heat the butter and in it cook the garlic and onion until transparent. Add the mushrooms and cook them until limp. Add the tomatoes and wine. Season the mixture with the thyme, salt, and pepper. Bring the sauce to the boil, reduce the heat, and simmer it, covered for 20 minutes.

At this point you may stop and continue later.

1½ pounds fish fillet cut in serving pieces or steak

In a lightly greased utensil large enough to accommodate the fish in a single layer, arrange the fillet or steaks. Return the sauce to the boil, pour it over the fish, and poach the fish, covered, according to the directions on page 59.

Fine-chopped parsley

If desired, you may remove the poached fish to a serving platter and keep it warm while reducing the sauce over high heat, stirring until it is somewhat thickened. Pour the sauce over the fish and garnish the dish with parsley.

Serve with casserole-baked bread, page 288.

POACHED CATFISH

4 servings
PREPARATION: about 10 minutes
COOKING: about 15 minutes

This Hoosier recipe yields a poached fat-fish dish that works very well. Simple and tasty.

> *3 cups water*
> *⅓ cup chopped parsley*
> *6 scallions, chopped, with as much green as is crisp*
> *1 teaspoon salt*
> *½ teaspoon white pepper*

In a large skillet, bring these five ingredients to the boil and cook them for 10 minutes.

> *2 pounds catfish, skinned, dressed, decapitated, and cut in 4-inch segments if necessary*

To the contents of the skillet, add the fish. When the water returns to a "shimmer," reduce the heat and poach the fish according to the directions on page 59. Remove the fish to a heated serving platter and keep it warm. Over high heat, reduce the broth to 1 cupful.

> *1 tablespoon soft butter*
> *1 tablespoon flour*
> *1 to 2 teaspoons curry powder, to taste*

In a small mixing bowl, blend thoroughly the butter, flour, and curry powder to make a *beurre manié*. Add it to the reduced bouillon, stirring constantly until the sauce is thickened and smooth. Pour the sauce over the fish.

Serve with rice, page 290.

FISH POACHED IN DRY VERMOUTH

4 servings
PREPARATION: about 40 minutes

*1½ pounds fish fillet cut in serving
pieces or steak
1¼ cups dry vermouth*

Poach the fillets in the vermouth, remove them to a warm serving platter, and keep them warm. Strain and reduce the vermouth to ½ cup.

*1 tablespoon soft butter
1 tablespoon flour
¾ cup cream*

In a small bowl, blend the butter and flour to make *beurre manié*. In a saucepan, add the cream to the reduced vermouth; bring the mixture to the boil, and to it add the *beurre manié*, stirring constantly until the sauce is thickened and smooth.

Fine-chopped parsley

Pour the sauce over the fish and garnish the dish with parsley.
    Serve with new potatoes, page 290.

POACHED EEL

4 servings
PREPARATION: about 40 minutes

You can get around the task of preparing the eel for cooking by befriending your fishmonger and convincing him to do the job for you; eels must be skinned, drawn, and cut in 2-inch sections before they are ready for cooking. My favorite composed eel dish, *Matelote* of Eel, Normandy Style, is found on page 142. For a simpler preparation, I recommend the following:

*2½ cups Court Bouillon, page 90
2 pounds eel, skinned, drawn, and cut
in 2-inch segments*

In a large saucepan, bring the *court bouillon* to the boil; add the eel, and when the liquid returns just to the boil, reduce the heat and simmer it, uncovered, for about 8 minutes or until it is tender. With a slotted spoon, remove it to a heated serving dish and keep it warm. Into a second saucepan, strain the *court bouillon,* and over high heat reduce it to 1 cup. Use the broth as the basis for the sauce of your choice in chapter eight.

Serve with casserole-baked bread, page 288.

MACKEREL IN WHITE WINE

4 servings
PREPARATION: about 30 minutes
COOKING: about 10 minutes
CHILLING TIME: 4 hours

An appetizing warm-weather dish that may also be made with bluefish.

> **1 cup (one 8-ounce bottle) clam juice**
> **3 tablespoons strained fresh lemon juice**
> **3 tablespoons olive oil**
> **1 medium onion, peeled and sliced thin**
> **1½ cups dry white wine**
> **2 bay leaves**
> **¼ teaspoon thyme**
> **1 teaspoon salt**
> **Grinding of white pepper**

In a large skillet, combine these nine ingredients. Bring the liquid to the boil and simmer the mixture, covered, for 10 minutes.

> **1½ pounds mackerel fillet cut in serving pieces**

Add the fish and poach it until it just barely begins to flake. Remove the skillet from the heat and allow the fish and broth to cool, uncovered.

At this point you may stop and continue later.

Transfer the fish to a chilled serving platter. Top it with the cooked onion slices. Strain the broth, reduce it by half, cool it, pour it over the fish, and chill the dish for 4 hours.

Serve with mixed green salad, page 295.

Sautéed or Pan-Fried Fish

To sauté is to cook and brown, uncovered, in a small quantity of hot fat in a frying pan. The best fat to use is a mixture of butter and oil, for the heat necessary to cook the fish quickly, thus sealing in its moistness, will cause butter alone to burn; oil acts as a fortifier. The fat must be very hot, but not smoky, before the fish is added to it, otherwise the juices will not be sealed in and the fish will not brown. Also, the fish should be dry, for dampness creates a layer of steam that prevents searing and browning. The skillet must not be crowded; air moving around each piece of cooking fish prevents steaming, which allows the juices to escape and burn in the pan. To assure yourself of crisply sautéed fish, fry a few pieces at a time, remove them to absorbent paper, and keep them warm; reheat the fat and proceed to fry a few more pieces.

Although sautéeing is a particularly tasty way of cooking freshwater fish, all fish named in the Lexicon may be sautéed. It is best, however, to use dressed small whole fish or fillet cut in serving pieces or steaks; large pieces of cooked fish are difficult to remove from the pan, without their breaking.

To ready it for the frying pan, wipe the fish dry with absorbent paper, dip it in milk, if desired, and then roll it lightly in seasoned flour, page 19, or a half-and-half combination of cornmeal (white or yellow) and seasoned flour. Sometimes beaten egg is used in place of milk, and sometimes neither milk nor egg is used; it depends upon your desire. Individual recipes, of course, present their own variations.

To Sauté: When ready to sauté the fish, heat to very hot about 4 table-spoons each of butter and oil. Fry the fish until golden brown on one side; then turn it and repeat the process. The total cooking time will equal about 10 minutes per inch of depth of the fish, following the Canadian Cooking Theory, page 15. When all the fish is sautéed and drained on absorbent paper, arrange it on a heated serving platter and garnish the dish with chopped parsley and lemon wedges.

A few garnishes are especially suited to sautéed fish. One of these is *sauce meunière:* add to the fat remaining in the skillet the strained juice of 1 small lemon and ⅓ cup fine-chopped parsley; stir to blend the mixture, and pour it over the fish. A second is *amandine,* sprinkling over the cooked fish thin-sliced or slivered almonds, about ¼ cup, which have been toasted in butter until golden brown. A third, *fines herbes,* calls for adding to the fat remaining in the skillet about 2 teaspoons each of fine-chopped chives, parsley, and fresh tarragon; stir to blend the mixture and pour it over the fish. Most of the sauces for hot fish in chapter eight are good with sautéed fish; your taste buds will reveal which ones are most appealing to you. My personal taste leads me away from much saucing of sautéed fish; the butter flavor, the taste of the fish itself, and its crispness require, from me, little further complement. Perhaps that is why I suggest these particular garnishes.

SAUTÉED FISH WITH ALMONDS AND CREAM

4 servings
PREPARATION: about 15 minutes
COOKING: about 10 minutes

> *1½ pounds fish fillet cut in serving*
> *pieces or steak*
> *Seasoned Flour, page 19*
> *4 tablespoons butter*
> *4 tablespoons oil*

Dust the fish with seasoned flour. In a skillet, heat the butter and oil to very hot and sauté the fish according to the directions on page 74. Remove it to absorbent paper, then arrange it on a serving platter and keep it warm.

> *½ cup slivered almonds*
> *½ cup heavy cream*
> *¼ teaspoon nutmeg*
> *Fine-chopped scallions*

To the fat remaining in the skillet, add the almonds and toast them until they are golden brown. Stir in the cream and nutmeg, deglazing the skillet, and simmer the sauce, stirring, for 2 minutes. Pour the sauce over the fish and garnish it with a sprinkling of scallions.

Serve with new potatoes, page 290.

SAUTÉED FISH WITH EGGPLANT

4 servings
PREPARATION: about 35 minutes
COOKING: about 10 minutes

    4 *tablespoons butter*
    1 *medium onion, peeled and chopped*
    1 *medium (about ¾-pound) eggplant,*
      peeled and diced
    3 *large ripe tomatoes, peeled, seeded,*
      and chopped
    ½ *teaspoon tarragon*
      Salt
      Grinding of pepper

In a skillet, heat the butter and in it cook the onion until translucent. Add the eggplant, stirring to coat it well; cook it for 5 minutes. Add the tomato and tarragon. Simmer the sauce for 20 minutes, or until the eggplant is very soft. Season it to taste with salt and pepper.

At this point you may stop and continue later.

   1½ *pounds fish fillet cut in serving*
      pieces **or** *steak*
      Seasoned Flour, page 19
    4 *tablespoons butter*
    4 *tablespoons oil*
      Fine-chopped parsley

Dust the fish with seasoned flour. In a skillet, heat the butter and oil to very hot and sauté the fish according to the directions on page 00. Remove it to absorbent paper, then arrange it on a serving platter and keep it warm. Spoon the prepared sauce over the fish and garnish the dish with parsley.

Serve with curried rice, page 291.

SAUTÉED FISH WITH TOMATO

4 servings
PREPARATION: about 20 minutes
COOKING: about 10 minutes

> **1½ pounds fish fillet cut in serving
> pieces or steak
> Seasoned Flour, page 19
> 6 tablespoons olive oil**

Dust the fish with seasoned flour. In a skillet, heat the oil to very hot and sauté the fish according to the directions on page 74. Remove it briefly to absorbent paper, then arrange it on a serving platter and keep it warm. Discard all but 3 tablespoons of the oil.

> **2 cloves garlic, peeled and chopped
> fine
> 1 medium onion, peeled and chopped
> fine
> 2 large ripe tomatoes, peeled, seeded
> and chopped
> 2 teaspoons strained lemon juice
> Salt
> Grinding of pepper
> ¼ cup fine-chopped parsley**

In the remaining oil cook the garlic and onion until barely golden. Add the tomatoes, and over high heat cook the mixture, stirring, for 5 minutes. Season the sauce with the lemon juice and salt and pepper to taste. Just before serving, stir in the parsley. Spoon the sauce over the fish.

Serve with casserole-baked bread, page 288.

Sautéed or Pan-Fried Fish / 77

SAUTÉED BLOWFISH

4 servings
PREPARATION: about 10 minutes
COOKING: about 10 minutes

Also called sea squab, the extremely ugly blowfish offers meat of exceptional sweetness and delicacy. It is equally recommended broiled. Read about blowfish, page 3.

> **20 to 24 dressed blowfish tails**
> **Seasoned Flour, page 19**
> **3 tablespoons butter**
> **3 tablespoons oil**
> **Lemon wedges**

Dust the fish with seasoned flour. In a skillet, heat the butter and oil until very hot and sauté the blowfish, a few at a time, according to the directions on page 74. Remove them to absorbent paper and then to a serving platter; keep them warm. Garnish the dish with lemon wedges.

Serve with new potatoes, page 290.

SAUTÉED CODFISH

4 servings
PREPARATION: about 15 minutes
COOKING: about 10 minutes

> **1½ pounds cod fillet cut in serving pieces**
> **Salt**
> **Grinding of pepper**
> **½ cup cornmeal**
> **1 egg, beaten with 1 tablespoon water**

With absorbent paper, wipe the fish dry. Season it to taste with salt and pepper. Dip it first in the cornmeal, then in the egg, and again in the cornmeal.

> **4 tablespoons butter**
> **4 tablespoons oil**
> **Fine-chopped parsley**
> **Lemon wedges**

In a skillet, heat the butter and oil to very hot and sauté the fish according to the directions on page 74. Remove the fish to absorbent paper and then to a heated serving platter. Garnish the dish with parsley and lemon wedges.

Serve with Brussels sprouts, page 293.

SAUTÉED PIKE WITH LEMON SAUCE

4 servings
PREPARATION: about 15 minutes
COOKING: about 10 minutes

6 tablespoons melted butter
3 tablespoons strained lemon juice
Grated rind of 1 medium lemon
1½ pounds pike fillet cut in serving pieces
3 tablespoons butter
3 tablespoons oil
Salt
Grinding of pepper
Fine-chopped parsley

In a mixing bowl, combine the melted butter, lemon juice, and lemon rind. Into the mixture, dip the fish. In a skillet, heat the butter and oil until very hot and sauté the fish according to the instructions on page 74. Remove it to absorbent paper and then arrange it on a serving platter and keep it warm. When all of the fish has been cooked, season it to taste with salt and pepper, sprinkle it with parsley, and pour any remaining lemon sauce over the dish.

Serve with new potatoes, page 290.

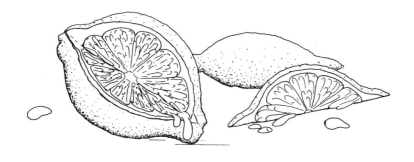

SAUTÉED SMELTS

4 servings
PREPARATION: about 15 minutes
COOKING: about 10 minutes

> 1½ **to 2 pounds dressed smelts**
> ½ **cup evaporated milk**
> ⅓ **cup cornmeal**
> ⅓ **cup flour**
> 2 **teaspoons salt**
> ¼ **teaspoon pepper**

Dip the fish in the evaporated milk. Combine and blend the dry ingredients and in the mixture, dredge the smelts.

> 4 **tablespoons butter**
> 4 **tablespoons oil**

In a skillet, heat the butter and oil until very hot and in the mixture sauté the smelts, a few at a time, according to the directions on page 74. Remove them to absorbent paper and then to a serving platter; keep them warm.

> **Fine-chopped parsley**
> **Lemon wedges**

Sprinkle the smelts with parsley and garnish the dish with lemon wedges.
   Serve with creamed spinach, page 295.
   A version of sautéed smelts from the Midwest: marinate the dressed smelts in beer, refrigerated, for 5 hours; dredge them, a few at a time, in Seasoned Flour, page 19; sauté them as directed and serve with Tartare Sauce, page 286.

SAUTÉED SQUID OR CALAMARI

4 servings
PREPARATION: about 30 minutes
COOKING: about 15 minutes

**2 pounds squid or calamari, prepared
for cooking, page 11
Seasoned Flour, page 19
Salt
Pepper**

Dredge the squid in seasoned flour; shake off any excess flour.

**Olive oil
3 large cloves garlic, peeled and sliced
lengthwise**

In a flameproof casserole (the high sides will prevent the oil from splattering), heat half an inch of olive oil and in it cook the garlic until it is browned; discard it. To the hot oil add the squid, a few pieces at a time, and sauté them for about 4 minutes, or until they are golden; turn them once. With a slotted spoon, remove them to absorbent paper and then to a heated serving plate; keep them warm until all the squid is fried.

**Fine-chopped parsley
Lemon wedges
Tartare Sauce, page 286, or other
sauce of your choice**

Serve the squid garnished with a sprinkling of parsley and accompanied by lemon wedges; offer the sauce separately.

Serve with new potatoes, page 290.

Steamed Fish

Steaming — my favorite way of cooking fish — is clean, uncomplicated, and kind to the calorie-conscious cook.

Steaming may well be a Chinese technique for cooking fish; in a country where fuel was scarce, steaming would have been economical and quick. In contemporary America, unfortunately, fish steamers are not easily found, although the Chinese and Japanese counterparts are often available in specialty stores. I use my fish poacher and raise the poaching rack about one inch above the level of the boiling water by putting two saucers under it. I also oil the rack to assure easy removal of the cooked fish.

Steamed fish is excellent as an ingredient in recipes calling for cooked fish: one pound of unsteamed fish yields two cupfuls of flaked cooked fish.

To Steam: bring the water in the steamer to a rolling boil. On the steaming rack, arrange the whole fish, the large fillet, fillets cut in serving pieces, or steaks. Measure the depth of the fish at its deepest point and allow 10 minutes of cooking time per inch of depth. Place the rack in the steamer, making sure that the boiling water does not touch the fish. Cover the steamer with a tight-fitting lid. Please note that in steaming fish it is important that the water boil briskly and that the cover of the utensil be carefully placed to retain the steam.

Serve steamed fish hot or chilled with a sauce of your choice from chapter eight.

STEAMED FISH IN CREAM SAUCE

4 servings
PREPARATION: about 20 minutes
COOKING: about 15 minutes

> *1½ pounds fish fillet cut in serving*
> *pieces or steak*
> *Salt*
> *Grinding of white pepper*

Season the fish to taste with salt and pepper. Over briskly boiling water, steam the fish, covered, according to the directions on page 82. Remove the fish to a serving platter and keep it warm. Reserve the liquid.

> *2 tablespoons butter*
> *1 scallion, trimmed and chopped fine,*
> *with some of the green*
> *1½ tablespoons flour*
> *1 cup light cream*
> *Reserved poaching liquid*
> *Salt*
> *Grinding of white pepper*
> *¼ cup fine-chopped parsley*

In a saucepan, heat the butter and in it cook the scallion until it is limp. Stir in the flour, and over gentle heat, cook the mixture for a few minutes. Gradually add the cream and then a little of the liquid, stirring constantly until the mixture is thickened and smooth and of your desired consistency. Season the sauce to taste with salt and pepper. Over the fish, pour the sauce; garnish the dish with parsley.

Serve with saffron rice, page 291.

STEAMED FISH WITH SPINACH
(Steamed Fish Florentine)

4 servings
PREPARATION: about 40 minutes
COOKING: about 15 minutes (partially in a 450° oven)

> **2 10-ounce packages fresh spinach with the woody stems removed, rinsed, wilted for 20 seconds in lightly salted boiling water to cover, pressed dry in a colander, and chopped or 2 10-ounce packages frozen chopped spinach, fully thawed to room temperature and pressed dry in a colander**

Prepare the spinach and reserve it.

> **3 tablespoons butter**
> **3 tablespoons flour**
> **½ teaspoon salt**
> **¼ teaspoon white pepper**
> **1¼ cups milk**
> **¼ cup heavy cream**

In a saucepan, heat the butter and in it, over gentle heat, cook the flour for a few minutes. Stir in the seasonings. Gradually add the milk and then the cream, stirring constantly until the mixture is thickened and smooth. Cover the sauce tightly so that it does not crust.

At this point you may stop and continue later.

> **1½ pounds fish fillet or steak**

Over briskly boiling water, steam the fish according to the directions on page 82 until it barely begins to flake. Remove it from the heat.

> **Reserved spinach**
> **Reserved sauce**
> **½ cup grated Parmesan cheese**

In a lightly buttered baking dish, arrange an even layer of the spinach. Over it, arrange the fish. Over all, spoon the sauce. Sprinkle the top with grated cheese. Bake the dish in a 450° oven for about 5 minutes, or until it has reached serving temperature and the cheese is melted.

Serve with rice, page 290.

FOUR

Fresh and Frozen Fish

Fresh fish cooked just at the time of serving, or — when a recipe permits — prepared ahead of time, affords us the greatest pleasure at table. A close runner-up, however, is frozen fish that has been given tender loving care. Both are flavorful and satisfying. In the following sections recipes are given for fresh and frozen fish; the instructions are only points of departure for your own culinary adventures. Enjoy them — fish cookery is particularly suited to experiment.

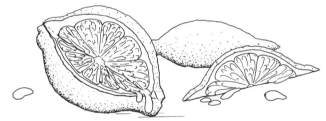

HORS D'OEUVRE AND FIRST COURSES

Hors d'oeuvre and first courses prepared from fish are attractive embellishments to the cocktail hour and tasty beginnings to the meal. In both instances they are light on the palate, stimulating rather than slaking the appetite. Many recipes offered here may be made with different kinds of fish so that a wide variety of tastes is possible. Other hors d'oeuvre and first courses are found in the sections on Canned Fish, Salted and Smoked Fish, and Clams and Mussels.

FISH AND BACON ROLLS

YIELD; about 24 rolls
PREPARATION: about 15 minutes
COOKING: about 10 minutes in a preheated broiler

1 pound fillet cut in bite-size pieces
Thin-sliced bacon

Wrap each piece of fish in a strip of bacon long enough to go around the fish twice. Arrange the rolls, seam side down, on a rack in a baking pan. Broil the rolls, turning them once, for about 10 minutes, or until the bacon is crisp. Serve this appetizer hot, speared with toothpicks to facilitate handling.

FISH CANAPÉS

YIELD: about 24 canapés
PREPARATION: about 20 minutes
COOKING: 3 minutes in a preheated broiler

The recipe may be made with any leftover cooked fish or with canned salmon or waterpack tuna.

2 tablespoons butter
2 tablespoons flour
⅔ cup Fish Stock, page 94, or clam
juice
¾ cup light cream

In a saucepan, heat the butter and in it, over gentle heat, cook the flour for a few minutes. Gradually add the fish stock, stirring constantly until the mixture is thickened and smooth. Gradually add the cream, stirring.

⅔ cup flaked cooked fish
Few drops of Tabasco sauce
2 egg yolks

To the contents of the saucepan, add the fish and Tabasco sauce, stirring to blend the mixture well. Beat in the egg yolks. Over moderate heat, cook the mixture until it thickens slightly more; do not allow it to boil.

6 to 8 slices buttered toast, cut into
squares

Spread the fish mixture on the toast pieces. Arrange them on a baking sheet and run them under the broiler for 3 minutes.

CHILLED PIKE COCKTAIL

4 to 6 servings
PREPARATION: about 25 minutes
CHILLING TIME: 3 hours

The recipe may also be made with any lean fillet.

> *2 cups water*
> *1 large clove garlic, chopped fine*
> *1 bay leaf, crumbled*
> *1½ teaspoons salt*
> *1½ pounds pike fillet*

In a saucepan, combine the water and seasonings. Bring the liquid to the boil, add the fish, reduce the heat, and simmer the fish, covered, for 8 minutes or until it flakes easily. Allow it to cool in the liquid. Remove the fish to absorbent paper; strain and reserve the liquid for use in another recipe. Flake the fish and chill it, covered, for 3 hours.

At this point you may stop and continue later.

> *Salad greens*
> *Green Mayonnaise, page 281, or Ravigote Sauce, page 285*

On individual beds of salad greens, arrange the flaked fish in equal portions. Over the fish, spoon some of the sauce of your choice; offer the remaining sauce separately.

ESCABECHE

4 to 6 servings
PREPARATION: about 30 minutes
CHILLING TIME: overnight

The recipe, of Spanish and French Provençal origin, may be made with any lean fillet.

> **2 pounds fish fillet cut in serving pieces**
> **Strained fresh lime juice**
> **Flour**
> **3 tablespoons butter**
> **3 tablespoons oil**

Dip the fish in the lime juice, turning to coat it on all sides. Reserve the lime juice. Dust the fish lightly with flour. In a skillet, heat the butter and oil; add the fish and sauté it on both sides until it is golden. Drain it on absorbent paper and then arrange it in a single layer in a baking dish two inches deep.

> **1 large clove garlic, put through a press**
> **Reserved lime juice plus additional juice to equal ⅓ cup**
> **⅓ cup olive oil**
> **⅓ cup strained fresh orange juice**
> **3 scallions, chopped fine, with as much green as is crisp**
> **Few drops of Tabasco sauce**
> **Salt**
> **Fine-chopped parsley**
> **Lemon wedges**

In a mixing bowl, combine the garlic, lime juice, olive oil, orange juice, scallions, and tabasco sauce. Stir to blend the mixture. Adjust the seasoning to taste with salt. Pour the marinade over the fish. Refrigerate the *escabeche,* covered, overnight. Serve it garnished with parsley and lemon wedges.

FISH QUICHE

6 to 8 servings as a first course
4 to 6 servings as a main dish for luncheon or supper
PREPARATION: about 25 minutes
(time does not include readying the pastry)
COOKING: 30 minutes, starting in a 450° oven

The recipe may be made with any lean fillet. If you use thawed frozen fish, pat it dry with absorbent paper and dust the bite-size pieces with flour.

> 1 unbaked 9-inch deep-dish pastry
> shell*
> Melted butter
> 1 pound fish fillet cut in bite-size pieces

Brush the pastry shell with melted butter and refrigerate it. Prepare the fish and arrange it over the bottom of the pastry shell; return it to the refrigerator.

> 5 eggs
> 1 cup light cream
> ¼ cup dry white wine
> ½ teaspoon salt
> Grinding of white pepper

In a mixing bowl, lightly beat the eggs; add the cream and blend the mixture well. Gradually add the wine, blending constantly. Stir in the salt and pepper.

> *At this point you may stop and continue later.*

> ¼ cup fine-chopped celery
> ¼ cup fine-chopped parsley
> ¼ cup grated Parmesan cheese

Over the fish, sprinkle the celery and parsley. Over all, pour the prepared custard. Sprinkle the top with the grated cheese. Bake the quiche in a 450° oven for 10 minutes; reduce the heat to 325° and continue to bake it for 20 minutes. Allow it to stand for 5 minutes before serving.

---

* Using your favorite recipe for a 9-inch quiche crust.

Fish soups and stews have a special place among my culinary favorites. They are easily made. They are flavorful. They are capable of elegance as a first course or of giving comfortable satisfaction as a main one. As meals in themselves, they are nourishing and sustaining. Accompanied by bread and salad or fruit, and perhaps a little cheese, they complete a menu leaving us well fed, but with no sense of satiety. It is for this reason that as a complement to many fish soups I suggest Casserole-baked Bread, page 288; I do so because the combination is one to which I return time and again with sure knowledge that the meal will be a pleasure. I hope you will agree.

Court Bouillon

Court bouillon is a liquid preparation for the poaching of fish and is designed to enhance the flavor of the completed dish. It also serves admirably as the basis for fish soups and sauces. When you have completed poaching fish, strain and reserve the *court bouillon,* and, if you do not intend using it in an accompanying sauce, save it for soup-making. *Court bouillon* will keep for a considerable period in the refrigerator and almost indefinitely in the freezer.

Herewith follow three *courts bouillons* that I hope you will find tasty and useful.

COURT BOUILLON I
(For fish to be served hot)

YIELD: about 4½ cups
PREPARATION: about 45 minutes

- 1 *medium carrot, scraped and sliced thin*
- 1 *large rib celery, chopped, with its leaves*
- 1 *medium onion, peeled and stuck with 2 cloves*
- 1 *bay leaf*
- 4 *parsley sprigs*
- 1½ *teaspoons tarragon*
- ½ *teaspoon thyme*
- 1 *tablespoon salt*
- 6 *peppercorns*
- 5 *cups dry white wine*

In a large saucepan, combine all of the ingredients. Bring the liquid to the boil, reduce the heat, and simmer the mixture, covered, for 30 minutes. Strain it for use as a poaching liquid, and afterward as the basis for a soup or sauce.

COURT BOUILLON II
(For fish to be served hot)

YIELD: about 6 cups
PREPARATION: about 45 minutes

- 2 medium carrots, scraped and sliced thin
- 1 clove garlic, peeled and chopped fine
- 12 scallions, trimmed and chopped, with some of the green part
- 8 sprigs parsley
- 2 bay leaves, crumbled
- ½ teaspoon thyme
- 1 tablespoon salt
- 8 peppercorns
- 5 cups water
- 1 cup dry white wine

In a large saucepan, combine all of the ingredients. Bring the liquid to the boil, reduce the heat, and simmer the mixture, covered, for 30 minutes. Strain it for use as a poaching liquid, and afterward as the basis for a soup or sauce.

COURT BOUILLON III
(For fish to be served chilled)

YIELD: about 8 cups
PREPARATION: about 1 hour

6 *cups water*
½ *cup malt vinegar*
2 *cups dry white wine*
2 *medium carrots, scraped and chopped*
1 *large rib celery, chopped, with its leaves*
2 *cloves garlic, peeled and chopped*
2 *medium onions, peeled and chopped*
1 *bay leaf*
5 *whole cloves*
4 *sprigs parsley*
½ *teaspoon thyme*
1½ *teaspoons salt*

In a large saucepan or soup kettle, combine all of the ingredients. Bring the liquid to the boil, reduce the heat, and simmer the mixture, covered, for 45 minutes. Strain it for use as a poaching liquid, and afterward as the basis for a soup or sauce.

FISH STOCK

YIELD: about 8 cups
PREPARATION: about 1 hour

A basis for fish soups and sauces.

> 2 *pounds lean fish with heads, bones, and trimmings*
> 1 *medium carrot, scraped and sliced thin*
> 1 *medium rib celery, chopped, with its leaves*
> 1 *large onion, peeled and chopped*
> **Bouquet Garni,** *page 17*
> 1 *4- or 5-inch piece of orange zest*
> 1 *teaspoon sugar*
> 2 *teaspoons salt*
> 6 *cups water*
> 2 *cups dry white wine*

In a soup kettle, combine all of the ingredients. Bring the liquid to the boil, reduce the heat, and simmer the mixture, uncovered, for 30 minutes. Strain the stock through two layers of cheesecloth; discard the residue. Allow the stock to cool before storing it.

Fumet (reduced wine-based fish stock): follow the recipe as written, using dry white wine in place of the water. Reduce the completed stock by half. Strain the *fumet* as directed and clarify it (see below). Use it as a basis for sauces and rich soups.

To Clarify Fish Stock and *Court Bouillon:* to the strained liquid, add 1 or 2 egg whites beaten with a fork in 2 tablespoons cold water; crush and add the eggshells. Over high heat, bring the liquid to the boil for 2 minutes; then, over the lowest possible heat, allow it to stand for 20 minutes. Strain the liquid through two layers of cheesecloth.

Clarifying stock and *court bouillon* is important in the making of clear soups and aspics; it is not necessary in the making of thick or cream soups and sauces.

BASQUE FISH SOUP

6 servings
PREPARATION: about 40 minutes
COOKING: 10 minutes

Soupe de poisson basquaise may be made with any lean fillet. I recommend one-half pound each of cod, haddock, halibut, and ocean perch.

¼ **cup olive oil**
3 **cloves garlic, peeled and chopped**
2 **leeks, thoroughly washed and
    chopped or 6 scallions, trimmed
    and chopped**
2 **large onions, peeled and chopped**

In a soup kettle, heat the oil and in it cook the garlic, leek, and onion until they are golden.

2 **large carrots, scraped and sliced thin**
3 **large ripe tomatoes, peeled, seeded,
    and chopped, with their liquid**
1 **bay leaf**
   Salt
   Pepper

To the contents of the soup kettle, add the carrots, stirring to coat them well. Add the tomatoes and bay leaf. Season the mixture to taste with salt and pepper.

4 **cups water**
2 **cups Fish Stock, page 94, or
    2 8-ounce bottles clam juice**
2 **cups dry white wine**

Add the water, stock, and wine. Bring the liquid to the boil, reduce the heat, and simmer the vegetables, covered, for 20 minutes.
At this point you may stop and continue later.

2 **pounds fish fillet cut in bite-size
    pieces**

Return the contents of the kettle to the boil, reduce the heat, add the fish and simmer it, covered, for 10 minutes or until it flakes easily.
Serve with casserole-baked bread, page 288.

AÏGO-SAU

6 to 8 servings
PREPARATION: about 1 hour
COOKING: 10 minutes

This Provençal soup-stew may be made with any lean fillet: it is traditionally made with cod.

> 4 *medium potatoes, peeled and cut into eighths*
> 4 *medium onions, peeled and sliced thick*
> 4 *medium carrots, scraped and cut in 1-inch rounds*
> 4 *large ribs celery, trimmed and cut in 1-inch pieces*
> 2 *green peppers, seeded and chopped coarse*
> 1 *32-ounce can Italian tomatoes*
> 1 *4-ounce jar pimientos, chopped*
> 3 *large cloves garlic, peeled and chopped fine*
> 2 *bay leaves*
> 6 *sprigs parsley*
> 1 *teaspoon oregano*
> *Grated rind of 1 orange*
> 1 *tablespoon sugar*
> 2 *teaspoons salt*
> ½ *teaspoon pepper*
> ⅓ *cup olive oil*
> *Boiling water*

In a large soup kettle, layer the ingredients in the order listed. Add boiling water to the top of the carrot layer. Bring the liquid to a second boil, reduce the heat, and simmer the vegetables, covered, for 40 minutes.

At this point you may stop and continue later.

> 2½ *pounds fish fillet cut in bite-size pieces*
> *Paprika*
> *Fine-chopped parsley*
> *Rouille, page 284*

To the contents of the kettle, add the fish and continue to simmer the *aïgo-sau*, covered, for 10 minutes, or until the fish flakes easily. Garnish the soup with a sprinkling of paprika and a generous amount of parsley. Serve it accompanied by a bowl of *rouille*.

Serve with casserole-baked bread, page 288.

BAKED FISH CHOWDER

6 servings
PREPARATION: about 25 minutes
COOKING: 1 hour in a 350° oven

4 *medium potatoes, peeled and cut in large dice*
4 *medium onions, peeled and chopped coarse*
2 *pounds fish fillet cut in bite-size pieces*

Prepare the potatoes and cover them with cold water to prevent their discoloring. Prepare the onions and fish. Ready the remaining ingredients and the casserole.

At this point you may stop and continue later.

Butter
1 **bay leaf**
½ **teaspoon celery seed**
Salt
Pepper
6 **cups hot milk**
Fine-chopped parsley

Butter a large casserole or baking dish. In it, arrange a layer of the potato, drained, and of onion; dot the onion with butter and season it with celery seed, salt, and pepper. Add the bay leaf. Arrange the fish in a single layer and season it with salt and pepper. Add, in order, the remaining potato and onion; dot the onion layer with butter and season it lightly with salt and pepper. Add the milk. Bake the chowder, uncovered, at 350° for 1 hour, or until the fish flakes easily and the potato is tender. Garnish the chowder with a sprinkling of parsley.

Serve with casserole-baked bread, page 288.

BOUILLABAISSE

6 to 8 servings
PREPARATION: about 40 minutes
COOKING: about 10 minutes

The celebrated soup-stew from Marseilles can only be made on Mediterranean shores, where important ingredients are native. Mentioned by Pliny and probably by every gastronome since, *bouillabaisse* is a delicious one-dish meal. This recipe is my adaptation of the famous dish, which I make with an assortment of any lean fillets.

> ⅓ *cup olive oil*
> 3 *large onions, peeled and chopped*
> 4 *large cloves garlic, peeled and put through a press*
> 1 *6-ounce can tomato paste*

In a soup kettle, heat the oil and in it cook the onion until it is barely golden. Add the garlic and tomato paste; cook the mixture, stirring, for 5 minutes.

> 2 *bay leaves*
> *Zest of 1 medium orange*
> 8 *parsley sprigs, tied together*
> 2 *pinches saffron*
> 2 *teaspoons sugar*
> 6 *cups Fish Stock, page 94, or 4 cups Fish Stock, 1 8-ounce bottle clam juice, and 1 cup dry white wine*
> *Salt*
> *Pepper*

Into the contents of the kettle, stir the seasonings. Add the liquid; bring it to the boil, reduce the heat, and simmer the mixture, covered, for 30 minutes. Season the broth to taste with salt and pepper.
At this point you may stop and continue later.

> 3 *to 4 pounds assorted fish fillet cut in bite-size pieces*

To the simmering broth, add the fish and cook it, uncovered, for about 10 minutes or until it flakes easily; do not overcook it.

> **Toasted rounds of French bread**
> **Rouille,** *page 284 (optional)*

Serve the soup over the toast; pass the *rouille* separately.

Serve with mixed green salad, page 295.

CODFISH STEW

6 servings

PREPARATION: about 45 minutes

The recipe may also be made with any lean fish. A delicately flavored soup suitable as a first or main course.

1½ pounds cod fillet steamed as di-
rected on page 82

With the tines of a fork, flake the fillets. Reserve the fish.

3 tablespoons butter
1 medium onion, peeled and chopped
fine

In the top of a double boiler over direct heat, melt the butter and in it cook the onion until it is golden

2 bay leaves
1¼ teaspoons paprika
1½ teaspoons Worcestershire sauce
2 cups (2 8-ounce bottles) clam juice

Add the bay leaves; stir in the paprika and Worcestershire sauce. Add the clam juice. Bring the liquid to the boil, reduce the heat, and simmer the mixture, covered, for 10 minutes.

At this point you may stop and continue later.

1 cup light cream or half-and-half
Reserved fish
Salt
Grinding of white pepper
Fine-chopped parsley

Place the top of the double boiler over boiling water. Add the cream, stirring. Add the reserved fish, stirring until the stew reaches serving temperature. Season it to taste with salt and pepper; garnish it with parsley.

Serve with muffins, page 289.

BOURRIDE
(France)

6 servings
PREPARATION: about 25 minutes
COOKING: 25 minutes

The celebrated stew from Provence may be made with any lean fillet. Because there are nearly as many recipes for *bourride* as there are for *bouillabaisse,* the present recipe does not pretend to be definitive.

> 1 *medium carrot, scraped and sliced thin*
> 1 *large onion, chopped*
> 4 *sprigs parsley*
> 2 *tablespoons cider vinegar*
> 4 *cups water*
> 1 *cup dry white wine*
> 1 *bay leaf*
> 1 *teaspoon salt*
> *Grinding of pepper*

In a soup kettle, combine these nine ingredients. Bring the liquid to the boil and cook the mixture, uncovered, for 10 minutes.

> 2 *pounds fish fillet cut in six serving portions*

Reduce the heat, add the fish, and cook it, uncovered, for 5 to 8 minutes, or until it just flakes; do not overcook it. With a slotted spoon, remove the fish; keep it warm. Over high heat, reduce the broth to 2½ cups.

> 3 *egg yolks*
> *Reduced broth*

In the top of a double boiler, lightly beat the egg yolks. Whisk in the reserved broth, and over simmering water stir it until the mixture thickens somewhat.

> 1 *cup* Aioli, *page 281*

Add the *aioli,* and with a rotary beater blend the mixture well.

> 6 *large slices French bread, toasted*
> *Additional* aioli

In each of six heated soup plates, arrange a slice of the toast, then a piece of the fish; ladle the broth over all. Offer additional *aioli* separately.
Serve with mixed green salad, page 295.

CIOPPINO

6 servings
PREPARATION: about 45 minutes
(time does not include readying the clams, page 232)
COOKING: 10 minutes

A Californian fish soup originating with the Portuguese fishermen living there, *cioppino* is subject to as many variations as there are cooks to prepare it. The present recipe, which may be made with any fillet, is simplified by the omission of the customary shellfish.

> **3 cloves garlic, peeled and chopped**
> **1 large onion, peeled and chopped**
> **¼ cup chopped parsley**
> **4 tablespoons olive oil**

In a large saucepan combine these four ingredients, and over moderate heat, cook them until the onion is golden.

> **½ cup dry sherry**
> **1 28-ounce can Italian tomatoes**
> **2 cups water**
> **½ teaspoon marjoram**
> **¾ teaspoon oregano**
> **1 teaspoon salt**
> **Grinding of pepper**

To the contents of the saucepan, add these seven ingredients. Bring the liquid to the boil, reduce the heat, and simmer the mixture for 20 minutes, stirring frequently to break up the tomatoes.

> *At this point you may stop and continue later.*

> **12 hard-shell clams, prepared for cooking**
> **2 pounds fish fillet cut in bite-size pieces**

To the simmering contents of the saucepan, add the clams and fish. Continue to simmer the *cioppino,* covered, for 10 minutes, or until the fish flakes easily and the clams have opened.

If desired, 2 6½-ounce cans minced clams and their liquid may be substituted for the fresh clams; add the canned clams just before serving the soup.

Serve with casserole-baked bread, page 288.

COTRIADE

14 servings
PREPARATION: about 45 minutes
COOKING: 16 minutes

The celebrated fish stew from Brittany cannot be made for only a few servings; because it is truly a one-dish meal, it is ideal for an informal supper party. When buying the fish, ask your fishmonger to fillet as many of them as possible; use the heads, tails, and bones to make another soup. The eel and sardines, of course, cannot be filleted.

> *1 pound each of the following fish:*
> *cod*
> *conger eel*
> *halibut*
> *mackerel*
> *mullet*
> *sardines*

The eel must be skinned; the sardines must be fresh. Cut the fish in bite-size pieces and reserve them.

> *½ cup lard*
> *3 large cloves garlic, peeled and chopped fine*
> *2 large onions, peeled and chopped*

In a soup kettle, melt the lard and in it cook the garlic and onion until the onion is golden.

> *6 medium potatoes, peeled and cut in quarters*
> *2 bay leaves*
> *6 sprigs parsley*
> *½ teaspoon thyme*
> *8 cups boiling water*

To the contents of the kettle, add the potato and seasonings. Pour in the boiling water and simmer the potato, covered, for 5 minutes.

> *At this point you may stop and continue later.*

(If you do so, remove the cover from the kettle to prevent the potato from going mushy.)

> *Reserved eel, halibut, mackerel, and mullet*

To the simmering contents of the kettle, add these four fish and cook them, uncovered, for 8 minutes.

Reserved cod and sardines

Add the cod and sardines and continue simmering the *cotriade* for 8 minutes, or until the fish flakes easily and the potato is tender. With a slotted spoon, remove the fish and potato to serving dishes. Strain the broth and offer it separately.

Strained juice of 2 lemons
½ cup olive oil
Salt
Pepper

Season the fish and potato with lemon juice, olive oil, and salt and pepper.
Serve with casserole-baked bread, page 288.

CREOLE FISH STEW

6 servings
PREPARATION: about 45 minutes
COOKING: 10 minutes

The recipe may be made with any fillet.

3 tablespoons butter
2 cloves garlic, peeled and chopped fine
3 medium onions, peeled and chopped

In a soup kettle or large saucepan, heat the butter and in it cook the garlic and onion until translucent.

2 tablespoons flour
2 teaspoons curry powder

Into the onion stir the flour, and over gentle heat, cook the mixture for a few minutes. Stir in the curry powder.

1 28-ounce can Italian tomatoes
2 bay leaves
6 cloves
½ teaspoons thyme
A few drops of Tabasco sauce
1 teaspoon salt
2 cups water

Add the tomatoes, seasonings, and water. Bring the liquid to the boil, reduce the heat, and simmer the mixture, covered, for 30 minutes.
At this point you may stop and continue later.

2 pounds fish fillet cut in bite-size pieces
½ cup dry sherry
Fine-chopped parsley

To the simmering contents of the kettle, add the fish; continue to simmer the stew, covered, for 10 minutes, or until the fish flakes easily. Gently stir in the sherry. Serve the stew garnished with parsley.

Serve with casserole-baked bread, page 288.

FISH SOUP WITH CURRY

6 servings
PREPARATION: about 45 minutes
COOKING: 10 minutes

> **3 tablespoons butter**
> **1 large onion, peeled and chopped fine**
> **1 tablespoon curry powder (preferably sweet Madras curry)**

In a large saucepan, heat the butter and in it cook the onion until it is translucent. Stir in the curry powder.

> **2 large ripe tomatoes, peeled, seeded, and chopped**
> **2 cups Fish Stock, page 94, or 1 cup (1 8-ounce bottle) clam juice and 1 cup dry white wine**

Add the tomatoes and fish stock. Bring the liquid to the boil, reduce the heat, and simmer the mixture, partially covered, for 15 minutes.

> **1½ cups half-and-half**
> **1 large potato, peeled and diced**

Add the cream and potato. Simmer the potato for 15 minutes, or until it is tender.

At this point you may stop and continue later.

> **2 pounds fish fillet cut in bite-size pieces**
> **Salt**
> **Pepper**
> **Fine-chopped parsley**

To the simmering contents of the saucepan, add the fish and continue to simmer the soup, covered, for 10 minutes, or until the fish flakes easily. Adjust the seasoning to taste with salt and pepper. Serve the soup garnished with chopped parsley.

Serve with muffins, page 289.

FISH-BALL SOUP

6 servings
PREPARATION: about 45 minutes
COOKING: 25 minutes

The recipe may be made with any lean fillet.

> *2 large ribs celery with their tops,*
> *chopped*
> *1 pound fish parts: heads, bones, etc.*
> *1 large onion, chopped*
> *6 sprigs parsley*
> *1 bay leaf*
> *½ teaspoon peppercorns*
> *4 cups water*

In a soup kettle, combine these seven ingredients. Bring the liquid to the boil, reduce the heat, and simmer the broth, covered, for 30 minutes. Strain it through a fine sieve and discard the residue. While the broth is simmering, prepare the fish balls, potato, and *béchamel.*

> *1½ pounds fish fillet cut into small*
> *pieces*

To the container of a food processor equipped with the steel blade, add the fish, a few pieces at a time, until it is reduced to a smooth paste.

> *2 tablespoons cracker crumbs*
> *1 egg*
> *¼ cup fine-chopped parsley*
> *¼ teaspoon ground mace*
> *1 teaspoon salt*

With the motor running, add to the contents of the processor these five ingredients. Whirl the mixture until it is well blended. Shape it into 12 balls.

> *3 large potatoes, peeled and diced*

Prepare the potatoes and cover them with cold water to prevent their discoloring.

> *3 tablespoons butter*
> *3 tablespoons flour*
> *4 cups milk*

In a saucepan, heat the butter and in it, over gentle heat, cook the flour for a few minutes. Gradually add the milk, stirring constantly until the mixture is thickened and smooth. Reserve the *béchamel*.

At this point you may stop and continue later.

Fine-chopped parsley

Return the strained broth to the boil. Add the fish balls and potato. Reduce the heat and simmer them for 20 minutes, or until the potato is tender. Stir in the *béchamel*, bring the soup to serving temperature, and garnish it with parsley.

Serve with muffins, page 289.

PORTUGUESE FISH SOUP

6 servings
PREPARATION: about 45 minutes
COOKING: 8 to 10 minutes

> ½ cup olive oil
> 3 large onions, peeled and chopped
> 6 large ripe tomatoes, peeled, seeded, and chopped
> 1 cup chopped parsley
> 2 cups Fish Stock, page 94, or 2 cups (2 8-ounce bottles) clam juice
> 1 cup dry white wine
> 1 bay leaf
> 1 teaspoon crushed red pepper flakes
> Salt
> Grinding of pepper

In a soup kettle, heat the oil and in it cook the onion until it is golden brown. Add the remaining ingredients, bring the liquid to the boil, reduce the heat, and simmer the mixture, covered, for 30 minutes. Season the mixture to taste with salt and pepper.

At this point you may stop and continue later.

> 2 pounds fish fillet cut in bite-size pieces

To the simmering contents of the kettle, add the fish and cook it, uncovered, for 8 to 10 minutes, or until it flakes easily.

Serve with casserole-baked bread, page 288.

HALIBUT AND PRUNE SOUP
(Ireland)

6 servings
PREPARATION: about 35 minutes

The recipe may also be made with any lean fillet.

24 tenderized pitted prunes
6 cups water
2 tablespoons cider vinegar
2 bay leaves, crumbled
¾ teaspoon powdered thyme
1 tablespoon salt

In a soup kettle, combine these 6 ingredients and boil them, covered, for 5 minutes.

4 tablespoons soft butter
4 tablespoons flour

In a small mixing bowl, combine the butter and flour to make *beurre manié,* blending with a fork until the mixture is homogenous. Bring the liquid in the saucepan to the boil, add the *beurre manié,* and stir constantly until the mixture is thickened and smooth.

2½ pounds halibut fillet cut in large bite-size pieces

To the boiling liquid, add the fish, reduce the heat, and simmer it for 5 minutes.

1 cup light cream or milk
Grated rind and strained juice of 1 small lemon
Sugar
Salt
White pepper

Into the contents of the saucepan, stir the cream and the lemon rind and juice. Stir the soup gently to blend it well. Adjust the seasoning to taste with sugar, salt, and pepper.

Serve with casserole-baked bread, page 288.

HUNGARIAN CARP SOUP

6 servings
PREPARATION: about 45 minutes
COOKING: 8 to 10 minutes

Ask the fishmonger to fillet a 2½-pound carp, reserving the head and bones.

> *Reserved fish head and bones*
> 2 *cloves garlic, peeled and chopped*
> 1 *green pepper, seeded and diced*
> 3 *onions, peeled and chopped*
> 4 *ripe tomatoes, quartered*
> 2 *bay leaves*
> 1½ *teaspoons salt*
> 8 *peppercorns*
> 8 *cups water*

In a soup kettle, combine these ten ingredients. Bring the liquid to the boil, reduce the heat, and simmer the mixture, covered, for 30 minutes. Strain the broth and return it to the kettle; discard the residue.

> 1 *tablespoon sweet Hungarian paprika*
> *Few drops of Tabasco sauce*
> *Salt*

To a little of the broth, add the paprika, stirring until the mixture is smooth; add it to the contents of the kettle, stirring. Season the broth to taste with Tabasco sauce and salt. Simmer the broth for 5 minutes to meld its flavors.

At this point you may stop and continue later.

> *Reserved carp fillet, cut in bite-size pieces*
> ¼ *cup fine-chopped parsley*

To the simmering broth, add the fish and cook it for 8 to 10 minutes, or until it flakes easily. Just before serving, stir in the parsley.

Serve with casserole-baked bread, page 288.

HUNGARIAN FISH CHOWDER

4 to 6 servings
PREPARATION: 1 hour
COOKING: about 10 minutes

The soup is traditionally made with any lean freshwater fish.

> **3 tablespoons butter**
> **2 medium carrots, scraped and sliced thin**
> **2 medium ribs celery, chopped**
> **3 medium onions, peeled and chopped**
> **¾ teaspoon sweet paprika**

In a soup kettle, heat the butter and in it cook the vegetables until the onion is translucent. Stir in the paprika and continue to cook the mixture for a few minutes.

> **2 pounds freshwater fish trimmings (heads, bones, etc.)**
> **Bouquet Garni, *page 17***
> **½ cup dry white wine**
> **Water**
> **Salt**

To the contents of the kettle, add the fish trimmings, *bouquet garni,* wine, and water to cover. Bring the liquid to the boil, reduce the heat, and simmer the mixture, covered, for 30 minutes. Strain the liquid and return it to a clean kettle; discard the residue. Season the broth to taste with salt.

> **½ cup cut green beans**
> **½ cup thin-sliced scraped carrots**
> **½ cup chopped onion**
> **½ cup green peas**

To the broth, add the vegetables and simmer them, uncovered, for 15 minutes, or until the carrot is tender.

> **1½ pounds freshwater fish fillet, cut in bite-size pieces**
> **Salt**
> **Pepper**
> **Fine-chopped parsley**

Add the fish and simmer the chowder for 10 minutes, or until the fish flakes easily. Adjust the seasoning to taste with salt and pepper. Serve the chowder garnished with chopped parsley.

Serve with casserole-baked bread, page 288.

MEXICAN FISH SOUP

6 servings
PREPARATION: about 1 hour
COOKING: 8 to 10 minutes

¼ cup olive oil
2 cloves garlic, peeled and chopped fine
4 large onions, peeled and chopped
1 32-ounce can Italian tomatoes
½ cup dry white wine
Bouquet Garni, page 17
1 tablespoon chili powder

In a soup kettle, heat the olive oil and in it cook the garlic and onion until golden brown. Add the tomatoes, wine, and seasonings, and cook the mixture, uncovered, until it is thick. Discard the *bouquet garni*.

3 cups water
4 tablespoons flour
3 cups (3 8-ounce bottles) clam juice

Into 1 cup of the water, stir the flour until the mixture is smooth. To the contents of the soup kettle, add the remaining water and clam juice. Add the flour mixture, and over high heat cook the soup, stirring, until it is slightly thickened.

At this point you may stop and continue later.

6 serving portions of fish fillet

To the simmering contents of the kettle, add the fish pieces; cook them, uncovered, for 8 to 10 minutes, or until they flake easily.

6 slices toast
Fine-chopped parsley

In heated bowls, arrange toast. With a slotted spoon, add a piece of the fish. Ladle the broth over the fish and garnish the soup with parsley.

Serve with mixed green salad, page 295.

NEW ENGLAND FISH CHOWDER

6 servings
PREPARATION: about 45 minutes
COOKING: 10 minutes

The recipe may be made with any lean fillet, saltwater or freshwater.

¼ pound salt pork, diced

In a 5-quart flameproof casserole, render the salt pork until it is golden and crisp. With a slotted spoon remove it to absorbent paper and reserve it.

2 large onions, peeled and chopped

In the fat, cook the onion until it is golden.

**2 large ribs celery, trimmed and
chopped**
3 medium potatoes, peeled and diced

Add the celery and potato, stirring to coat them well.

2 cups water
1 bay leaf
1 teaspoon salt
Grinding of pepper

Add the water and seasonings. Bring the liquid to the boil, reduce the heat, and simmer the vegetables, covered, for 10 minutes. Meanwhile, ready the milk and prepare the *beurre manié,* if desired.
At this point you may stop and continue later.

4 cups milk
2 tablespoons soft butter (optional)
2 tablespoons flour (optional)

Scald the milk. In a small mixing bowl, combine the butter and flour, blending them with a fork until the mixture is smooth. To the milk, add this *beurre manié,* stirring constantly until the mixture is slightly thickened and smooth. Return the contents of the casserole to the boil.

**2 pounds fish fillet cut in bite-size
pieces**
Reserved milk
Reserved salt pork
Fine-chopped parsley

To the casserole add the fish, reduce the heat, and simmer uncovered for 10 minutes, or until the fish flakes easily. Add the milk, stirring to blend the chowder. Serve the soup garnished with the salt pork and a generous sprinkling of parsley.

Serve with casserole-baked bread, page 288.

WEST INDIAN FISH CHOWDER

6 servings
PREPARATION: about 45 minutes
COOKING: about 10 minutes

½ cup olive oil
2 cloves garlic, peeled and chopped fine
2 medium onions, peeled and chopped
1 cup raw natural rice

In a soup kettle, heat the olive oil and in it cook the garlic and onion until translucent. Add the rice, stirring to coat each grain.

2 cups fine-shredded cabbage
3 medium potatoes, peeled and diced
2 large ripe tomatoes, peeled, seeded, and chopped
3 cups (3 8-ounce bottles) clam juice
3 cups water

To the contents of the kettle, add these ingredients. Bring the liquid to the boil, reduce the heat, and simmer the mixture, covered, for 20 minutes, or until the potato is tender; do not overcook it.

At this point you may stop and continue later.

2 pounds fish fillet cut in bite-size pieces
Salt
Grinding of pepper

To the simmering contents of the kettle, add the fish and cook it, uncovered, for 8 minutes, or until it flakes easily. Season the chowder to taste with salt and pepper.

Serve with casserole-baked bread, page 288.

FISH WITH PINEAPPLE
(Cambodia)

6 servings
PREPARATION: about 30 minutes
COOKING: 5 to 8 minutes

The stew may be made with any lean fillet. The subtle melding of flavors — fish, fruit, and spices — makes this soup rather elegant; traditionally it is served in deep bowls over cooked rice.

> *4 tablespoons vegetable oil*
> *2 cloves garlic, peeled and chopped fine*
> *2 medium onions, peeled and chopped fine*
> *1 small green pepper, seeded and diced*

In a flameproof casserole or wok, heat the oil and in it cook the garlic, onion, and pepper until the onion is translucent.

> *Grated rind and strained juice of 1 large orange*
> *1 20-ounce can unsweetened crushed pineapple, with its liquid*
> *½ cup sake (rice wine) or dry sherry*
> *6 cups water*
> *1 large bay leaf, crumbled*
> *½ teaspoon cumin seeds*
> *½ teaspoon dried pepper flakes*
> *¾ teaspoon saffron, crumbled*

To the contents of the casserole, add these nine ingredients. Bring the liquid to the boil, reduce the heat, and simmer the broth, covered, for 15 minutes.

> *At this point you may stop and continue later.*

> *2½ pounds fish fillet cut in bite-size pieces*

To the simmering broth, add the fish. Cook it, uncovered, for 5 to 8 minutes, or until it just begins to flake.

> *2½ tablespoons soy sauce*
> *3 tablespoons cornstarch*

Into the soy sauce, stir the cornstarch. When the mixture is smooth, add it to the contents of the casserole, stirring gently until the soup thickens slightly.

Serve with rice, page 290.

FISH SOUP WITH WATERCRESS

4 to 6 servings
PREPARATION: about 35 minutes

The recipe, of Philippine origin, may be made with any lean or fat fillet; it is traditionally made with mackerel.

> 1 large clove garlic, peeled and chopped fine
> 3 medium onions, peeled and sliced thin
> 1 bay leaf
> 1 teaspoon chili powder
> ½ to ¾ teaspoon red pepper flakes
> 3 cups (3 8-ounce bottles) clam juice
> 2 cups water

In a large saucepan, combine these seven ingredients; bring them to the boil, reduce the heat, and simmer them, covered, for 10 minutes.

> 1½ pounds fish fillet cut in bite-size pieces

Add the fish and simmer it, uncovered, for 10 minutes, or until it flakes easily.

> 1 large bunch watercress, the woody stems removed, rinsed, and chopped coarse
> Salt
> Grinding of pepper

Add the watercress and season the soup to taste with salt and pepper.
Serve with casserole-baked bread, page 288.

The greater part of fresh and frozen fish cookery, as we have seen, depends — with exception made for some specific recipes, of which, shamelessly, I give my favorites — upon preparing fish simply, by baking, broiling, deep frying, charcoal grilling, poaching, sautéing, and steaming. The cooked fish is embellished at your discretion by the addition of a sauce or by some garnish, such as chopped parsley or lemon wedges. Recipes using these various techniques are given in chapter three, under the section "The Methods Illustrated."

If I personally prefer this treatment, I readily add that fish lends itself deliciously to the making of composed dishes of various kinds: casseroles, loaves, soufflés, and so forth. I again admit to including here my favorite fish dishes; there are many others, variations on these as well as different ones entirely. Because the scope of the book does not permit an all-embracing catalog of recipes made with fish as the principal ingredient, they have had to be omitted. The recipes that I do offer I hope you will find easy and fun to make, and a pleasure to eat.

Flaked cooked fish is a principal ingredient in several of these composed recipes. Poached or steamed fish (I prefer the latter) is especially satisfactory used this way. One pound of raw fish yields two cups of flaked cooked fish. Prepare the fish according to the instructions for poaching, page 59, or steaming, page 82; cool and refrigerate it (it may be kept, well covered, for three or four days), and flake it just before using.

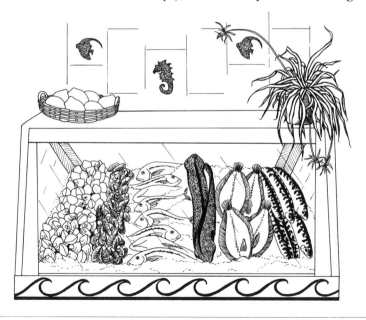

FISH-FILLED CRÊPES

4 servings
PREPARATION: about 30 minutes
(time does not include readying the crêpes, which may be made well in advance with the next recipe and frozen)
COOKING: about 12 minutes in a 400° oven

The recipe may be made with any lean fillet; it may also be offered as a first course.

> 2 *eggs*
> 1 *cup ricotta cheese*
> ½ *cup grated Parmesan cheese*
> 1 *small onion, peeled and grated*
> 2 *cups cooked flaked fish (1 pound uncooked)*
> *Salt*
> *Grinding of white pepper*

In a mixing bowl, beat the eggs lightly. Add the ricotta and Parmesan cheeses and blend the mixture well. When it is smooth, stir in the onion and prepared fish. Season the mixture to taste with salt and pepper.

> *12 prepared crêpes, see below*

Spread the filling in equal amounts on each crêpe. Roll and arrange crêpes seam side down in a lightly buttered ovenproof serving dish.

> *2 cups Mornay Sauce, page 281*

Prepare the sauce and spoon it evenly over the crêpes.
At this point you may stop and continue later.
(If you plan to continue later, cover the dish well with plastic wrap.)

Bake the crêpes, uncovered, at 400° for 12 minutes, or until the sauce is bubbly.

Serve with green peas, page 294.

If desired, ¼ to ⅓ cup fine-chopped parsley may be added to the fish filling.

CRÊPES

18 crêpes
PREPARATION: about 1 hour
STANDING TIME: 2 hours

2 *eggs*
¾ *cup milk*
¾ *cup water*
1½ *cups flour*
½ *teaspoon salt*
5 *tablespoons melted butter*

In the container of a blender, combine the first five ingredients. On medium speed, whirl them until the mixture is smooth. Use a rubber spatula to dislodge any flour that may stick to the sides of the container. With the motor running, add the butter and whirl the batter for an additional 20 seconds. Allow it to stand for 2 hours.

With soft butter, lightly grease a 5- or 6-inch skillet or crêpe pan. Set the skillet over medium-high heat. When it is very hot, add sufficient batter only to cover the bottom of the utensil (about 3 tablespoons); tilt the pan to spread the batter evenly. Cook the crêpe as you would a pancake, turning it once with a spatula.

To Store Crêpes: separate them with sheets of waxed paper, wrap the bundle in plastic, and place it in the freezer (crêpes may be kept this way for long periods).

FISH CROQUETTES

6 servings
PREPARATION: about 35 minutes
(time does not include readying the fish, page 59 or 82)
CHILLING TIME: 4 hours
COOKING: about 10 minutes in 375° deep fat

The recipe may be made with any lean fillet.

3 *cups flaked cooked fish (1½ pounds uncooked)*

Prepare the fish and reserve it.

5 *tablespoons butter*
5 *tablespoons flour*

¾ **teaspoon salt**
½ **teaspoon white pepper**
1½ **cups milk**
2 **tablespoons grated onion**
¼ **cup fine-chopped parsley**
1 **teaspoon vinegar**

In a saucepan, heat the butter and in it, over gentle heat, cook the flour for a few minutes. Stir in the salt and pepper. Gradually add the milk, stirring constantly until the mixture is thickened and smooth (this *béchamel* will be very thick). Stir in the onion, parsley, and vinegar.

Reserved fish

Add the fish and stir to blend the mixture well. Chill it for at least 3 hours. Shape the dough into twelve cone-shaped croquettes.

Bread crumbs
1 **egg, beaten with 2 tablespoons cold water**

Roll the croquettes in the bread crumbs, then in the egg and once again in the crumbs. Chill them for 1 hour.

Dill Sauce I, page 278, or Mousseline Sauce, page 282

Fry the croquettes in deep fat at 375° for 8 minutes, or until they are golden brown. Drain them on absorbent paper; keep them warm on a serving plate in the oven until all twelve have been cooked. Offer the sauce of your choice separately.

Serve with green peas, page 294.

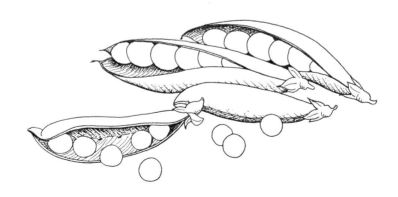

FISH FRITTERS

4 servings
PREPARATION: about 20 minutes
(time does not include readying the fish, page 59 or 82)
COOKING: about 5 minutes in 375° deep fat

1 cup flour
1½ teaspoons baking powder
½ teaspoon sweet paprika
1 teaspoon salt
Grinding of white pepper

In a mixing bowl, combine and blend the dry ingredients.

2 egg yolks
¾ cup milk
2 tablespoons melted butter
2 cups flaked cooked fish (1 pound uncooked)

Beat together the egg yolks and milk; add the mixture to the flour mixture above, stirring to assure a smooth batter. Stir in the butter and then the fish; stir to blend the mixture well.

At this point you may stop and continue later.

2 egg whites, beaten until stiff but not dry

Into the batter, fold the egg white. Cook the fritters by dropping table-spoonfuls of the batter into deep fat at 375°. Cook only a few at a time, allowing the fat to return to cooking temperature after each group of fritters. Drain the cooked fritters on absorbent paper and then keep them warm on a heated serving platter in a low oven.

Fine-chopped parsley
Marinara Sauce, page 280

When the cooking is completed, garnish the serving plate with parsley. Offer the marinara sauce separately.

Serve with spinach and mushroom salad, page 298.

FISH LOAF I

4 to 6 servings
PREPARATION: about 20 minutes
(time does not include readying the fish, page 59 or 82)
COOKING: about 40 minutes in a 375° oven

> 2 cups cooked flaked fish (1 pound uncooked)
> 1 cup bread crumbs
> 1 medium rib celery, chopped fine
> 1 medium onion, peeled and chopped fine
> ¼ cup fine-chopped parsley
> ½ medium green pepper, chopped fine
> ½ teaspoon tarragon, crumbled
> ¾ teaspoon salt
> Grinding of white pepper

In a mixing bowl, using two forks, lightly toss together these ingredients to blend them well.

> 2 egg yolks
> ½ cup milk
> 6 tablespoons melted butter

Beat together the egg yolks and milk. Add the mixture to the contents of the bowl, together with the melted butter; stir to blend the batter well.
At this point you may stop and continue later.

> 2 egg whites, beaten until stiff but not dry
> Cucumber Sauce, page 277

Into the batter, fold the egg whites. Using a rubber spatula, transfer the mixture to a well-buttered 9-by-5 loaf pan; set this in a pan of hot water and bake the fish loaf at 375° for 40 minutes, or until it is set. Allow it to stand for a few minutes before turning it onto a heated serving dish. Offer the cucumber sauce separately.

Serve with spinach and mushroom salad, page 298.

FISH LOAF II

4 to 6 servings
PREPARATION: about 25 minutes
(time does not include readying the fish, page 59 or 82)
COOKING: 35 minutes in a 375° oven

> **2 cups flaked cooked fish (1 pound uncooked)**
> **1 cup chopped toasted almonds (toast slivered almonds on a cookie sheet in a 350° oven for 5 to 8 minutes, or until they are a deep gold color; crush them once with a rolling pin)**
> **1 cup bread crumbs**
> **¼ cup fine-chopped parsley**
> **4 scallions trimmed and chopped fine, with as much green as is crisp**

In a mixing bowl, using two forks, toss these ingredients to blend them well.

> **3 egg yolks, lightly beaten**
> **Salt**
> **Grinding of white pepper**

Add the egg yolks, stirring to blend the mixture well. Season it to taste with salt and pepper.

At this point you may stop and continue later.

> **3 egg whites, beaten until stiff but not dry**

Into the batter, fold the egg whites. Using a rubber spatula, transfer the mixture to a well-buttered 1-quart mold. Set the mold in a pan of hot water and bake the fish loaf at 375° for 35 minutes, or until it is set. Allow it to stand for a few minutes before turning it onto a heated serving dish.

Serve with chopped spinach, page 294.

FISH LOAF III

4 servings
PREPARATION: about 20 minutes
(time does not include readying the fish, page 59 or 82)
COOKING: 25 minutes in a 375° oven

The recipe may be made with any lean fillet.

3 *tablespoons butter*
3 *tablespoons flour*
½ *teaspoon nutmeg*
1½ *teaspoons salt*
½ *teaspoon white pepper*
1 *cup milk*
2 *cups cooked flaked fish (1 pound uncooked)*
¼ *cup fine-chopped parsley*

In a saucepan, heat the butter and in it, over gentle heat, cook the flour for a few minutes. Stir in the seasonings. Gradually add the milk, stirring constantly until the mixture is thickened and smooth (it will be very thick). Stir in the fish and parsley.

1 *egg*
4 *egg yolks (refrigerate or freeze the whites for some other dish)*

Beat together the egg and egg yolks until light. Add them to the fish mixture, stirring to blend it well.

At this point you may stop and continue later.

Using a rubber spatula, transfer the mixture to a well-buttered straight-sided 1-quart casserole. Set the casserole in a pan of hot water and bake the fish loaf at 375° for 25 minutes, or until it is just set. Allow it to stand for a few minutes before turning it onto a heated serving dish.

Serve with Brussels sprouts, page 293.

FISH AND MACARONI CASSEROLE

4 to 6 servings
PREPARATION: about 45 minutes
COOKING: 20 minutes in a 425° oven

The recipe may be made with any lean fillet.

1 cup elbow macaroni

In lightly salted boiling water, cook the macaroni *al dente* according to the directions on the package; do not overcook it. Drain the pasta in a colander and rinse it with boiling water; reserve it.

1½ pounds fish fillet
2 cups Court Bouillon, *page 90*

Poach the fish in the *court bouillon* until it just barely flakes. Remove the poacher from the heat and allow the fish to cool, uncovered, in the liquid. Drain the fish and cut it in bite-size pieces; strain and reserve the liquid.

3 tablespoons butter
4 tablespoons flour
1 teaspoon salt
½ teaspoon white pepper
½ cup light cream
1½ cups reserved fish liquid
1 egg yolk

In a saucepan, heat the butter and in it, over gentle heat, cook the flour for a few minutes. Stir in the salt and pepper. Combine the cream and fish liquid. Gradually add the mixture, stirring constantly until the *béchamel* is thickened and smooth. Beat in the egg yolk.

Grated Parmesan cheese

In a lightly buttered 2-quart casserole, arrange a layer of the macaroni. Sprinkle it with grated cheese. Add a layer of the fish. Over it, spoon some of the sauce. Add a sprinkling of grated cheese. Repeat the layering, ending with macaroni, sauce, and a sprinkling of cheese.

At this point you may stop and continue later.

Bake the casserole at 425° for 20 minutes.

Serve with mixed green salad, page 295.

FISH-STUFFED PEPPERS

4 servings
PREPARATION: about 30 minutes
(time does not include readying the fish, page 59 or 82)
COOKING: 40 minutes in a 350° oven

4 large green peppers

In boiling water to cover, cook the peppers for 5 minutes. Drain and refresh them in cold water. Cut out the stem ends and seed them.

1 8-ounce can stewed tomatoes
1½ cups croutons
2 cups flaked cooked fish (1 pound uncooked)
1 clove garlic, peeled and chopped fine
8 pitted ripe olives, drained and chopped
¼ cup grated Parmesan cheese
¼ cup fine-chopped parsley
Salt
Grinding of pepper

In a mixing bowl, combine and toss together these first seven ingredients. Season the mixture to taste with salt and pepper. Stuff the peppers with the mixture, stand them in an ovenproof serving dish, and cover them until ready to bake.

At this point you may stop and continue later.

Marinara Sauce, page 280

Bake the peppers, uncovered, at 350° for 40 minutes. Offer the marinara sauce separately.

Serve with chopped spinach, page 294.

Fish Mousse and Quenelles

These recipes may be made with any lean fillet, but fillet of pike is strongly recommended.

Because both fish mousse and *quenelles,* those light and elegant fish dumplings from France, are made with fish forcemeat, we begin with this basic recipe, which yields about 4 cups.

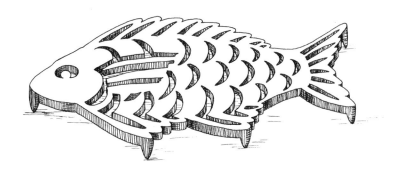

FISH FORCEMEAT
(Have all ingredients at refrigerator temperature)

4 to 6 servings
PREPARATION: about 25 minutes
CHILLING TIME: 2 hours
COOKING: for the mousse, about 30 minutes in a 375° oven;
for the *quenelles,* 8 to 10 minutes in simmering *court bouillon*

> **1 *pound lean fillet from which all bones***
> ***have been removed, chopped coarse***
> **2 *egg whites***
> **1 *teaspoon salt***
> **¼ *teaspoon white pepper***
> **2 *cups heavy cream***

In the container of a food processor, using the steel blade, reduce the fish to a smooth paste by dropping a few pieces at a time into the container with the motor running. Once all the fish is in the container, turn the motor on and off several times to assure the smoothness of the ground fish. Add singly the egg whites, then the seasonings, and finally the cream, in a slow, steady stream. Transfer the forcemeat to a chilled mixing bowl and allow it to sit, covered, in the refrigerator for at least 2 hours.

FISH MOUSSE

Butter a 5-cup ring mold and in it arrange 2 cups of fish forcemeat. Set the mold in a pan of hot water and bake the mousse at 375° for about 30 minutes, or until it is well puffed. Remove it from the oven and allow it to stand for 5 minutes. Turn the mousse onto a heated serving dish and garnish it with fine-chopped parsley. Offer Hollandaise Sauce, page 280, or Mornay Sauce, page 281, separately.

QUENELLES

Quenelles de brochet mousseline are a classic of French cuisine. The first time I ate them in Paris marks the beginning of a love affair between the City of Light and myself that endures happily to this day. *Quenelles* are light, delicate, and altogether delectably elegant. I offer them as a first course, for then I have no fear of their falling before being enjoyed; I also know that after the first course is eaten, my fame has been made!

Butter a large skillet. With large spoons, mold the *quenelles* from the chilled forcemeat; they should resemble duck eggs. Arrange them in the skillet with space between. Gradually add 4 cups lightly salted boiling water or mild boiling *court bouillon;* do not pour the liquid directly on the *quenelles.* Simmer them for 8 to 10 minutes, or until they are light and float on the surface of the liquid. With a slotted spoon, remove them briefly to absorbent paper. Arrange them on a warm serving platter and offer Hollandaise Sauce, page 280, or Mornay Sauce, page 281, separately.

Serve both mousse and *quenelles* with green peas, page 294.

FISH DUMPLINGS

4 to 6 servings
PREPARATION: about 35 minutes
COOKING: 8 to 10 minutes

A heartier dish than *quenelles,* but very good. The *pâte à chou* assures a well-risen if robust dumpling.

½ cup water
4 tablespoons butter
½ cup flour
½ teaspoon salt

In a saucepan bring the water to the boil, add the butter, and melt it. When the liquid is at a rolling boil, add the flour and salt all at one time. Stir the mixture until it forms a ball and no longer clings to the sides of the pan.

2 eggs

Away from the heat, beat in the eggs singly. Allow the *pâte à chou* to cool.

1 pound lean fish fillet from which all bones have been removed, chopped coarse

In the container of a food processor, using the steel blade, reduce the fish to a smooth paste by dropping a few pieces at a time into the container with the motor running. Once all the fish is in the container, turn the motor on and off several times to assure the smoothness of the ground fish. Add the fish to the *pâte à chou* and blend the mixture.

Nutmeg
Salt
White pepper
2 egg whites
1 cup heavy cream

Season the mixture to taste with nutmeg, salt, and pepper. Beat in the egg whites singly. Add the cream and blend the mixture well. Chill it overnight. Poach the dumplings according to the instructions on page 59. Offer them with Hollandaise Sauce, page 280, or Mornay Sauce, page 281.

Serve with Brussels sprouts, page 293.

FISH MOUSSE
(Made with cooked fish)

4 servings
PREPARATION: about 20 minutes
(time does not include readying the fish, page 59 or 82)
COOKING: 40 minutes in 375° oven

The recipe may be made with any lean fillet.

> **2 cups flaked cooked fish (1 pound uncooked)**
> **Grating of onion**
> **1 teaspoon Worcestershire sauce**
> **¾ teaspoon salt**
> **¼ teaspoon white pepper**
> **3 egg whites**

In the container of a food processor, using the steel blade, whirl the fish, onion, and seasonings to blend the mixture well. Add the egg whites singly. Transfer the mixture to a mixing bowl.

> **1 cup heavy cream, whipped**

Fold in the whipped cream. Into a buttered 1-quart casserole, spoon the mixture. Set the casserole in a pan of hot water and bake the mousse at 375° for 40 minutes, or until it is firm. Allow it to stand for a few minutes before turning it onto a heated serving plate.

> **Hollandaise Sauce, page 280**

Offer the sauce separately.
Serve with green beans, page 292.

Fish and Potato Casseroles

Fish and potato casseroles are popular dishes in nearly every part of the world. They may be made with fresh or salt fish (see page 217). While all fish and potato casseroles are of necessity variations on a single theme, sometimes the variation is sufficiently interesting to be given in detail. For this reason I have chosen five recipes, each from a different country. Let us start with one from America.

FISH AND POTATO CASSEROLE

4 servings
PREPARATION: about 45 minutes
COOKING: about 25 minutes

Traditionally cusk is used, but the recipe may be made with any lean fillet.

> 1½ *pounds fish fillet cut in large bite-size pieces*
> 3 *medium potatoes, peeled and diced*
> 1 *clove garlic, peeled and chopped fine*
> 2 *medium onions, peeled and chopped fine*
> 1 *bay leaf, crumbled*
> ½ *teaspoon celery seed*
> 4 *cloves*
> ¼ *teaspoon dill seed*
> 1½ *teaspoons salt*
> ½ *teaspoon pepper*
> 6 *tablespoons butter*

In a lightly buttered flameproof casserole, arrange layers of the fish, potato, garlic, and onion. Repeat the layering, ending with the remaining potato. Add the seasonings and dot with butter.

At this point you may stop and continue later.

> 2 *cups (2 8-ounce bottles) boiling clam juice or 1 cup water and 1 cup dry white wine, combined and brought to the boil*

Over the contents of the casserole, pour the clam juice. Cook the casserole, covered, over medium heat for 20 minutes, or until the potato is tender.

1 cup light cream, scalded
¼ cup fine-chopped parsley

Add the cream and continue to cook the casserole, uncovered, for 5 minutes. Garnish the dish with parsley.

Serve with spinach and mushroom salad, page 298.

FISH AND POTATO CASSEROLE, CANADIAN STYLE

4 servings
PREPARATION: about 30 minutes
(time does not include readying the fish, page 59 or 82)
COOKING: 45 minutes in a 375° oven

This Canadian dish may be made with any lean fillet.

4 medium potatoes, peeled and sliced thin
2 cups cooked flaked fish (1 pound uncooked)
1 large onion, peeled and chopped fine
½ cup fine-chopped parsley
Salt
Grinding of white pepper

In a well-buttered casserole, arrange layers of the ingredients in the order listed; season to taste with salt and pepper. End with a layer of potatoes.

Milk or light cream
Butter
4 strips bacon

To the contents of the casserole, add milk not quite to cover the top layer of potatoes. Dot with butter and add the bacon strips.

At this point you may stop and continue later.

Bake the casserole, covered, at 375° for 30 minutes; uncover it and continue to bake for 15 minutes, or until the potatoes are golden.

Serve with Brussels sprouts, page 293.

FISH AND POTATO CASSEROLE, DUTCH STYLE

4 servings
PREPARATION: about 30 minutes
COOKING: 45 minutes in a 350° oven

The recipe may be made with any lean fillet.

2 large potatoes, peeled

In lightly salted water to cover, boil the potatoes for 10 minutes. Drain and slice them thin.

3 tablespoons butter
2 medium onions, peeled and sliced thin

In a skillet, heat the butter and in it cook the onions until barely golden.

1½ pounds fish fillet
Dill
Salt
White pepper

In a lightly buttered baking dish arrange, in order, layers of potato, onion, and the fish. Season the fish with a sprinkling of dill, salt, and pepper. End with a layer of potato.

3 eggs
1 cup light cream
½ teaspoon salt

In a mixing bowl, beat together the eggs, cream, and salt.
At this point you may stop and continue later.

½ cup buttered bread crumbs

Over the contents of the casserole, pour the egg mixture. Add the bread crumbs in an even layer. Bake the dish at 350° for 45 minutes.

Serve with green bean salad, page 297.

FISH AND POTATO CASSEROLE, PORTUGUESE STYLE

4 servings
PREPARATION: about 30 minutes
COOKING: 25 minutes

The recipe may be made with any lean fillet.

> **4** *tablespoons olive oil*
> **2** *cloves garlic, peeled and chopped fine*
> **2** *large onions, peeled and sliced*
> **¼** *cup chopped parsley*
> **½** *teaspoon ground coriander seed*

In a flameproof casserole, heat the olive oil and in it cook the garlic and onion until translucent. Stir in the parsley and coriander.

> **4** *medium potatoes, peeled and sliced thin*
> **1½** *pounds fish fillet, cut in serving pieces if desired*
> **1** *16-ounce can Italian tomatoes with their liquid, the tomatoes broken up with the back of a spoon*
> **1** *bay leaf, crumbled*
> *Salt*
> *Pepper*
> **3** *tablespoons olive oil*

In the casserole, arrange a layer of half the potato, spooning the onion mixture over it. Add the fish and season to taste with salt and pepper. Pour half the tomatoes over this. Tuck in the bay leaf. Add the remaining potato and tomatoes and another sprinkling of salt and pepper. Over all, drizzle the olive oil.

At this point you may stop and continue later.

Over high heat, bring the contents of the casserole to the boil, reduce the heat, and simmer the dish, covered, for 25 minutes, or until the potatoes are tender.

Serve with Brussels sprouts, page 293.

FISH AND SWEET POTATO CASSEROLE
(France)

4 servings
PREPARATION: about 40 minutes
(time does not include readying the fish, page 59 or 82)
COOKING: 20 minutes in a 350° oven

This dish emerges from the first file of recipes I collected. It is labeled "Morue fraîche à la Bénédictine — a French classic." The index card offers no source for this information; I therefore experimented with the recipe itself to find that — un-French as the whole business seems — it can be made with fresh or prepared salt cod or with any lean fillet; it can also be made with yams or white potatoes. One version of the French *brandade* (page 222) calls for beating into the completed dish mashed white potato, *brandade à la Bénédictine* — but, alas, research reveals no other explanations for this name. Given these options, however, you may use the following instructions as a theme upon which to play your own variations.

> **6 medium sweet potatoes**
> **3 tablespoons butter**
> **1 tablespoon strained lemon juice**
> **Nutmeg**
> **Salt**
> **Pepper**
> **1 cup light cream**

In boiling water to cover, cook the sweet potatoes for 30 minutes, or until they are very tender. Skin and mash them with the butter and lemon juice. Add the cream and beat the mixture until it is light.

> **3 cups cooked flaked cod (1½ pounds uncooked)**
> **½ cup buttered bread crumbs**

Add the fish and blend the mixture well. In a buttered baking dish, arrange the sweet potato mixture. Over it, sprinkle the bread crumbs in an even layer.
At this point you may stop and continue later.
Bake the dish at 350° for 20 minutes, or until the crumbs are golden brown.
Serve with Brussels sprouts, page 293.

FISH PUDDING

6 servings as a main course; 8 servings as a first course
PREPARATION: about 30 minutes
COOKING: 1 hour in a 325° oven

This recipe of Danish origin may be made with any lean fillet. The pudding is light and delicately flavored, a rather elegant main dish.

*1 pound fish fillet from which all bones
 have been removed, chopped coarse*
2 eggs
1 cup milk
1 small onion, peeled and chopped
3 tablespoons potato flour
¼ teaspoon nutmeg
1 teaspoon salt
¼ teaspoon white pepper

In the container of a food processor, using the steel blade, reduce the fish to a smooth paste by dropping a few pieces at a time into the container with the motor running. Once all the fish is in the container, turn the motor on and off several times to assure the smoothness of the ground fish. Then, with the motor running, add the remaining ingredients. Transfer the mixture to a bowl.

1 cup heavy cream
½ cup dry white wine

Blend in the cream and white wine.

At this point you may stop and continue later.

Dill Sauce I, page 278

Into a buttered ring or other mold, spoon the pudding mixture. Set the mold in a pan of hot water and bake the pudding at 325° for 1 hour, or until a knife inserted at the center comes out clean. Offer the dill sauce separately.

Serve with green peas, page 294.

FISH AND RICE

4 servings
PREPARATION: about 35 minutes
COOKING: about 15 minutes

The recipe, with its overtones of Indian spicing, may be made with any lean fillet.

1 pound fish fillet cut in bite-size pieces

Prepare the fish and reserve it.

4 tablespoons butter
¼ teaspoon each of cardamom, chili powder, cinnamon, ground clove, cumin, pepper, and turmeric

In a skillet, heat the butter and to it add the spices, stirring to blend their flavors well. Remove the mixture from the heat and reserve it.

4 tablespoons butter
2 medium onions, peeled and chopped

In a large saucepan, heat the butter and in it cook the onion until it is golden.

1 cup raw natural rice

To the onion, add the rice and cook the mixture, stirring to coat the grains well, for about 3 minutes.

At this point you may stop and continue later.

2 cups clam juice
Strained juice of ½ medium lemon
⅓ cup fine-chopped parsley

To the rice, add the clam juice. Bring the liquid to the boil, stir the rice once with a fork, reduce the heat, and simmer it, covered, for 15 minutes, or until it is tender and the liquid is absorbed. While the rice is cooking, complete the recipe.

Heat the spice mixture until it is bubbly, add the prepared fish, reduce the heat somewhat, and cook the fish evenly, stirring it gently, for 3 minutes. Add the lemon juice and continue to cook the fish over gentle heat for 5 minutes, or until it just begins to flake.

To the cooked rice, add the fish, the spice mixture, and any juices accumulated in the skillet. Using two forks, gently toss the mixture. Transfer it to a heated serving dish and garnish it with the parsley.

Serve with mixed green salad, page 295.

FISH SOUFFLÉ

4 servings as a main course
6 servings as a first course
PREPARATION: about 20 minutes
(time does not include readying the fish, page 59 or 82)
COOKING: about 35 minutes in a 375° oven

The recipe may be made with any lean fillet.
Thoroughly butter a 2-quart soufflé dish.

> *4 tablespoons butter*
> *3 tablespoons flour*
> *¾ cup milk or light cream*
> *½ teaspoon salt*
> *¼ teaspoon white pepper*
> *1 cup cooked flaked fish (½ pound uncooked)*
> *4 egg yolks*

In a saucepan, heat the butter and in it, over gentle heat, cook the flour for a few minutes. Gradually add the milk, stirring constantly until the mixture is thickened and smooth. Stir in the salt and pepper. Add the fish and egg yolks and beat the mixture to blend it well.

At this point you may stop and continue later.

> *5 egg whites, beaten until stiff but not dry*

Into the soufflé batter, beat one-fifth of the egg white; fold in the remainder. Using a rubber spatula, transfer the mixture to the soufflé dish. Bake the soufflé at 375° for 35 minutes, or until it is well puffed and golden.

If desired, 1 teaspoon dill or ¼ cup fine-chopped parsley may be added to the *béchamel;* the strained juice of ½ medium lemon added to the *béchamel* gives a pleasantly fresh taste.

You may crust the soufflé by coating the buttered soufflé dish with a combination of 3 tablespoons fine bread crumbs and 4 tablespoons grated Parmesan cheese.

Serve with green peas, page 294.

KEDGEREE

6 servings
PREPARATION: about 40 minutes
COOKING: 30 minutes in a 300° oven

The English took *khichri* home with them from India, where it had originally been a rice, lentil, and onion dish. Now a classic offering for English breakfasts, kedgeree has come to mean fish and rice. A light dish, it is also pleasant for brunches, luncheons, or suppers. The recipe may be made with any lean fillet or with salt cod or finnan haddie prepared for poaching.

>   **6 tablespoons butter**
>   **2 teaspoons sweet curry powder (op-
>   tional)**
>   **1½ cups raw natural rice**

In a saucepan, heat the butter; stir in the curry powder. Add the rice, stirring to coat each grain. Set the rice aside and reserve it.

>   **2 pounds fish fillet**
>   **Court Bouillon, *page 90***

Poach the fish in *court bouillon* according to the directions on page 59. Remove the fish; strain and reserve the liquid. Flake the fish and reserve it. To the broth add water, if necessary, to equal 3 cups. Add the liquid to the rice and bring it to the boil; reduce the heat and simmer the rice, covered, for 15 minutes, or until it is tender and the liquid is absorbed.

>   **Strained juice of ½ medium lemon**
>   **4 hard-cooked eggs**
>   **½ cup fine-chopped parsley or water-
>   cress leaves**

Prepare the lemon juice. Chop the egg whites coarse; force the yolks through a coarse sieve. Reserve both separately. Prepare the parsley.
At this point you may stop and continue later.

>   **Reserved fish**
>   **Reserved rice**
>   **Reserved lemon juice**
>   **Reserved egg white**
>   **Reserved parsley**
>   **Worcestershire sauce**
>   **Salt**
>   **Grinding of white pepper**

In a large mixing bowl, using two forks, lightly toss together the fish and rice. Add the lemon juice, egg white, parsley, and a generous dash of Worcestershire sauce. Toss the mixture again and season it to taste with salt and pepper.

Light cream (optional)
Reserved egg yolk

Into a lightly buttered baking dish, spoon the kedgeree. If desired, add a little cream for extra moistness. Heat the dish, covered, in a 300° oven for 30 minutes. Garnish it with the egg yolk.

Serve with mixed green salad, page 295.

SCALLOPED FISH *AU GRATIN*

4 servings
PREPARATION: about 25 minutes
COOKING: about 15 minutes in a 425° oven

The recipe may be made with any lean fillet.

>   *3 tablespoons butter*
> *¼ cup fine-chopped celery*
> *1 small onion, peeled and chopped*
> *fine*
> *½ green pepper, chopped fine*
> *¾ teaspoon salt*
> *Grinding of white pepper*

In a saucepan, heat the butter and in it cook the celery, onion, and pepper until the onion is translucent. Season the vegetables with salt and pepper.

>   *3 tablespoons flour*
> *1½ cups light cream or milk*
> *Worcestershire sauce*

Into the contents of the saucepan, stir the flour, and over gentle heat cook the mixture for a few minutes. Gradually add the cream, stirring constantly until the mixture is thickened and smooth; season it to taste with Worcestershire sauce. Cover the sauce so that it will not crust and reserve it.

>   *1½ pounds fish fillet cut in bite-size*
> *pieces or in serving portions*
> *¼ cup fine-chopped parsley*
> *½ cup bread crumbs*
> *½ cup grated Cheddar cheese*

Prepare the fish and reserve it. Prepare and reserve the parsley. Combine and blend the bread crumbs and cheese; reserve the mixture.

At this point you may stop and continue later.

In a buttered ovenproof dish, arrange the fish. Into the sauce, stir the parsley; spoon the sauce over the fish. Over all, sprinkle the bread crumb mixture. Bake the dish at 425° for 15 minutes, or until the fish flakes easily.

Serve with saffron rice, page 291.

FISH AND VEGETABLE CASSEROLE

4 to 6 servings
PREPARATION: about 40 minutes
COOKING: 1 hour and 10 minutes

The recipe may be made with any lean fillet or steak.

> 1 *cup fine-shredded raw cabbage*
> 2 *medium carrots, scraped and cut in fine julienne*
> 1 *cup diced eggplant*
> 1 *medium onion, peeled and chopped fine*
> ½ *cup fresh peas*
> 1 *large potato, peeled and diced*
> 2 *large ripe tomatoes, peeled, seeded, and chopped, with their liquid*
>   *Sprinkling of thyme*
> 1½ *teaspoons salt*
>   *Grinding of pepper*
> ⅓ *cup olive oil*

In a large mixing bowl, combine the vegetables and seasonings. Over them pour the oil, and using two forks, toss the mixture to coat the vegetables well. Transfer them to a covered casserole or baking dish large enough to accommodate the fish (see below) in a single layer. Bake the vegetables, covered, at 400° for 1 hour, or until they are tender. While the vegetables are cooking, prepare the remaining ingredients.

> 1½ *pounds fish fillets cut in serving pieces* **or** *steak*
>   *Salt*
>   *Pepper*
>   *Olive oil*
>   *Fresh strained lemon juice*
>   *Fine-chopped parsley*

Season the fish with salt and pepper, brush it with olive oil, and sprinkle it with lemon juice. Reserve the parsley.

At this point you may stop and continue later.

On the surface of the vegetables, arrange the fish. Bake uncovered according to the directions on page 20. Garnish the dish with parsley.

Serve with casserole-baked bread, page 288.

MATELOTE OF EEL, NORMANDY STYLE

4 servings
PREPARATION: about 45 minutes
COOKING: about 10 minutes

¼ pound salt pork, diced
12 small white onions, peeled and boiled until tender

In a skillet, render the salt pork until it is golden and crisp; with a slotted spoon, remove it to absorbent paper and reserve it. In the remaining fat, glaze the onions until they are golden (a little sugar may be added to facilitate this step); remove them to absorbent paper and reserve them. Discard the fat.

2½ cups Court Bouillon, page 90
1½ cups cider
2 carrots, scraped and cut in fine julienne
3 medium ribs celery, diced
2 medium onions, peeled and chopped fine

In a large saucepan, combine the liquids and vegetables. Bring the liquid to the boil, reduce the heat, and simmer the vegetables for 15 minutes.

2 pounds fresh eel, skinned, drawn, and cut in 2-inch segments

Return the contents of the saucepan to the boil, add the eel, and when the liquid returns just to the boil, reduce the heat and simmer uncovered for 8 minutes. Remove the eel to a warmed flameproof serving dish, surround it with the onions, cover it well with plastic wrap, and keep it warm. Into a second saucepan, strain the broth, and over high heat reduce it to 1½ cups.

2 tablespoons soft butter
3 tablespoons flour

In a small mixing bowl, combine the butter and flour; using a fork, blend the mixture until it is a smooth *beurre manié*. Reserve it.

At this point you may stop and continue later.

Reserved beurre manié
½ cup heavy cream

Salt
Grinding of pepper

Return the broth to the simmer and to it add the *beurre manié,* stirring constantly until the mixture is thickened and smooth. Stir in the cream and season the sauce to taste with salt and pepper.

¼ *cup brandy (preferably apple brandy)*
Fine-chopped parsley
Reserved salt pork

Over the eel, pour the brandy and ignite it. When the flame dies, pour the hot sauce over the dish and garnish with parsley and salt pork.

Serve with casserole-baked bread, page 288.

Squid and Calamari

Once considered a poor man's food, squid and calamari are now enjoying increased popularity in restaurants and in the home. They are available fresh, frozen, and canned. I prefer them frozen, for this way they come cleaned and pan-ready; fresh squid and calamari require the removal of the ink sac and bone before being cut into bite-size pieces. (Refer to the Lexicon for complete instructions, p. 11) They may be deep fried in the same way as are clams, page 258, or sautéed, page 74. They are also very good in composed dishes, of which I offer two from Italy, where they are especially popular.

SQUID OR CALAMARI WITH PEAS

4 servings
PREPARATION: about 40 minutes
COOKING: about 15 minutes

4 *tablespoons olive oil*
2 *large cloves garlic, peeled and sliced lengthwise*
2 *pounds squid or calamari, prepared for cooking and cut in 1½-inch pieces*
¼ *cup fine-chopped parsley*
1 *teaspoon salt*
½ *teaspoon pepper*

In a skillet, heat the olive oil and in it cook the garlic until it turns brown; discard it. To the flavored oil, add the squid, parsley, and seasonings. Cook the squid, stirring, for 3 or 4 minutes, or until it starts turning pink.

1 *cup dry red wine*
1 *20-ounce can Italian tomatoes*

Add the wine and tomatoes and simmer the mixture, uncovered, for about 20 minutes, or until the squid is tender.
At this point you may stop and continue later.

1 *10-ounce package frozen peas*

Into the simmering sauce, stir the peas, and over gentle heat cook them, uncovered, for 15 minutes or until they are tender.
Serve with casserole-baked bread, page 288.

STUFFED SQUID OR CALAMARI

4 servings
PREPARATION: about 45 minutes
COOKING: 45 minutes in a 375° oven

**2 pounds small squid or calamari, pre-
pared for cooking, page 11, but not
cut up**

Remove the heads and tentacles, leaving the body intact. Force the heads and tentacles through the fine blade of a meat grinder. Reserve the bodies.

1 cup bread crumbs
**1 clove garlic, peeled and put through
a press**
4 tablespoons olive oil
¼ cup fine-chopped parsley
Salt
Grinding of pepper

In a mixing bowl, combine the ground squid with the bread crumbs, garlic, olive oil, and parsley; using a fork, blend the mixture well and season it to taste with salt and pepper. With it, stuff the reserved squid bodies, and if necessary skewer them with toothpicks. Arrange them in an oiled baking dish.

At this point you may stop and continue later.

4 tablespoons olive oil
½ cup dry white wine
1 cup Marinara Sauce, page 280

Over the squid, drizzle the oil, add the white wine, and bake the squid at 375° for 45 minutes, or until they are tender. Over them, pour the marinara sauce and heat it through.

Serve with casserole-baked bread, page 288.

Fresh or frozen fish, delectable and nourishing served hot, are also tasty and healthful offered chilled in various guises. A chilled poached whole fish, garnished with tomato wedges, hard-cooked egg, and watercress, and accompanied by a savory sauce, is a warm-weather meal in itself, needing perhaps only a bread (I often suggest muffins) to complement the main dish. Fish may also be made into refreshing salads in combination with vegetables and fruits. The following recipes, a selection from among many possible ones, make use of less expensive fish in dishes that I hope you will find attractive to the eye and palate. I hope, too, that making them will encourage you to experiment with fish salads of your creation.

ESCABECHE

You will find the recipe on page 88, in the section on hors d'oeuvre and first courses. *Escabeche,* however, is also excellent as a salad or as the main dish of a light meal. Serve it on a bed of leaf lettuce or watercress, dress it with Vinaigrette Sauce, page 287, and garnish each serving with tomato wedges and hard-cooked egg. Offer the *escabeche* with casserole-baked bread, page 288.

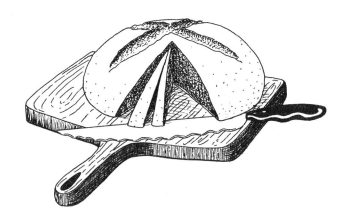

CHILLED FISH, SPANISH STYLE

4 servings
PREPARATION: about 50 minutes
COOKING: about 30 minutes in a 350 oven
CHILLING TIME: 3 hours

The recipe may be made with any lean fillet or steak.

> *Olive oil*
> *1½ pounds fish fillet cut in serving pieces or steak*
> *2 large cloves garlic, peeled and chopped fine*
> *1 bay leaf, crumbled*
> *Powdered cumin*
> *Large pinch of saffron, crumbled*
> *Thyme*
> *Salt*
> *Grinding of pepper*

With the olive oil, lightly coat a baking dish sufficiently large to accommodate the fish in a single layer. In the dish, arrange the fish. Add the garlic and bay leaf and a generous sprinkling of the other seasonings.

> *4 large ripe tomatoes, peeled, seeded, and chopped*
> *2¼ cups dry white wine*

Over the fish, spoon the tomatoes in an even layer. Add the wine. Bake the fish at 350° for about 30 minutes, or until it just flakes. Remove the dish from the oven and allow the fish to cool in the sauce (the fish will continue to cook for a few minutes in the hot sauce; for this reason it is important that you not overcook it in the oven). Chill the fish, covered, in the refrigerator for at least 3 hours.

> *Salad greens of your choice*
> *Vinaigrette Sauce, page 287 (optional)*
> *Lemon wedges*

On individual beds of salad greens, arrange the fish with its tomato topping. Add a little vinaigrette sauce and garnish each plate with a lemon wedge or two.

Serve with casserole-baked bread, page 288.

CHILLED SPICED FISH

4 servings
PREPARATION: about 30 minutes
CHILLING TIME: 24 hours

The recipe may be made with any lean fillet.

1½ pounds fish fillet

Poach or steam the fish according to the directions on pages 59 or 82, until it just flakes; do not overcook it. Allow it to cool briefly and then cut it in bite-size pieces.

Red onion slices (no more than ⅛-inch thick)

In a jar with a tight-fitting lid (a 1-quart mayonnaise jar is fine), arrange alternate layers of the onion and fish, ending with a layer of the onion.

1 cup white wine vinegar
½ cup dry white wine
1½ tablespoons pickling spice
3 tablespoons sugar
1 teaspoon salt
8 to 10 peppercorns

In a saucepan, combine these six ingredients; bring the liquid to the boil, reduce the heat, and simmer the mixture for 3 minutes. Allow it to cool and then add it to the contents of the jar. Cap the jar securely and refrigerate it for 24 hours, inverting it every once in a while.

Salad greens of your choice

On a bed of salad greens, arrange the fish and onion rings. Serve the salad well chilled.

Serve with muffins, page 289.

Chilled Whole Fish,
Large Fillets, or Steaks

Lean saltwater or freshwater fish, I feel, are more successful offered chilled than are fat fish. Although many people consider chilled poached catfish a delicacy, I must admit to not enjoying the oily feel of fat fish served cold. Serving it hot, on the other hand, enhances the rich texture and full flavor of the fish.

For chilled whole fish, large fillets, or steaks, I recommend carp, cod, flounder (very attractive if offered as flounder rolls), haddock, halibut, pike, pollock, and whitefish.

Whole fish, large fillets, and individual portions of fish steak may be poached or steamed according to the directions on pages 59 and 82. If you use a whole fish, peel off and discard from the cooked fish the upper half of the skin (as the fish lies flat); leave on the head and tail. Allow the fish, whether whole, fillet, or steaks, to cool quickly and then refrigerate it, covered to retain its moistness, for at least 3 hours.

Arrange the prepared fish on a bed of salad greens. You may garnish it with:

> *Aspic dice (see below)*
> *Avocado slices*
> *Caviar (black lumpfish roe or red salmon roe)*
> *Thin-sliced cucumber*
> *Hard-cooked egg*
> *Fine-chopped mixed fresh herbs (basil, chives, marjoram, parsley, summer savory, tarragon) or parsley alone*
> *Paper-thin slices of lemon, lime, or orange, or lemon or lime wedges, or a light sprinkling of fine-grated lemon rind*
> *Fine-chopped red onion or scallions*
> *Tomato wedges*

Decorate the fish with a little of the sauce you will offer with it and serve the larger quantity separately.

You may also coat the fish with aspic — an especially festive presentation:

FISH ASPIC

YIELD: 4 cups
PREPARATION: about 1 hour
CHILLING TIME: at least 6 hours

4 *cups water*
1 *cup dry white wine*
2 *pounds lean fish heads and bones*
2 *cloves garlic, peeled and chopped*
1 *large onion, peeled and chopped*
5 *sprigs parsley*
2 *bay leaves*
1½ *teaspoons salt*
½ *teaspoon peppercorns*

In a large saucepan, combine all of the ingredients. Bring the liquid to the boil, reduce the heat, and simmer the mixture, covered, for 30 minutes. Strain it, discarding the residue. Measure it and if necessary reduce it to 4 cups.

2 *envelopes unflavored gelatin, softened*
   for 5 minutes in ¼ cup cold water
2 *egg whites*
2 *eggshells, crushed*
2 *tablespoons cold water*

To the hot broth, add the gelatin, stirring until it is dissolved. In a small mixing bowl, combine the egg whites, eggshells, and water; using a fork, beat the mixture until it is slightly frothy and then stir it into the broth. Over high heat, bring the mixture to the boil, stirring constantly; immediately reduce the heat so that the liquid barely simmers. Leave it at this temperature, uncovered, for 20 minutes. In a sieve, arrange two layers of cheesecloth and through them strain the liquid into a mixing bowl. Cool and then chill the aspic.

To coat the fish with aspic, allow the aspic to chill until it is syrupy. With a spoon or rubber spatula, spread some of the aspic evenly over the chilled fish. Return the fish to the refrigerator until the aspic sets. Repeat the process until the fish is smoothly covered. Allow the remaining aspic to set until it is very firm (about 6 hours); cut it crosswise into small dice and use as garnish for the fish.

This same recipe will provide aspic with which to coat molds for chilled fish mousses. When the prepared aspic is syrupy (see above), pour some of it into a chilled mold. Turn the mold in different directions so that the aspic covers evenly. Return the mold to the refrigerator until the aspic sets. Repeat the process until the mold is smoothly covered to the depth you desire.

If desired, you may poach the fish in *court bouillon,* page 90, and when the fish is cooked, reduce the liquid until it is the flavor you wish. Strain and measure it; for each 2 cups of liquid, allow one envelope of unflavored gelatin softened for 5 minutes in ¼ cup of cold water. Add the gelatin, stirring to dissolve it; clarify the *court bouillon,* and proceed with the directions for aspic above.

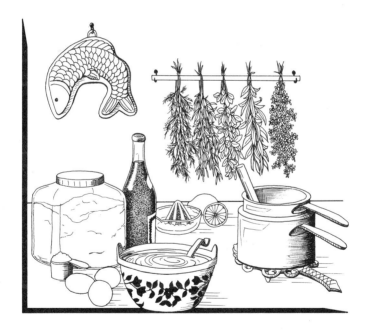

FISH, APPLE, AND GREEN PEA SALAD

6 servings
PREPARATION: about 30 minutes
(time does not include readying the fish, page 59 or 82)
CHILLING TIME: 3 hours

The recipe may be made with any lean fillet.

> *3 large apples, peeled, cored, and diced*
> *Strained juice of 1 medium lemon*

As you prepare the apples, toss them with lemon juice to prevent their discoloring. Drain the apples when you combine them with the other ingredients.

> *4 medium ribs celery, diced*
> *2 cups flaked cooked fish (1 pound uncooked)*
> *1 10-ounce package frozen small peas, fully thawed to room temperature*
> *½ green pepper, diced*
> *3 scallions, trimmed and chopped, with as much green as is crisp*
> *Mayonnaise, page 281*
> *Salt*
> *Grinding of white pepper*

In a large mixing bowl, toss together the prepared apples and the remaining ingredients. Add sufficient mayonnaise just to bind the mixture. Season it to taste with salt and pepper. Chill the salad for 3 hours.

> *Salad greens of your choice*

Arrange the salad on a bed of greens.
Serve with muffins, page 289.

FISH AND BEAN SALAD

6 servings
PREPARATION: about 40 minutes
(time does not include readying the fish, page 59 or 82,
or tenderizing the beans)
CHILLING TIME: 3 hours

The recipe, of Spanish origin, is traditionally made with cod, but you may use any lean fillet.

> 1 cup Great Northern or Navy pea beans
> ½ cup Vinaigrette Sauce, page 289
> 1 clove garlic, peeled

In 2 quarts of cold water, bring the beans rapidly to the boil and cook them, uncovered, for 5 minutes. Remove them from the heat and allow them to stand, covered, to tenderize for 1 hour. Return them to the boil, reduce the heat, and simmer them, uncovered, for about 20 minutes, or until they are tender but still retain their shape; do not overcook them. Drain them well, and while they are still warm, toss them with the vinaigrette sauce, into which the garlic clove has been pressed.

> 2 cups flaked cooked fish (1 pound uncooked)
> ½ cup pitted ripe olives, halved lengthwise
> ⅓ cup chopped parsley
> 3 scallions, trimmed and chopped, with as much green as is crisp
> 3 ripe tomatoes, peeled, seeded, and chopped
> Salad greens of your choice

Toss the remaining ingredients with the beans to blend the mixture well; more vinaigrette sauce may be added as necessary. Chill the salad for 3 hours and serve it on a bed of greens.

Serve with casserole-baked bread, page 288.

FISH, CAULIFLOWER, AND SNOW PEA SALAD

4 servings
PREPARATION: about 30 minutes
(time does not include readying the fish, page 59 or 82)
CHILLING TIME: 3 hours

The recipe may be made with any lean fillet.

***1 small cauliflower, cut in small
flowerets***

In lightly salted boiling water to cover, blanch the cauliflower for 1 minute. Drain and refresh it in cold water.

***½ pound snow peas, the strings re-
moved***

In lightly salted boiling water to cover, blanch the snow peas for 1 minute. Drain and refresh them in cold water.

⅓ cup Vinaigrette Sauce, page 287

With absorbent paper, pat both the cauliflower and snow peas as dry as possible. Toss them with the vinaigrette sauce.

***4 scallions, trimmed and chopped, with
as much green as is crisp***
***1 large bunch watercress with the
woody stems removed, rinsed and well
drained***

Prepare the scallions and watercress.

***2 cups flaked cooked fish (1 pound
uncooked)***
Vinaigrette Sauce

In a large bowl, toss together the cauliflower, snow peas, scallions, watercress, and fish; add vinaigrette sauce as needed. Chill the salad for 3 hours.

Salad greens of your choice

To facilitate serving, arrange the salad on individual beds of greens.
Serve with muffins, page 289.
The recipe may be made with frozen snow peas. Fully thawed and dried on absorbent paper, they should not require cooking. If you do blanch them, do not overcook them — their crunchiness is one of the attractive qualities of the salad.

FISH AND FRUIT SALAD

4 servings
PREPARATION: about 30 minutes
(time does not include readying the fish, page 59 or 82)
CHILLING TIME: 3 hours

The recipe may be made with any lean fillet

> *3 tablespoons preserved ginger,
> chopped fine*
> *2 tablespoons honey*
> *¼ cup strained lemon juice*
> *4 tablespoons Mayonnaise, page 281*
> *5 or 6 fresh mint leaves, chopped fine*
> *4 tablespoons sour cream*

In a small mixing bowl, combine and blend these six ingredients; allow
them to stand for several hours to meld the flavors.

> *2 cups flaked cooked fish (1 pound
> uncooked)*
> *1 cup seedless grapes, halved length-
> wise*
> *1 11-ounce can mandarin oranges,
> drained*
> *1 15½-ounce can pineapple chunks,
> drained*
> *Salad greens of your choice*

In a large bowl, toss the fish, grapes, mandarin oranges, and pineapple
with the prepared dressing. Chill for 3 hours before serving it on a bed of
salad greens.

Serve with muffins, page 289.

GEFILTE FISH

6 servings
PREPARATION: about 35 minutes
COOKING: 1½ hours
CHILLING TIME: 3 hours

The Jewish classic is traditionally made with carp, pike, and whitefish, but you may use any lean fish as an acceptable, if unauthentic, substitute.

1 pound each of carp, pike, and white-fish, filleted, the head, skin, and bones reserved

2 large carrots, scraped and sliced thin

2 large onions, peeled and sliced

6 cups water

2 teaspoons salt

½ teaspoon white pepper

In a saucepan, combine the fish heads, skin, and bones with the carrots, onions, water, salt and pepper. Bring the liquid to the boil, reduce the heat, and simmer the broth, covered, while you prepare the remainder of the recipe.

Reserved fish fillets, chopped coarse

2 eggs

6 tablespoons ice water

1½ tablespoons matzo or cracker meal

¾ teaspoon salt

½ teaspoon white pepper

In the container of a food processor, using the steel blade, reduce the fish to a smooth paste by dropping a few pieces at a time into the container with the motor running. Once all the fish is in the container, turn the motor on and off several times to assure the smoothness of the ground fish. Then, with the motor running, add the remaining ingredients.

With wet hands, form the mixture into 6 or 12 balls. Add them to the barely simmering stock to poach for 1 hour covered, then for ½ hour uncovered. Strain the stock over the gefilte fish, reserving the carrots as a garnish. Chill the gefilte fish for 3 hours and offer them with horseradish.

Serve with casserole-baked bread, page 288.

HADDOCK SALAD

4 servings
PREPARATION: about 30 minutes
CHILLING TIME: 2 hours

The recipe may also be made with cod or halibut.

This salad, remarkably simple to prepare, has a delicate refreshing taste, making it a welcome course for warm-weather meals.

1½ pounds haddock fillet, steamed, page 82

With the tines of a fork, flake the fish and reserve it.

1 5½-ounce can water chestnuts, drained and sliced thin or 1 cup fine-chopped celery
Strained juice of ½ medium lemon
1 tablespoon sweet paprika
1 teaspoon salt
Reserved fish

In a mixing bowl, toss together the water chestnuts, seasonings, and fish.

Mayonnaise, page 281, or Cucumber Sauce, page 277

Using only a sufficient quantity to bind the mixture, add the sauce of your choice and toss the salad lightly. Chill it, covered, for at least 3 hours.

Salad greens

Onto a bed of salad greens, spoon individual portions of the fish mixture.

To serve the salad as a light meal, use the fish mixture to stuff ripe tomatoes, arrange the tomatoes on salad greens, and garnish the platter with hard-cooked eggs; offer the dish with muffins, page 289.

CHILLED FISH MOUSSE

PREPARATION: about 30 minutes
(time does not include readying the fish, page 59 or 82)
CHILLING TIME: 6 hours

The recipe may be made with any lean fillet.
Lightly oil and chill a 6-cup ring or other mold.

> *1½ envelopes unflavored gelatin, soft-
> ened for 5 minutes in ½ cup cold
> water*
> *½ cup boiling water*

To the gelatin, add the boiling water, stirring until the gelatin is dissolved;
reserve it.

> *2 cups cream-style cottage cheese*
> *1 small onion, peeled and chopped
> coarse*
> *2 cups cooked flaked fish (1 pound
> uncooked)*
> *½ teaspoon paprika*
> *A few drops of Tabasco sauce*
> *1 teaspoon salt*
> *Reserved gelatin*

In the container of a food processor or blender, combine these seven ingredients. Whirl them until the mixture is smooth. Transfer it to a mixing
bowl.

> *⅓ cup fine-chopped gherkins*
> *⅔ cup Mayonnaise, page 281*

To the contents of the mixing bowl, add the gherkins and mayonnaise.
Blend the mixture well and chill it until it just begins to set.

> *1 cup heavy cream, whipped*

Fold in the whipped cream. Using a rubber spatula, transfer the mixture
to the prepared mold. Chill the mousse for 6 hours, or until it is
thoroughly set. Unmold the mousse onto a chilled serving plate. Fill the
center with Mixed Vegetable Salad, page 298.
Serve with muffins, page 289.

FISH AND POTATO SALAD

4 to 6 servings
PREPARATION: about 45 minutes
(time does not include readying the fish, page 59 or 82)
CHILLING TIME: 3 hours

The recipe may be made with any lean fillet.

> **3 large potatoes**
> **Vinaigrette Sauce, page 287**
> **2 cloves garlic, peeled**

In boiling water to cover, cook the potatoes until they are tender. Peel and cut them in large dice. Toss the dice with vinaigrette sauce (about ¼ cup) into which the garlic cloves have been pressed.

> **2 cups flaked cooked fish (1 pound uncooked)**
> **Prepared potatoes**
> **½ cup chopped parsley**
> **4 or 5 scallions, trimmed and chopped, with as much green as is crisp**
> **Mayonnaise, page 281**
> **Salt**
> **White pepper**

In a large bowl, toss together the fish, potatoes, parsley, and scallions. Add salt and pepper to taste and sufficient mayonnaise just to bind the mixture. Chill the salad for 3 hours.

> **Lettuce or watercress**
> **Hard-cooked eggs, cut in lengthwise quarters**
> **Tomato wedges**

Offer the salad arranged on lettuce or watercress and garnished with egg sections and tomato wedges.

Serve with muffins, page 289.

SEVICHE (CITRUS-MARINATED RAW FISH)
(*Latin America*)

4 servings
PREPARATION: about 30 minutes
MARINATING AND CHILLING: 6 hours

The recipe may be made with any lean white-fleshed fish.

Seviche (*ceviche, cebiche* — there are various spellings) may be served either as first course or main dish. Although the present recipe comes from the Western Hemisphere, fish "cooked" or cured in citrus juice is known also throughout the Pacific Islands and Southeast Asia.

1½ to 2 cups strained fresh lime juice **or**
half lime juice and half strained fresh lemon juice
1 teaspoon chili powder
1 medium clove garlic, chopped coarse
1 teaspoon sugar
1 teaspoon salt
Grinding of white pepper

In the container of a blender, combine and briefly whirl these six ingredients.

2 medium red onions, peeled, sliced thin, and separated into rings
1½ pounds fish fillet cut in 1-inch squares

In a flat glass or ceramic dish, arrange a layer of the onion; over the onion, arrange the fish; end with a layer of onion. Over all, pour the lime-juice mixture to cover. Marinate the fish, covered, in the refrigerator for at least 6 hours; it is "cooked" when it is opaque. Serve the *seviche* on a bed of salad greens.

To serve the *seviche* as a main dish, garnish it with green or red sweet pepper cut into julienne, tomato wedges, and halves of hard-cooked eggs. As a side dish offer boiled yams, the traditional accompaniment to *seviche* in Mexico.

FIVE

Canned Fish

More — much more — than tuna-and-noodle casserole or salmon salad or sardine sandwiches is possible when canned fish is used in cooking. Would you enjoy sardine soufflé? Salmon croquettes? Mackerel loaf? Tuna crêpes? Chilled herring mousse? These dishes are but a few of those that can be made with canned fish. Canned fish is indeed frugal fish. Everything contained in the can is usable, nourishing, and tasty. There is no waste.

In experimenting with these recipes, I became increasingly intrigued by the variety of dishes one can make with canned fish and also by their attractive appearance. The greater number call for salmon or tuna, largely because the preponderance of canned fish on supermarket shelves *is* salmon and tuna. In the recipes, salmon and tuna are most often interchangeable. A tuna soufflé, however, does not taste like one made with salmon, and salmon divan is quite a different dish from the same recipe made with tuna. Thus, you have virtually twice as many dishes to choose from as you have recipes.

Experimenting with dishes made from canned fish is fun and creative — and economical; I hope you do so with daring and pleasure. In cooking with canned fish I have discovered one rule of thumb that is helpful: if the fish is packed in oil, as much canned fish is, drain it thoroughly and set the fish for a few minutes on absorbent paper. Sometimes the oil is used as an ingredient in the recipe; therefore I suggest you read the recipe before draining the fish or discarding the oil. Unless a recipe directs otherwise, I recommend waterpack tuna.

The advantage in making appetizers and first courses with canned fish is that if you customarily stock your larder with a variety of them, you always have on hand necessary ingredients for original and flavorful dishes. Indeed, I urge you to go carefully over the canned fish display at your supermarket and to purchase several kinds — they come in handy, not only for appetizers and first courses, but also for the preparation of all recipes in this section of the book. Thus, you are able to offer with a minimum of effort and concern good foods for easy family dining or for unexpected guests.

ANCHOVY TOASTS

YIELD: 24 toasts
PREPARATION: about 15 minutes
COOKING: 5 minutes in a 350° oven
(if desired, the toasts may also be served unheated)

> *3 tablespoons melted butter*
> *2 egg yolks*
> *2 gratings of onion*
> *3 tablespoons anchovy paste*
> *2 tablespoons brandy*
> *½ teaspoon Worcestershire sauce*
> *Few grains of cayenne pepper*

In a small mixing bowl, whip together the first three ingredients. Add the rest, stirring to blend the mixture well.

> *6 large slices bread, toasted, the crusts removed*

Cut the toasts in quarters, arrange them on a baking sheet, and cook them at 350° for 5 minutes, or until they are heated through.

ANCHOVIES AND TOMATOES

4 servings
PREPARATION: about 15 minutes
COOKING (if desired): about 5 minutes in a preheated broiler.

> 8 *thin slices ripe tomato (if you are*
> *serving the first course chilled, peel*
> *the tomato before slicing it)*
> 8 *thin slices Mozzarella cheese*
> 24 *anchovy fillets*
> *Oregano*
> *Olive oil*
> *Grinding of pepper*

Top each tomato slice with one of Mozzarella; over the cheese, arrange the anchovies in a star pattern. Add a sprinkling of oregano, a delicate drizzle of olive oil, and a grinding of pepper. Serve the first course chilled *or* cook it in a preheated broiler for about 5 minutes, or until the cheese is melted.

CROSTINI

YIELD: 16 canapés
PREPARATION: about 15 minutes
COOKING: about 15 minutes in a 400° oven

An Italian hors d'oeuvre that may be prepared ahead of time and run into the preheated oven when you are ready to serve.

> 16 *thin slices Italian bread, the crusts*
> *removed*
> *Olive oil*
> 16 *thin slices Mozzarella cheese*
> 32 *anchovy fillets*

Brush one side of the bread with olive oil. On the reverse side, arrange the Mozzarella, trimming it to the shape of the bread slice. Over the Mozzarella, arrange the anchovies in a cross pattern. Before serving the *crostini,* toast them at 400° for about 5 minutes, or until the cheese is melted.

HERRING COCKTAIL DIP

YIELD: about 1½ cups
PREPARATION: about 12 minutes

3 pickled herring, chopped coarse
Strained juice of ½ small lemon
½ cup sour cream
1 tablespoon Dijon mustard
1 teaspoon prepared horseradish
A few drops of Tabasco sauce
1 teaspoon Worcestershire sauce

In the container of a food processor or blender, combine the seven ingredients and whirl them until they are thoroughly blended. Transfer the dip to a serving dish and chill it. Offer it with Melba toast.

HERRING AND APPLE COCKTAIL

6 servings
PREPARATION: about 20 minutes
CHILLING TIME: 3 hours

This first course also serves nicely as a salad.

1 cup sour cream
1 teaspoon salt
½ teaspoon white pepper
1 medium red onion, peeled and chopped fine

In a mixing bowl, whip together the sour cream, salt, and pepper until it is light. Fold in the onion. Reserve the mixture.

2 8-ounce jars plain herring fillets cut in bite-size pieces
3 medium apples, peeled, cored, and diced
Strained juice of 1 medium lemon

Prepare the herring and reserve it. Prepare the apples, tossing them with the lemon juice as you cut them to prevent their discoloring. Into the sour cream fold the herring, apple, and lemon juice. Chill the mixture.

Salad greens of your choice

Onto individual beds of salad greens, spoon equal amounts of the herring mixture.

BROILED SARDINES

4 servings
PREPARATION: about 20 minutes
COOKING: about 5 minutes in a preheated broiler

2 tablespoons butter
¼ cup bread crumbs
2 hard-cooked eggs, forced through a sieve
1 cup light cream
Salt
Grinding of pepper

In a saucepan, heat the butter and in it cook the bread crumbs, stirring, to toast them. Add the egg and cream, and over gentle heat cook the mixture for a few minutes. Season it to taste with salt and pepper. Reserve the sauce.

1 3¾-ounce can skinless sardines, well drained
4 slices toast, the crusts removed
Reserved sauce
Paprika

Arrange the sardines on the toast and run them under the broiler for about 5 minutes, or until they just begin to color. Arrange the toast slices on individual heated plates, spoon some of the hot sauce over them, and garnish each dish with a sprinkling of paprika.

SARDINE AND CHEESE SPREAD

YIELD: about 2 cups
PREPARATION: about 15 minutes

The spread may also be used as a filling for Miniature Puffs, page 299.

2   *3¾-ounce cans skinless sardines, well drained*
1   *cup cream-style cottage cheese*
1   *clove garlic, peeled and chopped*
1   *small onion, peeled and chopped*
1   *tablespoon brandy*
3   *tablespoons strained lemon juice*
¼   *teaspoon ground celery seed*
1   *tablespoon Worcestershire sauce*
    A few drops of Tabasco sauce
    Salt
    Melba toast

In the container of a food processor equipped with the steel blade, combine all but the final two ingredients. Whirl the mixture until it is smooth. Season the spread to taste with salt. Transfer it to a serving dish and offer it with Melba toast.

SARDINE AND CHIVE SPREAD

YIELD: about 1 cup
PREPARATION: about 10 minutes

The spread may also be used as a filling for Miniature Puffs, page 299.

2   *3¾-ounce cans skinless sardines, well drained*
1   *3-ounce package cream cheese, at room temperature*
1½ *tablespoons fine-chopped chives*
½   *teaspoon Worcestershire sauce*
    Melba toast

In a mixing bowl, combine and blend thoroughly all of the ingredients; transfer the spread to a serving dish and offer it with Melba toast.

SARDINE AND EGG SPREAD

YIELD: about 1 cup
PREPARATION: about 15 minutes

The spread may also be used as a filling for Miniature Puffs, page 299.

> 2 *3¾-ounce cans skinless sardines, well drained*
> 3 *tablespoons Mayonnaise, page 281*
> 1 *tablespoon Dijon mustard*
> 1 *tablespoon tarragon vinegar*
> 2 *hard-cooked eggs, forced through a sieve*
> ¼ *cup fine-chopped parsley*
> *Melba toast*

In a mixing bowl combine and blend the sardines, mayonnaise, mustard, and vinegar; stir in the sieved egg and parsley. Transfer the spread to a serving dish and offer it with Melba toast.

TUNA CANAPÉS

YIELD: about 24 canapés
PREPARATION: about 20 minutes
COOKING: 5 minutes in a 350° oven

> 2 *cups grated Cheddar cheese (mild or sharp, depending upon your taste)*
> 1 *(about 7-ounce) can waterpack tuna, drained and flaked*
> 2 *tablespoon dry vermouth*
> *Grinding of pepper*

In a mixing bowl combine and blend these four ingredients.

> 24 *toast squares (about 2 inches across)*

Spread the toast generously with the tuna mixture. Arrange the squares on a baking sheet and heat them in a 350° oven for 5 minutes, or until they are golden. Serve them hot.

TUNA AND HORSERADISH CANAPÉS

YIELD: about 32 canapés
PREPARATION: about 15 minutes
COOKING: 5 minutes in a 350° oven

1 (about 7-ounce) can waterpack tuna,
drained
6 tablespoons soft butter
3 tablespoons prepared horseradish,
drained
4 tablespoons Mayonnaise, page 281
1 scallion, trimmed and chopped fine,
with as much green as is crisp
½ teaspoon celery salt
Grinding of white pepper

In a mixing bowl, combine and blend all of the ingredients.

8 slices toast, the crusts removed and
cut in quarters

Spread the toasts with the tuna mixture. Arrange them on a baking sheet
and cook them at 350° for 5 minutes.

SALMON OR TUNA AND CHEESE CANAPÉS

YIELD: about 24 canapés
PREPARATION: about 25 minutes
COOKING: about 5 minutes in a preheated broiler

½ pound grated American or mild
Cheddar cheese
1 small onion, peeled and grated
1 (about 7-ounce) can salmon or
waterpack tuna, drained
5 tablespoons Mayonnaise, page 281
½ teaspoon sweet paprika
Grinding of white pepper

In a mixing bowl, combine and blend all of the ingredients.

6 slices thin-sliced bread, the crusts
removed and cut in quarters

Spread the bread with the fish mixture. Broil the canapés on a greased
cookie sheet for about 5 minutes, or until the cheese is melted and the
tops of the canapés are lightly browned.

SALMON OR TUNA RAREBIT

4 servings
PREPARATION: about 25 minutes
COOKING: about 2 minutes in a preheated broiler

The recipe may also be offered as a light main course.

> **2 cups coarsely grated Cheddar cheese**
> **1 tablespoon butter**
> **Few grains of cayenne pepper**
> **½ teaspoon dry mustard**
> **¼ teaspoon salt**

In the top of a double boiler, combine these five ingredients; over boiling water, cook them, stirring constantly, until the cheese begins to melt.

> **⅓ cup warm beer**
> **1 egg, lightly beaten**
> **¾ teaspoon Worcestershire sauce**

To the cheese mixture, add these three ingredients. Continue to cook the rarebit until it is smooth.

> *At this point you may stop and continue later.*

> **4 slices buttered toast or buttered English muffins**
> **1 (about 7-ounce) can salmon, drained, the skin and bones removed if necessary or 1 can waterpack tuna, drained**

Over the toast slices, distribute the fish in chunks. Over it, spoon the cheese sauce. Toast the rarebits under a hot broiler for 2 minutes, or until they are bubbly and lightly browned.

SALMON OR TUNA COCKTAIL SPREAD I

YIELD: about 3 cups
PREPARATION: about 20 minutes
CHILLING TIME: 3 hours

1 *16-ounce can salmon, drained, the skin and bones removed or 2 (about 7-ounce) cans waterpack tuna, drained*
1 *8-ounce package cream cheese, at room temperature*
1 *tablespoon prepared horseradish*
   Strained juice of ½ medium lemon
1 *small onion, peeled and grated*
½ *cup fine-chopped parsley*
   Salt

In a mixing bowl, combine and blend thoroughly all the ingredients except the salt. Season the spread to taste. Pack it into a lightly oiled mold and chill it for 3 hours, or until it is firm.

Melba toast

Onto a chilled serving plate, unmold the spread and offer it with Melba toast.

SALMON OR TUNA COCKTAIL SPREAD II

YIELD: about 2 cups
PREPARATION: about 20 minutes
CHILLING TIME: 3 hours

1 *(about 7-ounce) can salmon or waterpack tuna, drained*
1 *8-ounce package cream cheese, at room temperature*
1 *clove garlic, put through a press*
4 *tablespoons Mayonnaise, page 281*
1 *teaspoon Dijon mustard*
¼ *cup fine-chopped parsley*
2 *tablespoons dry white wine*
   Salt
   Melba toast

In a mixing bowl combine and blend thoroughly all the ingredients except the salt. Season the spread to taste. Transfer it to a serving bowl and chill it for 3 hours, or until it is firm. Offer it with Melba toast.

In the following selection of recipes, salmon and tuna are interchange-able — as they frequently are in this section of the book. The recipes, with the exception of the two chowders, are first-course soups. I include three bisque or bisque-type soups because, while they enjoy certain simi-larities, I felt that the directions for making them would be clearer if each were treated as a separate entity. I enjoy offering these soups to guests: they are easily prepared, they are economical, and they taste good.

CREAM OF SALMON OR TUNA SOUP

4 servings
PREPARATION: about 25 minutes

2 *tablespoons butter*
1 *tablespoon flour*
3 *cups milk, scalded*
1 *16-ounce can salmon, the skin and bones removed, with its liquid or 2 (about 7-ounce) cans waterpack tuna with their liquid*
   Salt
   Grinding of pepper
   Fine-chopped parsley

In a saucepan, heat the butter and in it, over gentle heat, cook the flour for a few minutes. Gradually add the milk, stirring constantly until the mixture is somewhat thickened and smooth. In the container of a food processor, using the steel blade, whirl the fish until it is smooth. Add it to the contents of the saucepan, stirring to blend the mixture well. Season the soup to taste with salt and pepper. Serve it garnished with parsley.

If desired, 4 scallions, trimmed and chopped fine, with as much green as is crisp, may be cooked until translucent in the butter before the addi-tion of the flour; complete the recipe as directed.

For a richer, bisque-type soup, add 3 tablespoons tomato paste to the *béchamel* before stirring in the fish.

SALMON OR TUNA BISQUE I

4 to 6 servings
PREPARATION: about 45 minutes

3 tablespoons butter
1 small carrot, scraped and grated
1 clove garlic, peeled and chopped fine
1 medium onion, peeled and chopped

In a saucepan, heat the butter and in it cook the carrot, garlic, and onion until the onion is translucent.

1 large ripe tomato, peeled, seeded, and
chopped

Stir in the tomato and simmer the mixture for 3 minutes.

2 cups water
1 cup dry white wine
1½ tablespoons raw natural rice

To the contents of the saucepan, add the water, wine, and rice. Bring the liquid to the boil, reduce the heat, and simmer the rice, covered, for 25 minutes, or until it is very tender. Allow the rice to cool somewhat. In the container of a food processor or blender, whirl the mixture, two cupfuls at a time, until it is smooth. Transfer it to a second, large saucepan.

1 (about 7-ounce) can salmon or water-
pack tuna, with its liquid

In the container of a food processor or blender, whirl the salmon or tuna until it is reduced to a smooth purée. Add it to the contents of the saucepan, stirring to blend the mixture well.

At this point you may stop and continue later.

1 cup heavy cream, scalded
2 teaspoons Worcestershire sauce
Salt
Grinding of white pepper
Thin-sliced scallions

Stir in the cream and bring the soup to serving temperature. Season it with the Worcestershire sauce and to taste with salt and pepper. Serve it garnished with scallions.

For *Curried Salmon or Tuna Bisque,* in step one add 1 to 1½ teaspoons curry powder.

SALMON OR TUNA BISQUE II

4 to 6 servings
PREPARATION: about 45 minutes

> **3 tablespoons butter**
> **1 small onion, peeled and chopped fine**
> **2 tablespoons flour**
> **4 cups milk**

In a large saucepan, heat the butter and in it cook the onion until translucent. Stir in the flour, and over gentle heat cook the mixture for a few minutes. Gradually add the milk, stirring constantly until the mixture is somewhat thickened and smooth.

> **1 16-ounce can salmon, broken up, with**
> **its liquid or 2 (about 7-ounce) cans**
> **waterpack tuna, with their liquid**

In the container of a food processor or blender, whirl the salmon or tuna until it is reduced to a smooth purée. Add it to the contents of the saucepan, stirring to blend the mixture well.

At this point you may stop and continue later.

> **1 cup light or heavy cream, scalded**
> **A few drops of Tabasco sauce**
> **Salt**
> **2 tablespoons dry sherry**
> **Fine-chopped parsley**

Stir in the cream and bring the soup to serving temperature. Season it to taste with Tabasco sauce and salt. At serving time, stir in the sherry and garnish the bisque with parsley.

SALMON OR TUNA BISQUE III

6 servings
PREPARATION: about 30 minutes

> **2 tablespoons butter**
> **1 small onion, peeled and grated**
> **2 tablespoons flour**

In a large saucepan, heat the butter and in it cook the onion for 3 minutes. Stir in the flour, and over gentle heat cook the mixture for a few minutes.

> **1 cup (1 8-ounce bottle) clam juice**
> **3 cups milk**

Gradually add the clam juice and milk, stirring constantly until the mixture is somewhat thickened and smooth.

> **1 16-ounce can salmon, broken up, with its liquid or 2 (about 7-ounce) cans waterpack tuna, with their liquid**

In the container of a food processor or blender, whirl the salmon and its liquid until it is reduced to a smooth purée. Add it to the contents of the saucepan, stirring to blend the mixture well.

> **1 cup light or heavy cream, scalded**
> **2 teaspoons Worcestershire sauce**
> **Salt**
> **Grinding of white pepper**
> **3 tablespoons dry sherry**
> **Fine-chopped parsley**

Stir in the cream. Season the bisque to taste with the Worcestershire sauce and salt and pepper. Stir in the sherry. Serve the soup garnished with parsley.

SALMON OR TUNA CHOWDER I

4 to 6 servings
PREPARATION: about 50 minutes

> 3 *tablespoons butter*
> 1 *rib celery, chopped fine*
> 1 *medium onion, peeled and chopped*
> ½ *green pepper, chopped*
> 3 *medium potatoes, peeled and diced*

In a large saucepan, heat the butter and in it cook the celery, onion, and pepper until the onion is barely golden. Add the potato, stirring to coat it well.

> 5 *cups Fish Stock, page 94, or 2 cups water and 3 cups clam juice (3 8-ounce bottles)*
> 3 *ripe tomatoes, peeled, seeded, and chopped or 1 16-ounce can tomatoes*
> ½ *teaspoon thyme*

To the contents of the saucepan, add the liquid, tomatoes, and thyme. Bring the liquid to the boil, reduce the heat, and simmer the mixture, covered, for about 15 minutes, or until the potatoes are tender.
At this point you may stop and continue later.

> 1 *16-ounce can salmon, the bones and skin removed, broken into chunks, with its liquid or 2 (about 7-ounce) cans waterpack tuna, broken into chunks, with their liquid*
> *Salt*
> *Grinding of pepper*
> *Dill*

Add the fish and its liquid, stirring gently to blend the chowder. Season it to taste with salt and pepper and serve it garnished with dill.
Serve with muffins, page 289.

SALMON OR TUNA CHOWDER II

6 servings
PREPARATION: about 35 minutes

A tasty and easy dish, based upon our traditional New England Fish Chowder, page 112.

¼ pound salt pork, diced

In a flameproof casserole or heavy saucepan, cook the salt pork until it is crisp and golden. With a slotted spoon, remove it to absorbent paper and reserve it.

2 medium onions, peeled and chopped
3 medium potatoes, peeled and diced
3 cups water

In the remaining fat, cook the onion until it is golden. Add the potato and cook it, stirring, for a few minutes to coat it well. Add the water. Bring the liquid to the boil, reduce the heat, and simmer the potato, covered, for 10 minutes.

1 16-ounce can salmon, drained (the liquid reserved) and flaked or 2 (about 7-ounce) cans waterpack tuna, drained (the liquid reserved) and flaked
3 cups milk or half-and-half

To the contents of the casserole, add the fish with its liquid and the milk. Bring the mixture to the simmer and continue cooking it, stirring, for 5 minutes, or until the potato is tender.

Salt
Grinding of pepper
Fine-chopped parsley
Reserved salt pork

Season the chowder to taste with salt and pepper. Stir in a generous quantity of parsley. Serve the soup garnished with the salt pork.

Serve with muffins, page 289.

MAIN DISHES

Main dishes made from canned fish are a comfort to the cook who suddenly discovers that family or friends are staying for a meal not planned. Most of the recipes in this section are readily prepared from ingredients already in your larder. I find them not only easily made but also so good tasting that I stock my kitchen shelves not necessarily for unexpected guests but for the pleasure I derive from these dishes.

ANCHOVY SAUCE FOR PASTA

6 servings
PREPARATION: about 25 minutes

> 1 **2-ounce can anchovy fillets, with their oil**
> 3 **cloves garlic, peeled and chopped coarse**
> 5 **large leaves fresh mint**
> ¾ **cup olive oil**

In the container of a food processor or blender, combine these four ingredients and whirl them until the mixture is smooth.

> 4 **teaspoons capers**
> 12 **pitted ripe olives, chopped fine**
> ½ **cup fine-chopped parsley**

Stir in the capers, olives, and parsley. Allow the sauce to sit at room temperature so that the flavors meld.

> *At this point you may stop and continue later.*

> 1½ **pounds spaghetti or linguine**

In a soup kettle, bring to the boil several quarts of lightly salted water; in it, cook the pasta according to the directions on the package until it is *al dente;* do not overcook it. Drain the cooked pasta and arrange it in a large heated serving bowl. Pour the sauce, which has been warmed while the pasta is cooking, over the spaghetti, and offer the dish accompanied by a dependable pepper grinder.

Serve with mixed green salad, page 295.

ANCHOVY SOUFFLÉ

4 servings
PREPARATION: about 30 minutes
COOKING: 30 minutes in a 350° oven

Butter and crumb a 2-quart soufflé dish.

3 2-ounce cans flat anchovy fillets

Drain the fillets, reserving 4 tablespoons of the oil; discard the remainder. Reserve the fillets.

1 cup milk

In a blender, combine the milk and fillets; whirl them until the mixture is smooth. Reserve it.

Reserved oil
4 tablespoons flour

In a saucepan, heat the reserved oil and in it, over gentle heat, cook the flour for a few minutes. Gradually add the milk, stirring constantly until the *béchamel* is thickened and smooth.

4 egg yolks
¼ cup fine-chopped parsley
4 scallions, trimmed and sliced thin, with a little of the crisp green
2 teaspoons Worcestershire sauce

Into the contents of the saucepan, beat the egg yolks. Stir in the parsley, scallions, and Worcestershire sauce.

At this point you may stop and continue later.

5 egg whites, beaten until stiff but not dry

Into the mixture, beat one-fifth of the egg white; fold in the remainder. Using a rubber spatula, transfer the batter to the prepared dish. Bake the soufflé at 350° for 30 minutes, or until it is well puffed and golden.

Serve with green beans, page 292.

For *Sardine or Mackerel Soufflé:* use 2 3¾-ounce cans skinless sardines *or* 2 4-ounce cans baby mackerel; drain them and use the oil as indicated above. With the tines of a fork, mash the fish until it is smooth; to the *roux*, add 1 small onion, peeled and grated; to the *béchamel*, add the fish. Complete the recipe as written.

MACKEREL LOAF

6 servings
PREPARATION: about 30 minutes
COOKING: 50 minutes in a 350° oven

The recipe may also be made with salmon or tuna.

 1 *15-ounce can mackerel, drained*
 (the liquid reserved) and flaked
 3 *tablespoons melted butter*
 1½ *cups cracker crumbs*
 2 *eggs, beaten*
 ⅓ *cup fine-chopped gherkins*
 Milk plus reserved fish liquid to
 equal ¾ cup
 1 *small onion, peeled and grated*
 ¼ *cup fine-chopped parsley*
 ½ *teaspoon salt*
 Grinding of pepper

In a mixing bowl, combine and blend these ingredients. Grease a 9-inch loaf pan with butter. Pack the pan tightly with the mackerel mixture.

At this point you may stop and continue later.

Bake the mackerel loaf for 50 minutes in a 350° oven. Offer it with Sauce Allemande, page 276.

Serve with Brussels sprouts, page 293.

SALMON OR TUNA CROQUETTES

Follow the directions for Fish Croquettes on page 118, using, in place of the 3 cups flaked cooked fish, 3 (about 7-ounce) cans salmon *or* water-pack tuna, drained, the skin and bones removed if necessary, and flaked with the tines of a fork. Complete the recipe as written.

Serve with green peas, page 294.

SALMON OR TUNA CRÊPES

4 servings as a main course
6 servings as a first course.
PREPARATION: about 30 minutes
(time does not include readying the crêpes, page 118,
which may be made well in advance and frozen)
COOKING: about 12 minutes in a 400° oven

2 eggs
1 cup ricotta cheese
½ cup grated Parmesan cheese
1 small onion, peeled and grated
1 16-ounce can salmon, drained, the skin and bones removed or 2 (about 7-ounce) cans waterpack tuna, drained
½ cup fine-chopped parsley
Salt
Grinding of white pepper

In a mixing bowl, beat the eggs lightly. Add the ricotta and Parmesan cheeses and blend the mixture well; stir in the onion. With a fork, flake the fish until it is smooth; blend it with the egg mixture and then stir in the parsley. Season the mixture to taste with salt and pepper.

12 prepared crêpes, page 118

Spread the filling in equal amounts on each crêpe. Roll and arrange them, seam side down, in a lightly buttered ovenproof serving dish.

2 cups Mornay Sauce, page 281

Prepare the sauce and spoon it evenly over the crêpes.
At this point you may stop and continue later.
(If you plan to continue later, cover the dish well with plastic wrap.)
Bake the crêpes, uncovered, at 400° for 12 minutes, or until the sauce is bubbly.
Serve with green peas, page 294.

An alternate filling: make a thick *béchamel* of 6 tablespoons butter, 6 tablespoons flour (add 1 teaspoon curry powder, if desired), and 2 cups milk. Add 1 small onion, peeled and grated, and your choice of flaked fish, as directed above. Add 1 10-ounce package frozen mixed vegetables cooked, according to the directions on the package, until the vegetables are just tender — do not overcook them. Complete the recipe as written.

SALMON OR TUNA WITH GRAPES
(*VÉRONIQUE*)

4 servings
PREPARATION: about 25 minutes

---

4 tablespoons butter
1 small onion, peeled and chopped fine
4 tablespoons flour
   Liquid from 2 (about 7-ounce) cans salmon or waterpack tuna plus milk to equal 1 cup; flake the fish and reserve it
1 cup milk
   Salt
   Grinding of white pepper

In a saucepan, heat the butter and in it cook the onion until translucent. Stir in the flour, and over gentle heat cook the mixture for a few minutes. Gradually add the tuna liquid and milk, stirring constantly until the mixture is thickened and smooth. Season the *béchamel* to taste with salt and pepper.

At this point you may stop and continue later.

4 to 8 slices buttered toast or toasted English muffins
1½ cups   seedless   grapes,   rinsed, drained on absorbent paper, and sliced lengthwise

Top the toast with the reserved fish. Bring the sauce to serving temperature; add the grapes and heat them through. Spoon the sauce over the fish.

Serve with Brussels sprouts, page 293.

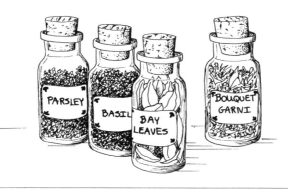

SALMON OR TUNA LOAF WITH SPINACH

4 to 6 servings
PREPARATION: about 30 minutes
COOKING: 1 hour in a 350° oven

> *2 eggs*
> *Liquid from 1 (about 7-ounce) can salmon or waterpack tuna, plus milk to equal ½ cup*
> *Fish from the 7-ounce can, the skin and bones removed if necessary, broken into chunks*

In the container of a food processor or blender, combine the eggs, milk, and fish. Whirl them until the mixture is smooth; transfer it to a mixing bowl.

> *½ cup bread crumbs*
> *2 medium ribs celery, chopped fine*
> *1 medium onion, peeled and chopped fine*
> *1 10-ounce package fresh spinach with the woody stems removed, rinsed, wilted for 20 seconds in boiling water to cover, pressed dry in a colander, and chopped or 1 10-ounce package frozen chopped spinach, fully thawed to room temperature and pressed dry in a colander*
> *1 tablespoon strained lemon juice*
> *2 teaspoons Worcestershire sauce*
> *Salt*
> *Grinding of pepper*

To the contents of the mixing bowl, add the bread crumbs, celery, onion, spinach, lemon juice, and Worcestershire sauce. Blend the mixture well before seasoning it to taste with salt and pepper.

Into a well-buttered 8- or 9-inch loaf pan, spoon the mixture evenly.

At this point you may stop and continue later.

Bake the fish loaf at 350° for 1 hour. Unmold it onto a heated serving platter and slice it at table. Cucumber Sauce, page 277, or Dill Sauce I, page 278, is a pleasant accompaniment to this dish.

Serve with broccoli, page 292.

SALMON OR TUNA WITH MACARONI AND MUSHROOMS

6 servings
PREPARATION: about 40 minutes
COOKING: 30 minutes in a 375° oven

>   *2 cups elbow macaroni*

Cook the macaroni according to package directions; do not overcook it. Drain and reserve.

>   *3 tablespoons butter*
>   *1 clove garlic, peeled and chopped fine*
>   *1 medium onion, peeled and chopped fine*
> *1½ teaspoons paprika*
>   *1 teaspoon salt*
>   *¼ teaspoon pepper*
>   *Liquid from 2 (about 7-ounce) cans salmon or waterpack tuna, plus milk to equal 3 cups; separate the fish into chunks and reserve it*

In a saucepan, heat the butter and in it cook the garlic and onion until translucent. Stir in the seasonings. Gradually add the milk, stirring constantly until the mixture is thickened and smooth.

>   *Reserved macaroni*
>   *¼ pound small mushrooms, sliced*
>   *¼ cup chopped parsley*
>   *Reserved fish*
>   *⅓ cup grated Parmesan cheese*

Into the contents of the saucepan, fold the macaroni, mushrooms, parsley, and fish. Using a rubber spatula, transfer the mixture to a buttered 2-quart casserole. Sprinkle the cheese over the dish.
At this point you may stop and continue later.
Bake the casserole at 375° for 30 minutes, or until it is heated through and the top is golden.

Serve with green bean salad, page 297.

SALMON OR TUNA WITH MUSHROOMS, MORNAY

4 servings
PREPARATION: about 35 minutes
COOKING: 20 minutes in a 350° oven

> **3 tablespoons butter**
> **1 pound mushrooms, wiped with a damp cloth, the stems removed (but reserved for another recipe)**

In a skillet, heat the butter and in it cook the mushroom caps, covered, until they are slightly wilted.

> **2 (about 7-ounce) cans salmon or waterpack tuna, drained and broken into chunks**
> **Strained lemon juice**
> **2 cups Mornay Sauce, page 281**
> **Grated Parmesan cheese**

In a buttered baking dish, arrange the mushrooms stem side up. Over them, arrange the fish; sprinkle it with lemon juice. Add the Mornay sauce and a sprinkling of Parmesan cheese.

At this point you may stop and continue later.

Bake the dish at 350° for 20 minutes, or until it is thoroughly heated through and the top is golden.

Serve with rice, page 290.

For *Salmon or Tuna Florentine:* omit the mushrooms and line the baking dish with 2 10-ounce packages fresh spinach, the woody stems removed, rinsed, wilted for 20 seconds in boiling water to cover, pressed dry in a colander, and chopped *or* 2 10-ounce packages frozen chopped spinach, fully thawed to room temperature and pressed dry in a colander. Complete the recipe as written.

Serve with green peas, page 294.

Sardines Florentine are a pleasant variation on this recipe: in place of the salmon or tuna, use 2 3¾-ounce cans skinless and boneless sardines, well drained on absorbent paper. Complete the recipe as written.

SALMON OR TUNA MOUSSE

4 to 6 servings
PREPARATION: about 40 minutes
COOKING: 40 minutes in a 375° oven

Butter a 6-cup ring mold.

> 2 *(about 7-ounce) cans salmon or*
> *waterpack tuna, drained, boned if*
> *necessary, and mashed until smooth*
> *with the tines of a fork*
> 1 *small onion, peeled and grated*
> *Strained juice of 1 small lemon*
> ¾ *teaspoon salt*
> ¼ *teaspoon white pepper*

In a mixing bowl, combine and blend these five ingredients.

> 3 *egg whites*

Into the fish mixture, beat the egg whites singly.
> *At this point you may stop and continue later.*

> 1 *cup heavy cream, whipped*

Fold in the whipped cream. Using a rubber spatula, transfer the mixture to the prepared mold. Place the mold in a pan of hot water and bake the mousse at 375° for 40 minutes, or until a sharp knife inserted at the center comes out clean. Allow the mousse to stand for about 5 minutes before unmolding it onto a heated serving plate.

Serve with green peas, page 294.

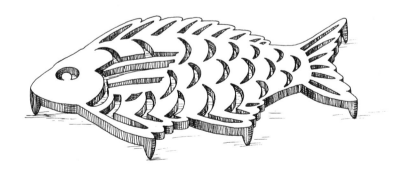

SALMON OR TUNA NEWBURG ON RICE

4 servings
PREPARATION: about 25 minutes
COOKING: 5 minutes under a preheated broiler

A dish easily made with ingredients at hand, in the event of unexpected guests.

1 tablespoons butter
1 cup raw natural rice
2 cups water
½ teaspoon salt

In a saucepan, heat the butter and in it cook the rice for a few minutes, stirring to coat each grain. Add the water and salt. Bring the liquid to the boil, reduce the heat, and simmer the rice, covered, for 15 minutes, or until it is tender and the liquid is absorbed.

2 (about 7-ounce) cans salmon or wa-
terpack tuna, drained, boned if neces-
sary, and broken into chunks
2 cups Newburg Sauce, page 282

In an ovenproof serving dish, make a bed of the cooked rice and over it, arrange the fish. Over all, spoon the sauce. Put the dish under the broiler for 5 minutes, or until the sauce is slightly glazed.

Serve with broccoli, page 292.

SALMON OR TUNA *QUENELLES*

4 to 6 servings
PREPARATION: about 25 minutes
CHILLING TIME: at least 2 hours
COOKING: 8 to 10 minutes

Quite unorthodox and certainly of more stalwart flavor than *quenelles* made with fresh lean fillet — but very good.

Follow the recipe for Fish Mousse and *Quenelles* on page 127, using in the forcemeat, in place of the lean fillet, 2 (about 7-ounce) cans of salmon *or* waterpack tuna, drained, boned if necessary, and chopped coarse. Follow the recipes for fish forcemeat and for cooking the *quenelles*.

Serve with green peas, page 294.

SALMON OR TUNA QUICHE

4 servings as a main course
6 servings as a first course
PREPARATION: about 20 minutes
(time does not include readying the pastry)
COOKING: 30 minutes, starting in a 450° oven

4 strips bacon, diced

Cook the bacon until crisp; with a slotted spoon, remove it to absorbent paper to drain; reserve it.

2 tablespoons butter
1 medium onion, peeled and chopped fine

In the butter, cook the onion until translucent.

3 eggs
1 16-ounce can salmon or 2 (about 7-ounce) cans waterpack tuna, drained (reserve the liquid), boned if necessary, and broken into chunks
1½ cups light cream
Salt

In a mixing bowl, lightly beat the eggs. Add the fish liquid and cream, stirring to blend the mixture. Season it to taste with salt.
At this point you may stop and continue later.

1 9-inch unbaked pastry shell*

Over the bottom of the pastry shell, distribute the bacon, the onion, and the fish. Over all, pour the custard. Bake the quiche at 450° for 10 minutes; reduce the heat to 325° and continue baking it for 20 minutes, or until a knife inserted at the center comes out clean. Allow the quiche to stand for 5 minutes before serving it.

Serve with mixed green salad, page 295.

If desired, you may add ⅓ cup fine-chopped parsley to the custard before pouring it over the fish, and you may sprinkle the custard with grated Parmesan cheese just as you put the quiche in the oven.

---

* Using your favorite recipe for a 9-inch quiche crust.

SCALLOPED SALMON OR TUNA

4 servings
PREPARATION: about 35 minutes
COOKING: 30 minutes in a 350° oven

3 large potatoes

In lightly salted boiling water to cover, cook the potatoes for 20 minutes, or until they are just tender; do not overcook them. Drain, peel, and slice them. Reserve.

3 tablespoons butter
1 medium onion, peeled and chopped
3 tablespoons flour
1 teaspoon salt
¼ teaspoon white pepper
2 cups milk
¼ cup chopped parsley

In a saucepan, heat the butter and in it cook the onion until translucent. Add the flour, and over gentle heat cook the mixture for a few minutes. Stir in the salt and pepper. Gradually add the milk, stirring constantly until the mixture is thickened and smooth. Stir in the parsley.

2 (about 7-ounce) cans salmon or waterpack tuna, drained, boned if necessary, and broken into chunks
½ cup grated cheese

In a buttered dish, arrange layers of the potatoes, fish, and sauce; repeat. Sprinkle the top with grated cheese.

At this point you may stop and continue later.

Bake the dish at 350° for 30 minutes, or until it is thoroughly heated through and the cheese is melted.

Serve with spinach and mushroom salad, page 298.

SALMON OR TUNA SOUFFLÉ

4 servings
PREPARATION: about 25 minutes
COOKING: 30 minutes in a 350° oven

Butter and crumb a 2-quart soufflé dish.

> *1 (about 7-ounce) can salmon or water-pack tuna, drained (reserve the liquid) and mashed with a fork*
> *Milk*

Combine the fish liquid and milk to equal 1 cup; reserve.

> *Reserved fish*
> *Reserved milk*
> *1 small onion, peeled and chopped*
> *¾ teaspoon salt*
> *¼ teaspoon white pepper*

In the container of a food processor or blender, combine the fish, milk, onion, and seasonings. Whirl them until the mixture is smooth.

> *4 tablespoons butter*
> *4 tablespoons flour*

In a saucepan, heat the butter and in it, over gentle heat, cook the flour for a few minutes. To the *roux,* add the salmon mixture, stirring constantly until it is thickened and smooth.

> *4 egg yolks*
> *¼ cup fine-chopped parsley*

Into the mixture, beat the egg yolks; stir in the parsley.
> *At this point you may stop and continue later.*

> *5 egg whites, beaten until stiff but not dry*

Beat in one-fifth of the egg white; fold in the remainder. Using a rubber spatula, transfer the batter to the prepared dish. Bake the soufflé at 350° for 30 minutes, or until it is well puffed and golden.

Serve with green peas, page 294.

CURRIED TUNA ON RICE

6 servings
PREPARATION: about 30 minutes
COOKING: about 20 minutes

  8 *tablespoons butter*
  1 *large clove garlic, peeled and chopped*
    fine
  4 *medium onions, peeled and chopped*
  3 *apples, peeled, cored, and diced (toss*
    the apple with strained fresh lemon
    juice to prevent its discoloring)
  2 *tablespoons flour*
  1 *tablespoon (or more, to taste) sweet*
    curry powder
  1 *16-ounce can Italian tomatoes*
  2 *teaspoons sugar*
    Salt
    Grinding of pepper

In a saucepan, heat the butter and in it cook the garlic and onion until translucent. Add the apple, stirring to coat the dice. Over the contents of the saucepan, sprinkle the flour and curry powder, stirring. Add the tomatoes and sugar, breaking the tomatoes against the sides of the saucepan with a large spoon. Season the sauce to taste with salt and pepper. Bring it to the boil, reduce the heat, and simmer it, covered, for 20 minutes.

At this point you may stop and continue later.

  1½ *cups raw natural rice*
   3 *cups water*
   ¾ *teaspoon salt*

In a saucepan combine the rice, water, and salt. Bring the liquid to the boil, stir the rice once with a fork, reduce the heat, and simmer covered for 15 minutes, or until it is tender and the liquid is absorbed. While the rice is cooking, complete the sauce.

  2 *(about 7-ounce) cans waterpack tuna,*
    drained and broken into chunks

Over medium heat, bring the sauce to serving temperature. Add the tuna and heat it through. Serve the rice and curried tuna separately. If desired, offer small bowls of condiments for curried dishes: mango chutney, shredded coconut, peeled and diced cucumber, crushed unsalted peanuts, golden raisins, and chopped scallions.

Serve with mixed green salad, page 295.

TUNA AND BEAN CASSEROLE

6 servings
PREPARATION: about 20 minutes
COOKING: 25 minutes in a 425° oven

A hearty dish made from convenience foods at hand.

> **2 16-ounce cans kidney beans, drained
> and rinsed with cold water**
> **2 medium onions, peeled and chopped**
> **1 20-ounce can Italian tomatoes, with
> their liquid**
> **2 (about 7-ounce) cans undrained oil-
> pack tuna broken in chunks**
> **2 teaspoons chili powder**
> **A few drops of Tabasco sauce**
> **Salt**

In a mixing bowl, combine and blend the first five ingredients. Season the mixture to taste with Tabasco sauce and salt. Transfer it to an ovenproof casserole or baking dish.

At this point you may stop and continue later.

Bake the casserole, uncovered, at 425° for 25 minutes, or until it is heated through and the top is slightly crusty.

Serve with mixed green salad, page 295.

TUNA DIVAN (TUNA WITH BROCCOLI)

6 servings
PREPARATION: about 35 minutes
COOKING: 12 minutes in a 450° oven

The recipe may also be made with canned salmon; in making the sauce, substitute 4 tablespoons butter for the tuna oil.

> **2 pounds fresh broccoli with the coarse
> outer leaves removed, the woody stems
> peeled and split or 2 or 3 10-ounce
> packages frozen broccoli**

In 1 inch of boiling salted water, cook the broccoli for 15 minutes, or until it is tender-crisp; do not overcook it. (If you use frozen broccoli, cook it according to package directions.) Drain and arrange the vegetable over the bottom of a buttered baking dish.

> **2 (about 7-ounce) cans oilpack tuna
> (the oil reserved), broken into chunks**

Prepare the fish and reserve it.

> **Reserved tuna oil
> 4 tablespoons flour
> 2 chicken bouillon cubes, powdered
> 2 cups milk
> ⅓ cup grated Parmesan cheese
> 1 tablespoon strained fresh lemon
> juice
> Salt
> Grinding of pepper**

In a saucepan, heat the tuna oil and in it, over gentle heat, cook the flour for a few minutes. Stir in the bouillon powder. Gradually add the milk, stirring constantly until the mixture is thickened and smooth. Blend in the cheese. Season the sauce with the lemon juice and salt and pepper, to taste. Reserve.

> **Reserved tuna**

Over the broccoli layer, distribute the tuna.

At this point you may stop and continue later.

> **Reserved sauce
> ⅓ cup buttered bread crumbs**

Over the tuna and broccoli, pour the prepared sauce. Over the sauce, sprinkle the bread crumbs. Bake the dish at 450° for 12 minutes, or until it is well heated and the sauce is bubbly.

Serve with green peas, page 294.

TUNA SAUCE FOR PASTA

4 servings
PREPARATION: about 25 minutes
COOKING: 10 minutes

> 2 (about 7-ounce) cans oilpack tuna, drained (reserve the oil) and broken into chunks
> Olive oil
> 3 cloves garlic, peeled and chopped fine
> 3 large ripe tomatoes, peeled, seeded, and chopped
> ¼ cup fine-chopped parsley
> ½ teaspoon oregano
> Salt
> Grinding of pepper

Combine the tuna and olive oils to equal ½ cup. In a saucepan, heat the oil mixture and in it cook the garlic for 5 minutes. Add the tomatoes and cook them for 5 minutes. Add the reserved fish, parsley, and oregano, stirring to blend the sauce well. Season it to taste with salt and pepper.

At this point you may stop and continue later.

> 1 pound spaghetti or linguine
> Grated Parmesan cheese

In a soup kettle, bring to the boil several quarts of lightly salted water; in it, cook the pasta according to package directions until it is *al dente;* do not overcook it. Meanwhile, over gentle heat, bring the sauce to serving temperature. Drain the cooked pasta and arrange it in a large heated serving bowl. Pour the hot sauce over it; offer the grated cheese separately.

Serve with mixed green salad, page 295.

TUNA IN GINGER SAUCE

4 servings
PREPARATION: about 30 minutes

> *3 tablespoons butter*
> *4 scallions, trimmed and cut in ½-inch segments, with as much green as is crisp*
> *3 medium ribs celery, diced*
> *1 8-ounce can water chestnuts, drained and sliced*
> *1 13½-ounce can pineapple chunks, drained (reserve the liquid)*
> *2 (about 7-ounce) cans waterpack tuna, drained (reserve the liquid) and flaked*

In a saucepan, heat the butter and in it cook the scallions until they are limp. Add the celery and continue to cook the mixture, stirring often, for 5 minutes. Add the water chestnuts, pineapple chunks, and tuna, stirring to blend the mixture.

> *Reserved pineapple liquid*
> *Reserved tuna liquid*
> *2 teaspoons cornstarch*
> *1 teaspoon powdered ginger*
> *2 tablespoons soy sauce*

In a second saucepan, combine the pineapple and tuna liquids. In a small mixing bowl, combine and blend the cornstarch and ginger. Add the soy sauce and a little of the liquid, stirring until the mixture is smooth. Add the cornstarch mixture to the pineapple and tuna liquids.
At this point you may stop and continue later.

> *1 cup raw natural rice*
> *2 cups water*

In a saucepan, combine the rice and water. Bring the liquid to the boil, stir the rice once with a fork, reduce the heat, and simmer covered for 15 minutes, or until it is tender and the liquid is absorbed. While the rice is cooking, ready the tuna-vegetable mixture and the sauce.

Over gentle heat, bring the tuna and vegetables to serving temperature; cover to keep them moist. Stir the sauce (the cornstarch will have settled to the bottom); over high heat, bring the sauce to the boil, stirring constantly until it is thickened and smooth.

On a heated serving platter, arrange a bed of the rice. Over it, distribute the tuna mixture. Over all, spoon the sauce.

Serve with green bean salad, page 297.

For *Tuna in Sweet-and-Pungent Sauce:* follow step one, using 1 20-ounce can pineapple chunks. In step two, to make the sauce, combine in a saucepan 3 tablespoons sugar, ¾ teaspoon ground ginger, and 3 tablespoons cornstarch; add 1 cup chicken broth, the liquid from the can of pineapple, 4 tablespoons cider vinegar, and 3 tablespoons soy sauce (if desired, you may also add the grated rind of 1 medium orange). Complete steps three through five.

TUNA AND VEGETABLE CASSEROLE

6 servings
PREPARATION: about 40 minutes
COOKING: 15 minutes in a 425° oven

3 large carrots, scraped and sliced thin
3 medium potatoes, peeled and diced

In boiling water just to cover, cook the carrots and potatoes for 15 minutes, or until they are tender. Drain them, reserving the liquid.

2 (about 7-ounce) cans waterpack tuna, drained (reserve the liquid) and flaked
Reserved vegetable liquid
Heavy cream

Combine the tuna and vegetable liquids and to them add heavy cream to equal 2 cups. Reserve the mixture.

4 tablespoons butter
1 medium onion, peeled and chopped
2 tablespoons flour
¼ teaspoon powdered thyme
Reserved cream mixture
Salt
Grinding of white pepper

In a saucepan, heat the butter and in it cook the onion until translucent. Stir in the flour, and over gentle heat cook the mixture for a few minutes. Stir in the thyme. Gradually add the liquid, stirring constantly until the mixture is thickened and smooth. Season the sauce to taste with salt and pepper.

Reserved carrots and potatoes
Reserved fish
1 10-ounce package frozen small peas, fully thawed to room temperature

Into the contents of the saucepan, fold the carrots, potatoes, fish, and peas. Into a buttered 10-by-6 baking dish, spoon the mixture.
At this point you may stop and continue later.

½ cup butter-toasted bread crumbs

Over the contents of the baking dish, sprinkle the crumbs. Bake the casserole, uncovered, at 425° for 15 minutes, or until it is heated through and the crumbs are golden brown.

Serve with mixed green salad, page 295.

TUNA-STUFFED EGGPLANT

4 servings
PREPARATION: about 40 minutes
COOKING: 30 minutes in a 375° oven

2 small eggplants

Cut the eggplant in lengthwise halves. Scoop out the pulp, leaving a ½-inch shell. Chop the pulp; reserve the shells.

4 tablespoons olive oil
1 clove garlic, peeled and chopped fine
1 medium onion, peeled and chopped fine
Reserved eggplant pulp
1½ cups tomato purée
¼ cup fine-chopped parsley
Few drops of Tabasco sauce
Salt

In a skillet, heat the oil and in it cook the garlic and onion until translucent. Add the eggplant pulp and cook it until it is brown. Stir in the tomato purée and parsley. Season the sauce to taste with Tabasco and salt. Reserve.

1 (about 7-ounce) can waterpack tuna, drained and flaked
2 slices bread, soaked in water and squeezed dry
½ teaspoon Dijon mustard
¼ teaspoon thyme
Reserved eggplant shells

In a mixing bowl, combine and blend the tuna, bread, mustard, and thyme. Spoon the mixture into the eggplant shells. In a lightly oiled baking dish, arrange the shells.

At this point you may stop and continue later.

Reserved sauce
⅔ cup water

Into the sauce, stir the water. Bring the mixture to the boil, pour it over the eggplant, and bake at 375° for 30 minutes, or until the shells are tender.

Serve with green beans, page 292.

SARDINE-STUFFED PEPPERS

4 servings
PREPARATION: about 30 minutes
COOKING: 30 minutes in a 350° oven

⅔ cup raw natural rice
1⅓ cups water

In a saucepan, combine the rice and water. Bring the liquid to the boil, stir the rice once with a fork, reduce the heat, and simmer covered for 15 minutes, or until the rice is tender and the water is absorbed. Reserve.

4 large green peppers

In boiling water to cover, cook the peppers for 5 minutes. Drain and refresh them in cold water. Remove the stem ends and seed them. Reserve.

2 3¾-ounce cans skinless and boneless
sardines, drained (reserve the oil) and
flaked
1 medium onion, peeled and chopped
fine

In a saucepan, heat the sardine oil and in it cook the onion until translucent.

Reserved rice
Reserved sardines
1 egg, beaten
¼ cup fine-chopped parsley
½ cup Marinara Sauce, page 280, or
canned tomato sauce
Salt
Grinding of pepper
¼ cup buttered bread crumbs

To the contents of the saucepan, add the rice, sardines, egg, parsley, and marinara sauce, stirring to blend the mixture well. Season it to taste with salt and pepper. With the mixture, fill the peppers; top them with the bread crumbs.

At this point you may stop and continue later.

Arrange the peppers in a baking pan; add water to a depth of ¼ inch. Bake the peppers at 350° for 30 minutes, or until they are tender.

Serve with spinach and mushroom salad, page 298.

For *Tuna-stuffed Peppers:* substitute 2 (about 7-ounce) cans of oilpack tuna for the sardines.

SALADS AND CHILLED DISHES

The larder in my home always contains a variety of canned fish — salmon and tuna, of course, and anchovies, mackerel, and sardines of several kinds. Not only are they useful as the principal ingredients of various hot dishes, as we have seen in the previous section of the book, but they may also be used in a variety of salads and chilled dishes attractive to the eye and pleasing to the taste. How comforting for the cook to know that with a minimum of fuss a salad or cold plate can be offered to family or friends who happen to drop by!

Canned fish salads are appetizing served on fresh greens of your choice or in avocado halves or tomato shells. Accompanied by muffins, page 289, which are almost as rapidly produced as the salads themselves, these dishes constitute a colorful and satisfying light meal.

All recipes in this section may be used as main dishes, and can be prepared for the most part without cooking on a summer's day. They also serve, however, as side dishes or salad courses, depending upon how you choose to present them.

ANCHOVY AND LENTIL SALAD

4 to 6 servings
PREPARATION: about 35 minutes

1 cup quick-cooking lentils

In lightly salted boiling water to cover, cook the lentils for 25 minutes, or until they are tender but still hold their shape. Drain and transfer them to a mixing bowl.

> *1 2-ounce can anchovy fillets, drained
> on absorbent paper and chopped*
> *⅓ cup fine-chopped dill pickles*
> *⅓ cup fine-chopped parsley*
> *5 scallions, trimmed and chopped fine,
> with a little of the crisp green
> Vinaigrette Sauce, page 289*

To the lentils, add the anchovy, dill pickles, parsley, and scallions. Add sufficient vinaigrette sauce to coat the mixture; toss the salad with two forks. The salad should not be wet with dressing. Chill before serving.

HERRING MOUSSE

6 to 8 servings
PREPARATION: about 25 minutes
CHILLING TIME: 6 hours

Lightly oil and chill a 5-cup ring or other mold.

> *1½ envelopes unflavored gelatin, soft-*
> *ened for 5 minutes in ½ cup cold*
> *water*
> *½ cup boiling water*

To the gelatin, add the boiling water, stirring until the gelatin is dissolved; reserve it.

> *2 8-ounce jars herring in cream sauce*
> *1 cup cream-style cottage cheese*
> *Reserved gelatin*

In the container of a food processor or blender, combine these three ingredients; whirl them until the mixture is smooth. Transfer it to a mixing bowl and chill it until it just begins to set.

> *⅓ cup fine-chopped parsley*
> *½ green or red sweet pepper, diced*
> *3 scallions, trimmed and chopped fine,*
> *with as much green as is crisp*
> *Salt*
> *Grinding of white pepper*
> *1 cup heavy cream, whipped*

Into the contents of the mixing bowl, fold the parsley, pepper, and scallions. Season the mixture to taste with salt and pepper. Fold in the whipped cream. Using a rubber spatula, transfer the mixture to the prepared mold. Chill the mousse for 6 hours, or until it is thoroughly set. Unmold it onto a chilled serving plate. Fill the center with Mixed Vegetable Salad, page 298.

Serve with casserole-baked bread, page 288.

HERRING SALAD, DANISH STYLE
(*SILDESALAT*)

6 servings
PREPARATION: about 30 minutes
CHILLING TIME: 3 hours

> **2 *tart apples, peeled and cored***
> ***Strained juice of 1 medium lemon***
> **1 *medium dill pickle, diced***
> **2 *8-ounce jars herring in wine sauce,***
> ***drained (reserve the liquid) and cut***
> ***in bite-size pieces***

Dice the apple into the lemon juice; stir the fruit to prevent its discoloring.
Add the dill pickle and herring, stirring to blend the mixture.

> **1 *tablespoon butter***
> **1½ *tablespoons flour***
> **½ *cup reserved herring liquid***
> **¾ *cup chicken broth***
> **¾ *teaspoon Dijon mustard***

In a small saucepan, heat the butter and in it, over gentle heat, cook the
flour for a few minutes. Add the herring liquid and chicken broth, stirring
constantly until the mixture is thickened and smooth. Stir in the mustard.
To the herring mixture, add the sauce and blend the ingredients well. Chill
the salad for 3 hours.

> ***Salad greens of your choice***
> ***Fine-chopped parsley***

On a bed of salad greens, arrange the herring mixture. Garnish it with
parsley.

Serve with muffins, page 289.

MACKEREL OR SARDINE AND HORSERADISH MOUSSE

6 servings
PREPARATION: about 35 minutes
CHILLING TIME: 6 hours

Lightly oil and chill a 5-cup ring or other mold.

> *1½ envelopes unflavored gelatin, soft-*
> *ened for 5 minutes in ½ cup cold*
> *water*

Over simmering water, dissolve the gelatin and reserve it.

> *2 3¾-ounce cans skinless sardines,*
> *drained or 2 4-ounce cans baby*
> *mackerel, drained*
> *2 cups cream-style cottage cheese (16*
> *ounces)*
> *Reserved gelatin*

In the container of a food processor or blender, combine these three ingredients and whirl them until the mixture is smooth. Transfer it to a mixing bowl.

> *4 tablespoons prepared horseradish*
> *1 small clove garlic, peeled and put*
> *through a press*
> *⅓ cup fine-chopped parsley*
> *½ teaspoon salt*
> *¼ teaspoon white pepper*

To the contents of the mixing bowl, add these five ingredients. Blend the
mixture well and then chill it until it just begins to set.

> *1 cup heavy cream, whipped*

Fold in the whipped cream. Using a rubber spatula, transfer the mixture
to the prepared mold. Chill the mousse for 6 hours, or until it is
thoroughly set. Unmold the mousse onto a chilled plate. Fill the center
with Mixed Vegetable Salad, page 298.

SALMON OR TUNA SALAD

6 servings
PREPARATION: about 20 minutes
CHILLING TIME: 3 hours

1 large rib celery, diced
1 large cucumber, peeled, seeded, and diced
¼ cup fine-chopped gherkins or sweet pickle
2 or 3 gratings onion
1 16-ounce can salmon or 2 (about 7-ounce) cans waterpack tuna, drained, the skin and bones removed if necessary, and broken into chunks
Mayonnaise, page 281
Salad greens of your choice
Hard-cooked egg wedges

In a mixing bowl, combine the first five ingredients. Add sufficient mayonnaise just to bind the mixture, and chill it for 3 hours. Arrange it on salad greens and garnish with the egg wedges.

Serve with muffins, page 289.

For *Salmon or Tuna in Tomato Shells:* prepare the salad as directed above. Peel and remove the stems and centers from 6 large ripe tomatoes; season the cavities lightly with salt and pepper. Arrange them hollow side down on a plate, cover them with plastic wrap, and refrigerate them. Fill the tomatoes with the fish mixture, arrange them on salad greens, and garnish with the egg wedges.

SALMON OR TUNA AND APPLE SALAD

4 to 6 servings
PREPARATION: about 25 minutes

3 *large tart apples, peeled and diced*
Strained juice of 1 large lemon
2 *medium ribs celery, chopped fine*
1 *11-ounce can mandarin orange sec-*
tions, drained (optional)
1 *(about 7-ounce) can waterpack tuna,*
drained and broken into small pieces
Mayonnaise, page 281
Salt
Grinding of pepper

In a mixing bowl, combine the apple and lemon juice, stirring the apple to prevent its discoloring. To the apple, add the celery, mandarin orange sections, and tuna. Add only sufficient mayonnaise to bind the mixture. Using two forks, toss the salad lightly. Season it to taste with salt and pepper. Chill and serve it on salad greens of your choice.

For *Salmon or Tuna and Grape Salad:* in place of the apple use 2 cups of seedless grapes, rinsed, drained on absorbent paper, and halved lengthwise; for the celery, substitute 1 5½-ounce can water chestnuts, drained and sliced thin; and for plain mayonnaise, substitute Curried Mayonnaise, page 281.
Serve with muffins, page 289.

SALMON OR TUNA,
APPLE, AND GREEN PEA SALAD

See the recipe for Fish, Apple, and Green Pea Salad, page 152; for the flaked cooked fish, substitute 2 (about 7-ounce) cans salmon or waterpack tuna, drained, the skin and bones removed if necessary, and broken into chunks. Complete the recipe.

For *Herring, Apple, and Green Pea Salad:* see the recipe for Fish, Apple, and Green Pea Salad, page 152; for the flaked cooked fish, substitute 12 ounces herring in wine sauce, drained, rinsed, and cut in bite-size pieces.

SALMON OR TUNA WALDORF SALAD

6 servings
PREPARATION: about 40 minutes
CHILLING TIME: 3 hours

The classic apple-and-celery salad is very good with the addition of salmon or tuna.

> **3 large tart apples, peeled, cored, and
> diced**
> **Strained fresh lemon juice**

As you prepare the apples, toss them with lemon juice to prevent their discoloring.

> **3 medium ribs celery, diced**
> **Mayonnaise, page 281**
> **Salt**
> **Grinding of white pepper**

In a mixing bowl, combine the apples and celery. Add sufficient mayonnaise just to bind the mixture and toss to blend it well. Season the salad to taste with salt and pepper. Chill it for 3 hours.

> **2 (about 7-ounce) cans salmon or wa-
> terpack tuna, drained, the skin and
> bones removed if necessary, broken
> into chunks, and chilled**
> **¾ cup chopped walnuts**
> **Salad greens of your choice**
> **Fine-chopped parsley**

Into the salad, fold the fish and walnuts; add mayonnaise as necessary for a moist consistency. Arrange the salad on a bed of greens and garnish it with parsley.

Serve with muffins, page 289.

SALMON OR TUNA AND GRAPEFRUIT SALAD

4 servings
PREPARATION: about 30 minutes
CHILLING TIME: 3 hours

- 3 *medium ribs celery, diced*
- 1 *large grapefruit, halved, sectioned, the seeds removed*
- 1 *small red onion, peeled, sliced thin, and separated into rings*
- ½ *medium green pepper, diced*
- 2 *(about 7-ounce) cans salmon or tuna, drained, the skin and bones removed if necessary, and broken into chunks*
  Mayonnaise, page 281
  Strained juice of ½ small lemon
  Salt
  Grinding of white pepper

In a large mixing bowl, combine the first five ingredients. Add the mayonnaise (about ½ cup, just enough to bind the mixture) and lemon juice. Gently toss the salad. Season it to taste with salt and pepper and toss it briefly once again. Chill it for at least 3 hours.

Salad greens of your choice
Fine-chopped parsley

Arrange the salad on a bed of greens and garnish it with a sprinkling of parsley.

Serve with muffins, page 289.

HERBED SALMON OR TUNA SALAD

4 to 6 servings
PREPARATION: about 25 minutes
CHILLING TIME: 3 hours

- 2 *scallions, trimmed and chopped fine, with as much green as is crisp*
- 3 *tablespoons strained lemon juice*
- ½ *teaspoon ground cloves*
- ½ *teaspoon crumbled rosemary*
- ½ *teaspoon powdered thyme*
- ½ *teaspoon salt*
- 1 *cup sour cream*

In a mixing bowl, combine and blend these ingredients. Allow the sauce to stand for some time at room temperature, so that the flavors meld, before refrigerating it for 3 hours.

> 2 *(about 7-ounce) cans salmon or waterpack tuna, drained, the skin and bones removed if necessary, and broken into chunks*
> *Salad greens of your choice*

Arrange the fish on the salad greens. Garnish it with the sauce or offer the sauce separately.

Serve with muffins, page 289.

SALMON OR TUNA AND PINEAPPLE SALAD

4 servings
PREPARATION: about 25 minutes
CHILLING TIME: 3 hours

> 2 *(about 7-ounce) cans salmon or tuna, drained, the skin and bones removed if necessary, and broken into chunks*
> ½ *medium green pepper, diced*
> 1 *20-ounce can unsweeted pineapple chunks, drained*
> 4 *scallions, trimmed and sliced thin, with as much green as is crisp*
> ½ *cup thin-sliced water chestnuts*
> *Mayonnaise, page 281*
> *Salt*
> *Grinding of white pepper*

In a mixing bowl, combine the first five ingredients. Add sufficient mayonnaise just to bind them (about ½ cup) and gently toss the mixture to blend it. Season the salad to taste with salt and pepper and toss it briefly once again. Chill it for 3 hours.

> *Salad greens of your choice*
> *Fine-chopped sweet gherkins*

Arrange the salad on a bed of greens and garnish it with a sprinkling of sweet gherkins.

Serve with muffins, page 289.

Two cups coarse-chopped fresh pineapple may be substituted for the canned chunks — a delicious, if costlier, variation.

SALMON OR TUNA MOUSSE I

6 to 8 servings
PREPARATION: about 35 minutes
CHILLING TIME: 6 hours

Lightly oil and chill a 6-cup ring or other mold.

> *1 envelope plus 1 teaspoon unflavored*
> *gelatin softened for 5 minutes in ½*
> *cup cold water*
> *½ cup boiling water*

To the softened gelatin, add the boiling water, stirring until the gelatin is dissolved.

> *Dissolved gelatin*
> *1 16-ounce can salmon, drained (the*
> *liquid reserved), the skin and bones*
> *removed, broken into small pieces or*
> *2 (about 7-ounce) cans waterpack*
> *tuna (the liquid reserved), broken*
> *into small pieces*
> *Grated rind and strained juice of 1*
> *medium lemon*
> *1 teaspoon salt*
> *½ teaspoon white pepper*

In the container of a food processor or blender, combine the gelatin, the salmon and its liquid, the lemon rind and juice, and salt and pepper. Whirl them until the mixture is smooth. Transfer to a mixing bowl.

> *¼ cup fine-chopped gherkins*
> *¼ cup fine-chopped parsley*

Into the contents of the mixing bowl, stir the gherkins and parsley.

> *½ cup Mayonnaise, page 281*
> *2 cups cream-style cottage cheese*

In the container of a food processor or blender, combine the mayonnaise and cottage cheese. Whirl them until the mixture is smooth; add it to the contents of the mixing bowl, stirring to blend the ingredients well. Chill the mixture until it just begins to set.

> *1 cup heavy cream, whipped*
> *3 egg whites, beaten until stiff but not*
> *dry (optional)*

Fold in the whipped cream. For an airier mousse, fold in the egg white as well. Using a rubber spatula, transfer the mixture to the prepared mold. Chill the mousse for at least 6 hours, or until it is thoroughly set. Unmold the mousse onto a chilled serving plate. Fill the center with Mixed Vegetable Salad, page 298.

Serve with muffins, page 289.

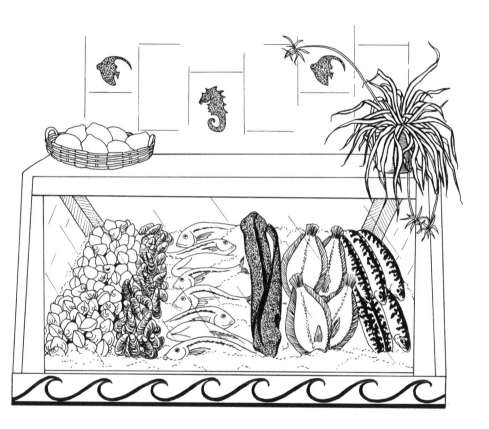

SALMON OR TUNA MOUSSE II

6 to 8 servings
PREPARATION: about 30 minutes
CHILLING TIME: 6 hours

Lightly oil and chill a 6-cup ring or other mold.

> *1½ envelopes unflavored gelatin, soft-*
> *ened for 5 minutes in ½ cup cold*
> *water*
> *½ cup boiling water*

To the gelatin, add the boiling water, stirring until the gelatin is dissolved; reserve it.

> *2 cups cream-style cottage cheese*
> *1 small onion, peeled and chopped*
> *coarse*
> *2 (about 7-ounce) cans salmon or*
> *waterpack tuna, drained, boned if*
> *necessary, and broken into chunks*
> *½ teaspoon paprika*
> *A few drops of Tabasco sauce*
> *1 teaspoon salt*
> *Reserved gelatin*

In the container of a food processor or blender, combine these seven ingredients. Whirl them until the mixture is smooth. Transfer it to a mixing bowl.

> *⅓ cup fine-chopped gherkins*
> *⅔ cup Mayonnaise, page 281*

To the contents of the mixing bowl, add the gherkins and mayonnaise. Blend the mixture well and chill it until it just begins to set.

> *1 cup heavy cream, whipped*

Fold in the whipped cream. Using a rubber spatula, transfer the mixture to the prepared mold. Chill the mousse for 6 hours, or until it is thoroughly set. Unmold the mousse onto a chilled serving plate. Fill the center with Mixed Vegetable Salad, page 298.

Serve with muffins, page 289.

SARDINE AND POTATO SALAD

6 servings
PREPARATION: about 40 minutes
CHILLING TIME: 3 hours

2 *3¾-ounce cans skinless, boneless sardines, drained*
1 *teaspoon Dijon mustard*
½ *cup sour cream*
½ *teaspoon salt*
¼ *teaspoon white pepper*

In a mixing bowl, mash the sardines. Add the mustard, sour cream, salt, and pepper, and blend the mixture until it is smooth. Reserve it.

3 *large potatoes, peeled and cut in large dice*
1 *large rib celery, diced*
1 *medium red onion, peeled, sliced thin, and separated into rings*
½ *cup fine-chopped parsley*
   Vinaigrette Sauce, page 287

In lightly salted boiling water to cover, cook the potatoes for 12 minutes, or until they are just tender; do not overcook. Drain them thoroughly. In a mixing bowl, combine the potato with the celery, onion, and parsley. Toss the mixture with about ¼ cup vinaigrette sauce. Cover and chill the salad for 3 hours.

At this point you may stop and continue later.

   Hard-cooked eggs
1 *3¾-ounce can skinless, boneless sardines, drained*

Over the potato salad, pour the sardine–sour cream mixture; toss the salad lightly and garnish it with hard-cooked egg halves and whole sardines.

Serve with casserole-baked bread, page 288.

6 servings
PREPARATION: about 40 minutes
CHILLING TIME: 3 hours

The well-known French combination of tuna and vegetables offers a satisfying one-dish warm-weather meal.

> *3 medium potatoes, boiled for 20 minutes or until tender, peeled and sliced*
>
> *1 pound green beans, trimmed, cooked in lightly salted boiling water to cover for 12 minutes or until tender-crisp, refreshed in cold water, and drained*

Prepare the two vegetables and chill them.

> *3 medium ribs celery, diced*
>
> *1 medium clove garlic, peeled and put through a press*
>
> *12 pitted ripe olives, cut in lengthwise quarters*
>
> *1 medium onion, peeled and chopped fine*
>
> *½ medium green pepper, diced*
>
> *½ teaspoon thyme*

In a mixing bowl, toss together these six ingredients. Cover and chill them.

> *2 (about 7-ounce) cans oilpack tuna, broken in chunks, with their oil*
> *Vinaigrette Sauce, page 287*

To the contents of the mixing bowl, add the potatoes, beans, and tuna. Toss the mixture with sufficient vinaigrette sauce to coat and season the ingredients. Cover and chill the salad.

> *Salad greens of your choice*
>
> *1 2-ounce can anchovy fillets, drained on absorbent paper*
>
> *3 hard-cooked eggs, halved*
>
> *3 ripe tomatoes, peeled and cut in wedges*

Arrange the salad on a bed of greens and garnish it with the anchovy fillets, hard-cooked egg halves, and tomato wedges.

Serve with casserole-baked bread, page 288.

TUNA AND RICE SALAD

6 servings
PREPARATION: about 30 minutes
CHILLING TIME: 3 hours

> ¾ **cup raw natural rice**
> 1½ **cups water**
> ¾ **teaspoon salt**

In a saucepan, combine the rice, water, and salt. Bring the liquid to the boil, stir the rice once with a fork, reduce the heat, and simmer the rice, covered, for 15 minutes, or until it is tender and the liquid is absorbed.

> 1 **large rib celery, diced**
> 1 **10-ounce package frozen small peas,**
> **fully thawed to room temperature**
> 1 **5½-ounce can pineapple tidbits,**
> **drained (reserve the liquid)**
> 3 **scallions, trimmed and chopped fine,**
> **with as much green as is crisp**
> 2 **(about 7-ounce) cans waterpack tuna,**
> **drained and broken in chunks**
> **Mayonnaise, page 281**
> **Salt**
> **Grinding of white pepper**

In a mixing bowl, combine the cooked rice with the next five ingredients. Toss the mixture with sufficient mayonnaise barely to bind them; add a little of the pineapple liquid and gently toss the mixture again. Season the salad to taste with salt and pepper, and if necessary add more mayonnaise to assure the binding. Chill the salad for 3 hours.

> **Salad greens of your choice**
> **Unpeeled thin-sliced cucumber**

Arrange the salad on a bed of greens and garnish it with cucumber slices.

Serve with muffins, page 289.

TUNA IN TOMATO ASPIC

6 to 8 servings
PREPARATION: about 1 hour
CHILLING TIME: 6 hours

Lightly oil and chill a 2-quart mold.

> *4 tablespoons butter*
> *3 medium ribs celery, with their leaves,*
> *chopped*
> *1 large clove garlic, peeled and*
> *chopped*
> *2 medium onions, peeled and chopped*

In a large saucepan or soup kettle, heat the butter and in it, over medium heat, cook the celery, garlic, and onion for 10 minutes.

> *5 ripe medium tomatoes, chopped*
> *coarse*
> *3 cups tomato juice*
> *1 tablespoon tomato paste*
> *Zest and strained juice of 1 medium*
> *lemon*
> *1 tablespoon Worcestershire sauce*
> *1 tablespoon dried basil, or several*
> *leaves of fresh*
> *1 bay leaf*
> *3 cloves*
> *2 teaspoons sugar*
> *1 teaspoon salt*
> *8 peppercorns*

To the contents of the saucepan, add these twelve ingredients. Bring the liquid to the boil, reduce the heat, and simmer the mixture, covered, for 40 minutes.

> *2 envelopes plus 1 teaspoon unflavored*
> *gelatin, softened for 5 minutes in 1*
> *cup of tomato juice*

Into a mixing bowl, strain the contents of the saucepan. To the liquid, add the gelatin, stirring until it is dissolved. Allow the mixture to cool and then chill it until it just begins to set.

> *1 large cucumber, peeled, seeded, and*
> *diced*

**2 (about 7-ounce) cans waterpack tuna,
drained and broken in chunks**

Into the aspic, fold first the cucumber and then the tuna. Using a rubber spatula, transfer the mixture to the prepared mold. Chill the aspic for 6 hours, or until it is thoroughly set.

**Salad greens of your choice
Hard-cooked eggs**

Onto a chilled serving dish, unmold the aspic; garnish it with salad greens and hard-cooked egg halves.

Serve with casserole-baked bread, page 288.

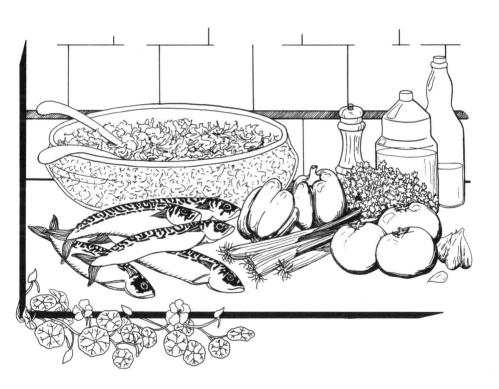

TUNA AND BEAN SALAD

6 servings
PREPARATION: about 30 minutes
CHILLING TIME: 3 hours

1 cup Great Northern or Navy pea
beans

In 2 quarts of cold water, bring the beans rapidly to the boil and cook them, uncovered, for 5 minutes. Remove them from the heat and allow them to stand, covered, for 1 hour. Return them to the boil, reduce the heat, and simmer them, uncovered, for 20 minutes, or until they are tender but still retain their shape; do not overcook. Drain well and reserve.

2 green peppers, seeded and chopped
8 scallions, trimmed and chopped, with
as much green as is crisp
2 (about 7-ounce) cans oilpack tuna,
broken into chunks, with their oil
Reserved beans
Vinaigrette Sauce, page 287

In a mixing bowl, combine the peppers, scallions, tuna, and beans. Toss them with sufficient vinaigrette sauce to moisten the mixture well. Chill the salad for 3 hours.

Salad greens of your choice
Pitted black olives, sliced lengthwise
¼ cup fine-chopped parsley
Lemon wedges

On a bed of salad greens, arrange the fish mixture. Garnish the salad with the olives, sprinkle with parsley, and add the lemon wedges.

Serve with muffins, page 289.

For *Tuna and Lentil Salad:* use 2 cups quick-cooking lentils, preparing them as directed on the package; do not overcook. When cooking them, add to the water 1 medium onion stuck with 2 cloves, and 1 bay leaf. Add to the cooked lentils 4 scallions, trimmed and chopped fine, with as much green as is crisp. Toss the lentils with vinaigrette sauce (about ½ cup); add the tuna and toss again lightly.

SIX

Salt and Smoked Fish

The recipes in this section are selected for use with salt cod, finnan haddie, and salt herring, all readily available. Salt cod, once it is prepared for cooking, and finnan haddie, which usually requires no preparation, are interchangeable in these recipes; as a matter of fact, they may be used in many of the recipes for composed dishes of fresh and frozen fish. Salt herring, to be sure, is a bit more special; strong tasting and *very* salty, it had best be restricted to the recipes suggested for it.

To Prepare Salt Cod for Cooking: rinse the skinned fillets, cut in serving pieces, under cold running water; then soak the fish in water to cover overnight (cover the container well and place it in the refrigerator). *Or,* in a large saucepan, cover the fish with cold water and bring it *very slowly* to the boil; discard the first water and rinse the fish in cold water. Unless it is particularly salty, finnan haddie will not require soaking.

To Prepare Salt-cured Herring: rinse it well under cold running water, cover it with buttermilk, and place it in the refrigerator overnight (cover the container well). Drain the herring and rinse it under cold running water; dry it with absorbent paper.

HERRING DIP

YIELD: about 1½ cups
PREPARATION: about 15 minutes
(time does not include readying the herring, page 217)
CHILLING TIME: 3 hours

3 salt herring fillets, prepared for cooking and chopped coarse
1 cup sour cream
1 tablespoon Dijon mustard
1 teaspoon prepared horseradish
   Few drops of Tabasco sauce
1 teaspoon Worcestershire sauce

In the container of a food processor equipped with the steel knife, combine all the ingredients. Whirl them until the mixture is smooth. Transfer the dip to a serving bowl and chill it for 3 hours. Offer it with Melba toast rounds.

HERRING IN OIL

6 to 8 servings
(time does not include readying the herring, page 217)
CHILLING TIME: 24 hours

At a charming outdoor restaurant in the court of the Palais Royal in Paris, I ate greedily of *hareng à l'huile;* when I returned the next day to repeat the performance, the proprietor graciously gave me this recipe.

1 pound salt herring fillets prepared for cooking
4 medium carrots, scraped and sliced thin
3 medium onions, peeled, sliced, and separated into rings
3 bay leaves, crumbled
   Vegetable oil

In a shallow dish, arrange layers of the fish, carrots, and onions; end with a layer of onion. Tuck in the bay leaf. Over all, pour vegetable oil to cover. Cover the dish tightly with plastic wrap and refrigerate it for 24 hours. (The herring will keep well for several days.) Offer the herring, if desired, on a bed of salad greens; I must admit to preferring it unadorned.

MARINATED HERRING, DANISH STYLE

YIELD: about 1 quart
PREPARATION: about 30 minutes
CHILLING TIME: 24 hours

1 pound herring fillets in brine

In a glass or stainless steel container, arrange the fillets. Add cold water to cover and soak the fish, refrigerated, overnight; change the water occasionally. Drain and cut the fillets crosswise in 1-inch pieces.

2 medium carrots, scraped and sliced thin
2 medium red onions, peeled and sliced thin

In a tall, wide-mouthed glass jar with tight-fitting lid, arrange alternate layers of the fish, carrot, and onion.

1½ cups cider vinegar
10 whole allspice berries, crushed
4 bay leaves, crumbled
12 peppercorns, bruised
¾ cup sugar

In a saucepan, combine these ingredients. Bring the mixture to the boil, reduce the heat, and simmer for 5 minutes. Allow to cool somewhat before pouring it over the contents of the jar. Allow the jar to cool to room temperature and then refrigerate it for 24 hours. Serve the herring, if desired, on a bed of salad greens or with Cucumber Sauce, page 277, *or* Dill Sauce II, page 278.

SALT COD SOUP, ITALIAN STYLE

4 to 6 servings
PREPARATION: about 35 minutes
(time does not include readying the salt cod for cooking, page 217)
COOKING: 1 hour

This *zuppa di baccalà* from Umbria is a satisfying one-dish meal.

> ½ *cup olive oil*
> 1 *large rib celery, diced*
> 3 *large cloves garlic, peeled and*
> *chopped*
> 2 *large onions, peeled and sliced thin*

In a soup kettle, heat the olive oil and in it cook the celery, garlic, and onion until the onion is translucent.

> 3 *large ripe tomatoes, peeled, seeded,*
> *and chopped* or 1 16-ounce can Ital-
> *ian tomatoes*
> ½ *cup chopped parsley*
> 1 *bay leaf*
> ½ *teaspoon thyme*
> 1 *cup dry white wine*

To the contents of the soup kettle, add these ingredients. Bring the liquid to the boil, reduce the heat somewhat, and cook the mixture, uncovered, for 10 minutes.

> 5 *cups cold water*
> 4 *medium potatoes, peeled*
> 2 *pounds salt cod prepared for cooking*
> *and cut in bite-size pieces*
> ¼ *cup olive oil*

Into the measured water, quarter the potatoes. Ready the fish and measure the olive oil.

At this point you may stop and continue later.

To the contents of the soup kettle, add the potatoes and their water, the cod, and olive oil. Bring the liquid to the boil, reduce the heat to low, and cook the soup, uncovered, for 1 hour, or until the potatoes are very tender and the cod flakes easily. The soup may be diluted as necessary with additional water.

Salt
Grinding of pepper
Fine-chopped parsley
Slices of Italian bread fried crisp in
   olive oil (optional)

Season the soup to taste with salt and pepper. Serve it garnished with parsley over the fried bread.

Serve with mixed green salad, page 295.

SALT COD AND SPINACH SOUP

6 to 8 servings
PREPARATION: about 30 minutes
(time does not include readying the salt cod, page 217)
COOKING: 35 minutes

½ **cup olive oil**
6 **large potatoes, peeled and sliced**
2 **10-ounce packages fresh spinach**
   with the woody stems removed, rinsed
   and well drained
6 **large cloves garlic, peeled and**
   chopped fine
2 **teaspoons ground coriander seed**
¾ **teaspoon thyme**

In a soup kettle, heat the oil and to it add the potatoes, stirring to coat the slices well. Add the spinach, garlic, and seasonings. Over high heat cook the mixture, stirring, for 2 minutes or until the spinach is wilted. Reduce the heat.

2 **pounds salt cod prepared for cooking**
   and cut in bite-size pieces
1 **cup dry white wine**
   Water
   Salt
   Grinding of pepper

Over the spinach, arrange the fish in a layer. Pour the wine over the fish and then add water to cover. Bring the liquid to the boil, reduce the heat, and simmer the soup for 35 minutes, or until the potatoes are tender. Season the soup to taste with salt and pepper.

Serve with casserole-baked bread, page 288.

BRANDADE OF SALT COD

6 servings
PREPARATION: about 1 hour
(time does not include readying the salt cod, page 217)

This famous dish from the Carmargue region of France is traditionally served with crusty bread.

> 2 *pounds salt cod, prepared for cook-*
> *ing, cut in chunks, and wrapped in*
> *cheesecloth*
> 1 *large bay leaf*
> 2 *cloves garlic, peeled and split*
> 6 *sprigs parsley*
> ½ *teaspoon thyme*
> *Water*

In a large saucepan or kettle, combine the fish and seasonings; add cold water to cover. Bring the liquid to the boil, reduce the heat, and simmer the fish for 20 minutes, or until it is tender. Drain, cool, and flake the fish, discarding any bones.

> ½ *cup olive oil*
> 1¼ *cups evaporated milk or heavy*
> *cream*
> 3 *tablespoons strained lemon juice*
> ½ *teaspoon nutmeg*
> ½ *teaspoon white pepper*

Transfer the fish to the container of a food processor equipped with the steel knife. Whirl the fish by turning the motor on and off, until it is virtually a paste. Separately heat to lukewarm the olive oil and evaporated milk. With the motor running, add the oil and milk alternately, 1 tablespoon at a time. When the addition is complete, add the lemon juice and seasonings. Transfer the *brandade* to the top of a double boiler for reheating over simmering water.

Serve with casserole-baked bread, page 288.

CODFISH CAKES

4 to 6 servings
PREPARATION: about 45 minutes
(time does not include readying the salt cod, page 217)
COOKING: about 12 minutes

The recipe may also be made — and very tastily — with finnan haddie.

**½ pound salt cod prepared for cooking
and cut in chunks**
2½ cups potato cubes
Boiling water

In a large saucepan, combine the fish and potato cubes; add boiling water just to cover. Over medium-high heat, cook the ingredients for 15 minutes, covered, or until the potatoes are soft. Drain the fish and potatoes.

1 tablespoon soft butter
1 egg, beaten
Grinding of pepper

Mash the fish and potato together until the mixture is quite smooth. Beat in the butter and then the egg. Season to taste with pepper. With a fork, beat the mixture until it is smooth and light, about 2 minutes. Shape the dough into 12 flat patties.

At this point you may stop and continue later.

Butter

In a skillet, heat a little butter and in it brown the codfish cakes. Remove them briefly to absorbent paper and then to a heated plate.

Serve topped with a poached egg (a recollection from my childhood, when Saturday night's supper was not infrequently codfish cakes served in this manner).

SALT COD WITH GREEN OLIVES
(Italy)

4 to 6 servings
PREPARATION: about 45 minutes
(time does not include readying the salt cod, page 217)
COOKING: 15 minutes in a 325° oven

2 pounds salt cod, prepared for cook-
ing and cut in 2-inch squares
Flour
¾ cup olive oil

Dry the fish and dredge it in flour. In a skillet, heat the oil and brown the fish, a few pieces at a time. Remove the fish to absorbent paper and then arrange it in a baking dish.

Olive oil
1 medium onion, peeled and chopped
1 16-ounce can Italian tomatoes,
chopped, with their liquid
Salt
Grinding of pepper

To the oil remaining in the skillet, add more to equal about 3 tablespoons. In it, cook the onion until golden. Add the tomatoes and salt and pepper to taste. Over medium-high heat, cook the mixture, uncovered, for 20 minutes or until it is slightly thickened.

1½ tablespoons capers
1 cup pitted green olives, sliced
⅓ cup chopped parsley

Into the sauce, stir the capers, olives, and parsley.
At this point you may stop and continue later.
Over the fish, spoon the sauce. Bake the dish at 325° for 15 minutes, or until it is bubbly.

A Sicilian variation of this dish is called *pescestocco alla gliotta* (Glutton's Stockfish). It adds to the ingredients of the sauce 3 medium potatoes, peeled and diced, 3 tablespoons pine nuts, and ½ cup white raisins. The sauce is cooked until the potato is tender. Complete the recipe.

Serve with mixed green salad, page 295.

SALT COD, PORTUGUESE STYLE

4 servings
PREPARATION: about 40 minutes
(time does not include readying the salt cod, page 217)
COOKING: 35 minutes in a 350° oven

This dish is a relative of the *brandade* on page 222.

**1½ pounds salt cod prepared for cook-
ing and cut in small pieces**

In a saucepan, cover the fish with water. Bring it to the boil, reduce the
heat, and simmer for 20 minutes, or until it flakes easily. Drain and cool
the fish.

4 medium potatoes, peeled

Boil the potatoes for 25 minutes, or until they are very tender. Chop them
coarse.

¼ cup heavy cream
½ cup olive oil
**3 cloves garlic, peeled and put through
a press**

In the container of a food processor equipped with the steel knife, combine the fish and potato. Whirl them by turning the motor on and off, until
the mixture is smooth. Add the cream and whirl the mixture to blend it.
With the motor running, add the olive oil and garlic. Transfer the mixture
to a buttered baking dish.

At this point you may stop and continue later.

Bake the dish at 350° for 35 minutes.

Serve with mixed green salad, page 295.

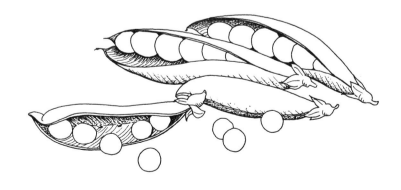

SALT COD WITH TOMATOES I

4 servings
PREPARATION: about 1 hour
(time does not include readying the salt cod, page 217)
COOKING: 15 minutes in a 350° oven

Codfish Provençal is a popular French dish.

> *4 tablespoons butter*
> *4 tablespoons olive oil*
> *3 large cloves garlic, peeled and chopped*
> *3 medium onions, peeled and chopped*

In a saucepan, combine and heat the butter and olive oil. In the mixture, cook the garlic and onion until they are barely golden.

> *1 28-ounce can solid-pack tomatoes*
> *1 6-ounce can tomato paste*
> *2 cups dry red wine*
> *1 bay leaf*
> *¼ teaspoon fennel seed*
> *1 teaspoon rosemary, crumbled*

To the contents of the saucepan, add the ingredients. Bring the mixture to the boil, reduce the heat, and simmer it, uncovered for 20 minutes, or until it is slightly thickened.

> *2 pounds salt cod prepared for cooking and cut in serving pieces*
> *Flour*
> *Olive oil*

Dredge the fish in flour. In a skillet, heat sufficient oil to cover the bottom generously and in it sauté the fish, a few pieces at a time, until it is golden. Remove it to absorbent paper and then arrange it in a single layer in a lightly oiled baking dish.

> *2 tablespoons capers*
> *1 cup black pitted olives, sliced thin*
> *Salt*
> *Grinding of pepper*

To the tomato sauce, add the capers and olives; season it to taste with salt and pepper.

At this point you may stop and continue later.

Bring the sauce to the boil, spoon it over the fish, and bake the dish at 350° for 15 minutes, or until it is thoroughly heated.

Serve with new potatoes, page 290.

For *Salt Cod with Tomatoes, Spanish Style:* in step one, add 2 green peppers, seeded and chopped; in step two, add 12 pitted green olives, chopped, and omit the fennel seed and rosemary. Complete the recipe.

SALT COD WITH TOMATOES II

4 servings
PREPARATION: about 40 minutes
(time does not include readying the salt cod, page 217)
COOKING: 30 minutes in a 375° oven

A much simplified version of the preceding Cod Provençal, this recipe may also be made with finnan haddie.

> **2 pounds salt cod prepared for cooking
> and cut in serving pieces**
> **1 bay leaf**
> **2 sprigs parsley**
> **½ teaspoon thyme**

In a large skillet, combine the fish and seasonings. Add water to cover and bring it to the boil. Remove the skillet from the heat and allow the fish to stand, covered, for 20 minutes.

> **2 cloves garlic, peeled and chopped**
> **2 medium onions, peeled and chopped**
> **3 ripe tomatoes, peeled, seeded, and
> chopped**
> **Salt**
> **Grinding of pepper**

In a mixing bowl, combine the garlic, onions, and tomatoes. Season the mixture to taste with salt and pepper and blend it well. On the bottom of an oiled baking dish, arrange half of the vegetable mixture. Drain the fish on absorbent paper and add it in a single layer to the baking dish. Over the fish, spread the remaining vegetables.

> *At this point you may stop and continue later.*

> **¼ cup olive oil**

Over the contents of the baking dish, drizzle the oil. Bake the fish at 375° for 30 minutes, or until the fish flakes easily.

Serve with new potatoes, page 290.

SALT COD WITH TOMATO-AND-RAISIN SAUCE

6 servings
PREPARATION: about 40 minutes
(time does not include readying the salt cod, page 217)
COOKING: about 15 minutes

This Roman dish is traditionally served with *polenta,* the Italian counterpart of our cornbread.

> **4 tablespoons olive oil**
> **3 large onions, peeled and sliced thin**

In a skillet, heat the olive oil and in it cook the onions until they are golden.

> **1 20-ounce can Italian tomatoes**
> **¾ teaspoon oregano**
> **¾ teaspoon pepper**

Stir in the tomatoes and seasonings. Bring the liquid to the boil, reduce the heat, and simmer sauce for 15 minutes, or until it is somewhat reduced.

> **2 pounds salt cod prepared for cooking**
>   **and cut in bite-size pieces**
> **⅓ cup white raisins**
>   **Salt**

To the contents of the skillet, add the fish, spooning the sauce over it; add the raisins. Simmer the fish for about 15 minutes, or until it flakes easily. Adjust the seasoning to taste with salt.

Serve with casserole-baked bread, page 288.

If desired, you may add to the cooking onion 3 green peppers, seeded and chopped; in this case, increase the olive oil to ⅓ cup.

SALT COD OR FINNAN HADDIE SOUFFLÉ

4 servings as a main dish
6 servings as a first course
PREPARATION: about 30 minutes
(time does not include readying the salt cod, page 217)
COOKING: 30 minutes in a 350° oven

Thoroughly butter a 2-quart soufflé dish.

> **¾ pound salt cod prepared for cooking
> or finnan haddie**

In simmering water, poach the fish, page 59, until it flakes easily; drain and mash it with the tines of a fork. Reserve it.

> **4 tablespoons butter
> 4 tablespoons flour
> 1 cup milk
> Grating of nutmeg
> Grinding of white pepper**

In a saucepan, heat the butter and in it, over gentle heat, cook the flour for a few minutes. Gradually add the milk, stirring constantly until the mixture is thickened and smooth. Season it to taste with nutmeg and pepper.

> **Reserved fish
> ¼ cup fine-chopped parsley
> 4 egg yolks**

Into the contents of the saucepan, stir the fish and parsley; beat in the egg yolks.

> *At this point you may stop and continue later.*

> **5 egg whites, beaten until stiff but not
> dry**

Into the soufflé batter, beat one-fifth of the egg white; fold in the remainder. Using a rubber spatula, transfer the mixture to the prepared dish. Bake the soufflé at 350° for about 30 minutes, or until it is well puffed and golden.

Serve with green peas, page 294.

BAKED FINNAN HADDIE

4 servings
PREPARATION: about 10 minutes
COOKING: 20 minutes in a 350° oven

The recipe may also be made with salt cod prepared for cooking as described on page 217.

Butter
2 *pounds finnan haddie cut in serving pieces*
½ *cup milk*
½ *cup light cream*
Grinding of pepper

Butter a baking dish and in it arrange the pieces of finnan haddie in a single layer. Pour the milk and cream over it. Season the fish with pepper and dot it with butter. Cover the dish tightly with foil. Bake the fish at 350° for 20 minutes, or until it flakes easily.

Serve with new potatoes, page 290.

FINNAN HADDIE IN CREAM SAUCE

4 servings
PREPARATION: about 45 minutes
COOKING: 15 minutes in a 350° oven

The recipe may be made with salt cod prepared for cooking as on page 217, or with any fresh lean fillet.

2 *pounds finnan haddie cut in serving or bite-size pieces*
2 *cups milk*
1 *bay leaf*
1 *slice onion*
10 *peppercorns*

In a large skillet arrange the fish, over it pour the milk, and add the seasonings. Marinate the fish for 1 hour. Bring the milk barely to the boil, reduce the heat, and poach the fish for 10 minutes. Remove the fish to a lightly buttered baking dish. Strain and reserve the marinade.

4 tablespoons butter
4 tablespoons flour
   Reserved marinade
¼ cup light cream
   Few drops of Tabasco sauce

In a saucepan, heat the butter and in it, over gentle heat, cook the flour for a few minutes. Gradually add the reserved marinade, stirring constantly until the mixture is thickened and smooth. Stir in the cream. Season to taste with Tabasco sauce. Over the fish, spoon the sauce.
    At this point you may stop and continue later.

    ¼ cup fine-chopped parsley

Bake the fish at 350° for 15 minutes, or until the sauce is bubbly. Garnish the dish with parsley.
   Serve with saffron rice, page 291.
   If desired, in step two you may add to the sauce 2 teaspoons Dijon mustard, 2 tablespoons prepared horseradish, and the strained juice of ½ medium lemon (see also Horseradish Sauce, page 280); in this case, serve the dish with plain rice, page 290.

POACHED SALT COD OR FINNAN HADDIE

4 servings
PREPARATION: about 10 minutes
(time does not include readying the salt cod, page 217)
COOKING: about 15 minutes

    Water or equal parts milk and water
2 pounds salt cod prepared for cook-
    ing or finnan haddie, cut in serving
    pieces

Bring the liquid to the boil and to it add the fish. When the liquid barely returns to the boil, reduce the heat and poach the fish according to the directions on page 59 until it flakes easily. With a slotted spoon, remove it to a heated dish.

    Potato and Garlic Sauce, page 284

Offer the fish accompanied by the sauce.
   Serve with chopped spinach, page 295.

SEVEN

Clams and Mussels, Fresh and Canned

Clams and mussels, those delectable bivalve mollusks, the most reasonably priced of shellfish, may be used in *hors d'oeuvre* and soups, in main dishes and selected salads. They are available fresh and canned, and in the case of mussels, frozen.

When buying clams and mussels in the shell, you should select those that are tightly closed — the surest indication that they are fresh. With a stiff brush, scrub them under running water, discarding those with crushed shells or those that do not remain tightly shut. Remove the "beards" from the mussels, those fringes of sea vegetation adhering to their hinged sides. In cold water to cover, soak them for several hours; the addition of cornmeal to the water encourages their flushing out of sand or silt. Drain and rinse them in a colander under cold water.

One method of opening fresh clams and mussels — and a very convenient way — calls for steaming them in a large pot or kettle in water sufficient only to start the steam (usually about ¼ cup); the pot, tightly covered, should be placed over high heat. The clams or mussels will open in 5 or 6 minutes; discard any that remain closed. Over a bowl (to collect the liquid), remove them from their shells. They are now ready for use in any recipe of your choosing.

Clams and mussels may also be opened in the oven, if they are not to be used raw. In a baking pan, arrange them in a single layer. Heat them in a preheated 450° oven for 3 to 5 minutes, or until they open; discard any that remain closed. Remove the clams or mussels from their shells as directed above.

Clams may be shucked open: over a bowl (to collect the liquid), hold the clam in your hand with the hinged edge of the shell against the heel of your palm. With a strong, thin, sharp knife inserted between the two shells, cut around the inside edges to sever the connecting muscles; then twist the knife to open the shells. Remove the clams from their shells as directed above.

HORS D'OEUVRE AND FIRST COURSES

BAKED CLAMS CASINO

4 to 6 servings
PREPARATION: about 50 minutes
(time does not include readying clams, page 232)
COOKING: 5 minutes in a 450° oven

24 hard-shell clams prepared for cooking

Shuck the clams. Wash the deep half of the shells; discard the remainder. Place a clam in each of the reserved shells.

4 slices bacon, diced

Render the bacon and drain it on absorbent paper; reserve it.

4 tablespoons soft butter
1 small rib celery, chopped fine
½ small green pepper, chopped fine
**3 scallions, trimmed and chopped fine
(the white part only)**

In a mixing bowl, combine and blend these four ingredients.

Reserved clams
Strained lemon juice
Reserved bacon
Butter-toasted bread crumbs

Top each of the clams with about one tablespoon of the vegetable mixture. Add a drop or two of lemon juice and a sprinkling of the bacon and bread crumbs. In a shallow pan, arrange a bed of rock salt or of crumpled foil (to enable the clams to sit flat) and place clams on this layer. Bake the clams at 450° for 5 minutes, transfer them to individual dishes, and serve.

For *Broiled Clams:* follow step one as directed; arrange the clams on rock salt or foil. Add a drop or two of Worcestershire sauce and a 1-inch piece of bacon. Cook the clams in a preheated broiler for about 5 minutes, or until the bacon is crisp. Offer the clams with lemon wedges.

6 servings as a first course
4 servings as a main course
PREPARATION: about 20 minutes
(time does not include readying clams or mussels, page 232)

48 hard- or soft-shell clams or mussels
prepared for cooking

In a soup kettle, arrange the clams. Add just enough water to start the steam (about ⅔ cup). Over high heat, steam the clams, tightly covered, for 5 to 8 minutes, or until they open; do not overcook them. If you use soft-shell clams, remove the skin from the neck. Arrange the clams in soup plates. Strain the broth and offer it separately. Offer the clams with

Melted butter
Lemon wedges

For *Steamed Clams or Mussels, Italian Style:* in the soup kettle, heat 4 tablespoons olive oil and in it cook 3 large cloves garlic, split lengthwise, until they are golden; discard them. Add the prepared clams *or* mussels and ¼ cup water; steam the clams as directed above, and when they have opened, sprinkle over them the strained juice of 1 medium lemon and 1 cup fine-chopped parsley. Off heat, shake the kettle to distribute the parsley. Arrange the clams in soup plates and offer the broth separately, without straining it (any sediment will rapidly find its way to the bottom of the cup).

Offer the clams with

Lemon wedges

For *Steamed Clams or Mussels Oreganata* (another Italian way of preparing them): in the soup kettle, heat 4 tablespoons olive oil and in it cook 1 large onion, peeled and chopped fine, until translucent. Stir in 1 cup dry white wine, 2 tablespoons oregano, and ¾ teaspoon salt. Bring the liquid to the boil, reduce the heat, and simmer the mixture, uncovered, until it is reduced by half. Add the prepared clams or mussels and complete the basic recipe as written.

Serve steamed clams or mussels with casserole-baked bread, page 288.

CLAM CANAPÉS

16 canapés; 4 servings as a first course
PREPARATION: about 25 minutes
COOKING: 5 minutes in a preheated broiler

½ *pound American cheese, shredded*
2 *6½-ounce cans minced clams,*
   drained
1 *small onion, peeled and grated*
¼ *cup fine-chopped parsley*
   Few drops of Tabasco sauce
   Salt

In a mixing bowl, combine the first four ingredients; with a fork, stir the mixture to blend it well. Season it to taste with Tabasco sauce and salt.

4 *large slices bread*

Toast the bread and remove the crusts. Spread each slice with one-quarter of the clam mixture. If you are serving canapés, cut each slice of toast in quarters; if you are offering the recipe as a first course, leave the toast slices whole. On a baking sheet, arrange the toasts and run them under the broiler for 5 minutes, or until the cheese is melted.

CREAMED CLAMS

6 servings

PREPARATION: about 25 minutes

> **3 6½-ounce cans minced clams, drained**
> **(reserve the liquid)**
> **Milk**

To the clam liquid, add milk to equal 2 cups. Reserve the clams and liquid.

> **6 tablespoons butter**
> **1 medium onion, peeled and chopped**
> **fine**

In a saucepan, heat the butter and in it cook the onion until it is barely golden.

> **6 tablespoons flour**
> **¾ teaspoon salt**
> **½ teaspoon white pepper**
> **Reserved clam-milk liquid**
> **1 5-ounce can bamboo shoots, drained**
> **and diced**

Into the onion, stir the flour, and over gentle heat, cook the mixture for a few minutes. Stir in the salt and pepper. Gradually add the liquid, stirring constantly until the mixture is thickened and smooth. Stir in the bamboo shoots.

> **Reserved clams**
> **¼ cup fine-chopped parsley**
> **2 tablespoons dry sherry**

Stir in the clams, parsley, and sherry. Serve the creamed clams on crisp buttered toast *or* a toasted English muffin half *or* in patty shells.

CLAM-STUFFED MUSHROOMS

YIELD: 24 mushrooms or 4 first-course servings
PREPARATION: about 25 minutes
COOKING: 5 minutes in a preheated broiler

> **24 large mushrooms, stemmed (reserve the stems) and wiped with a damp cloth**

Prepare and reserve the mushroom caps.

> **6 tablespoons butter**
> **2 cloves garlic, put through a press**

In a small saucepan, heat the butter and to it add the garlic. Into the mixture, dunk the mushroom caps; remove them to absorbent paper, top side down, to drain.

> **Reserved mushroom stems**
> **Liquid from 1 6½-ounce can minced clams (reserve the clams)**

Chop the mushroom stems fine, add them to the remaining butter, stirring to coat well. Add the clam liquid and cook them, uncovered, until they are tender.

> **½ cup bread crumbs**
> **⅓ cup fine-chopped parsley**
> **2 tablespoons fine-chopped green pepper**
> **½ teaspoon salt**
> **¼ teaspoon pepper**

Combine and blend these five ingredients with the mushroom-stem mixture. With it, mound each of the mushroom caps. Arrange the caps on a baking sheet and run them under the broiler for 5 minutes.

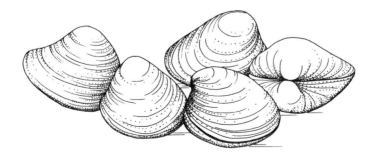

CLAM DIP

YIELD: 1½ cups
PREPARATION: about 20 minutes

1 6½-ounce can minced clams, drained (reserve the liquid)
1 3-ounce package cream cheese, at room temperature
1 small clove garlic, peeled and put through a press
2 tablespoons strained lemon juice
¼ cup fine-chopped parsley
A few drops of Tabasco sauce
1 teaspoon Worcestershire sauce
Salt

In a mixing bowl combine, and using a fork blend thoroughly, all of the ingredients except the salt. Add some of the clam liquid as necessary for the desired consistency. Season the mixture to taste with salt. Transfer it to a serving dish.

Assorted raw vegetables or Melba toast

Offer the dip with raw vegetables or Melba toast.

HOT CLAM DIP

YIELD: about 4 cups
PREPARATION: about 25 minutes

Excellent with crisp fresh vegetables and also good as a sauce.

2 6½-ounce cans minced clams, drained (reserve the liquid)
Dry white wine

To the clam liquid, add white wine to equal 1 cup. Reserve the clams and liquid.

3 tablespoons butter
1 small onion, peeled and grated
3 tablespoons flour
1 cup milk or half-and-half
Reserved clam liquid

In a saucepan, heat the butter and in it, over gentle heat, cook the onion for a few minutes. Stir in the flour and continue to cook the mixture for a few minutes. Gradually add the milk and then the clam liquid, stirring constantly until the mixture is thickened and smooth.

3 cups shredded mild cheese
Reserved clams

To the contents of the saucepan, add the cheese, stirring constantly until it is melted. Stir in the clams. Transfer the dip to a warm bowl and serve it at once. It will thicken as it cools but may be thinned again by reheating.

CLAM PUFFS

YIELD: about 2½ cups of filling (about 24 puffs)
PREPARATION: about 15 minutes
(time does not include readying the miniature puffs,
page 299, which may be made well in advance and frozen)

24 Miniature Puffs

Cut the pastry puffs in half crosswise and reserve them.

½ cup crumbled blue cheese
*1 8-ounce package cream cheese, at
room temperature*
*1 small onion, peeled and grated
A few drops of Tabasco sauce
Salt*
*1 6½-ounce can minced clams, drained
(reserve the liquid)*

In a mixing bowl, combine the first three ingredients. With a fork, beat to blend well. Season the mixture to taste with Tabasco sauce and salt. Blend in the clams, adding a little of the liquid, if necessary, for the desired consistency.

On the bottom half of each miniature puff, arrange a little of the clam mixture. Add the top half of the puff. The puffs may be served at room temperature, or you may heat them for about 8 minutes in a 350° oven.

STUFFED MUSSELS

4 servings
PREPARATION: about 40 minutes
(time does not include readying the mussels, page 232)
CHILLING TIME: 3 hours

16 large mussels prepared for cooking

Without separating the two halves of shell, pry the mussels open. Soak them in cold water while you make the stuffing.

¼ cup olive oil
1 medium onion, peeled and chopped fine
¼ teaspoon saffron, crumbled
½ cup raw natural rice (preferably Italian)

In a saucepan, heat the oil and in it cook the onion until it is golden. Stir in the saffron and then the rice. Over gentle heat, cook the mixture, stirring, for a few minutes.

3 tablespoons currants
Grinding of pepper
1 cup (1 8-ounce bottle) clam juice

Stir in the currants and pepper. Add the clam juice. Bring the liquid to the boil, stir the rice once with a fork, reduce the heat, and simmer the mixture, covered, for 15 minutes or until the rice is tender and the liquid is absorbed.

3 tablespoons fine-chopped parsley

Away from the heat, stir in the parsley. Allow the mixture to cool. Drain the mussels and stuff each with some of the mixture. Close each mussel with a rubber band.

On a rack in a large saucepan or soup kettle, arrange the mussels. Add boiling water to reach not quite to the level of the rack. Over the lowest possible heat, steam the mussels, covered, for 20 minutes. Allow them to cool and then chill them at least 3 hours.

Lemon wedges

To serve the stuffed mussels, remove the rubber bands and arrange the mussels on individual plates; garnish them with lemon wedges.

Soups and stews made of clams and mussels are among the most subtle and satisfying I know. They deservedly demand our attention and trial. I offer here ten of my favorites; all of them are easily prepared and, I feel, are at their best when made with fresh clams or mussels. The liquid expelled by the mollusks as they are steamed open is an important ingredient of these soups, giving them their individual and elusive flavor. (The possibility of using canned clams is also indicated.) Some of these soups and stews serve well as the main dish of a light meal — a good bread and a salad, followed perhaps by fresh fruit and cheese, will complete your menu. Other recipes, such as Chilled Cream of Mussel Soup (Billi Bi) and Clam or Mussel Purée, are more suitable as the first course of an elegant dinner.

CLAM SOUP

6 servings
PREPARATION: about 40 minutes

This Roman recipe may also be made with fresh mussels.

> ½ **cup olive oil**
> 3 **cloves garlic, peeled and split**

In a soup kettle, heat the oil and in it cook the garlic until it is browned; discard the garlic.

> 1 **6-ounce can tomato paste**
> 2 **cups water** or **clam juice (2 8-ounce bottles)**
> 2 **cups dry white wine**
> ½ **cup fine-chopped parsley**
> 1 **teaspoon oregano**
> 1 **teaspoon red pepper flakes**
>   **Salt**

To the contents of the kettle, add the first six ingredients, stirring to blend the mixture well. Bring the liquid to the boil, reduce the heat, and simmer it, covered, for 15 minutes. Season the mixture to taste with salt.

At this point you may stop and continue later.

> 6 **dozen cherrystone or littleneck clams, well scrubbed**

Return the broth to the boil, add the clams, and steam them, covered, for 8 to 10 minutes or until they are opened. In six heated soup plates, distribute the clams; pour the broth over them.

Serve with casserole-baked bread, page 288.

CREAM OF CLAM AND VEGETABLE SOUP

6 servings
PREPARATION: about 40 minutes
(time does not include readying the clams, page 232)

4 strips bacon, diced
2 medium onions, peeled and chopped

In a large saucepan or soup kettle, render the bacon; with a slotted spoon, remove it to absorbent paper and reserve it. In the remaining fat, cook the onion until translucent.

2 medium carrots, scraped and chopped
    fine
1 large potato, peeled and chopped
    fine
3 medium zucchini, sliced thin
3 cups clam juice (3 8-ounce bottles)

To the contents of the saucepan, add these ingredients. Bring the liquid to the boil, reduce the heat, and simmer the vegetables, covered, for 20 minutes.

24 large cherrystone clams, steamed
    open, removed from their shells,
    their liquid reserved or 3 6½-ounce
    cans minced clams, drained, their
    liquid reserved

Add the clams and their liquid. In the container of a food processor or blender, whirl the mixture, two cupfuls at a time, until it is reduced to a smooth purée. Transfer it to a second saucepan.

Light cream
Salt
Grinding of white pepper
Reserved bacon

Add cream to the consistency you desire. Season the soup to taste with salt and pepper. Bring it to serving temperature and garnish it with the reserved bacon.

Serve with muffins, page 289.

4 to 6 servings
PREPARATION: about 45 minutes
(time does not include readying the clams, page 232)
COOKING: 30 minutes

> 24 *razor clams, steamed open, removed*
> *from their shells, their liquid re-*
> *served or 2 6½-ounce cans chopped*
> *clams, drained, their liquid reserved*

If you use fresh clams, whirl them briefly in the container of an electric blender to chop them fine.

> 1 *cup clam juice (1 8-ounce bottle)*
> *Reserved clam liquid*
> *Chopped clams*
> ¼ *cup chopped parsley*
> 1 *medium onion, peeled and chopped*
> 3 *whole allspice berries, crushed*
> 2 *whole cloves*
> ¼ *teaspoon ground mace*

In a saucepan, combine these ingredients. Bring the liquid to the boil, reduce the heat, and simmer the mixture, covered, for 30 minutes.

> 4 *cups milk*
> 4 *tablespoons flour*
> *Salt*
> *Grinding of white pepper*
> 2 *tablespoons dry sherry*
> *Paprika*

In ½ cup of the milk, stir the flour until the mixture is smooth. In a saucepan, combine the flour paste and the remaining milk. Over medium heat, cook the mixture, stirring constantly, until it is thickened and smooth. Through a sieve lined with two thicknesses of cheesecloth, strain the clam mixture, pressing against the sides of the sieve to extract all the liquid. Add the liquid to the milk mixture; discard the residue. Season the soup to taste with salt and pepper. Bring the bisque to serving temperature, stir in the sherry, and garnish each portion with a sprinkling of paprika.

NEW ENGLAND CLAM CHOWDER

6 to 8 servings
PREPARATION: about 45 minutes
(time does not include readying the clams, page 232)
COOKING: 30 minutes

> 24 *large cherrystone clams, steamed*
> *open, removed from their shells,*
> *their liquid reserved or 3 6½-ounce*
> *cans minced clams, drained, their*
> *liquid reserved*
> *Water*

To the reserved clam liquid, add water to equal 4 cups.

> ¼ *pound salt pork, diced*
> 3 *medium onions, peeled and chopped*
> 4 *large potatoes, peeled and diced*

In a soup kettle, render the salt pork; remove it to absorbent paper and reserve it. Discard all but ⅓ cup of the fat; in it, cook the onion until golden. Add the potato, stirring to coat it well. Add the clam liquid, bring it to the boil, reduce the heat, and simmer the potatoes, covered, for 20 minutes or until they are tender.

At this point you may stop and continue later.

> *Reserved clams*
> 2 *cups milk*
> 2 *cups light cream*
> 3 *tablespoons soft butter*
> *Salt*
> *Grinding of white pepper*
> *Reserved salt pork*
> *Fine-chopped parsley*

Add the clams, milk, and cream. Bring the chowder to serving temperature; do not let it boil. Stir in the butter and season the soup to taste with salt and pepper. Serve it garnished with the salt pork and parsley.

Serve with casserole-baked bread, page 288.

MANHATTAN CLAM CHOWDER

6 to 8 servings
PREPARATION: about 45 minutes
(time does not include readying the clams, page 232)
COOKING: 30 minutes

> **24 large cherrystone clams, steamed open, removed from their shells, their liquid reserved or 3 6½-ounce cans minced clams, drained, their liquid reserved**
> **Water**

To the clam liquid, add water to equal 4 cups; reserve the mixture.

> **4 slices bacon, diced**
> **1 medium rib celery, diced**
> **1 large onion, peeled and chopped**
> **1 small green pepper, seeded and chopped**

In a soup kettle, render the bacon; remove it to absorbent paper and reserve it. In the fat, cook the celery, onion, and pepper until the onion is golden.

> **2 large carrots, scraped and sliced thin**
> **4 medium potatoes, peeled and diced**
> **2 medium white turnips, scraped and diced**
> **½ teaspoon thyme**

Add the three vegetables, stirring to coat them well. Add the thyme. Add the clam liquid, bring it to the boil, reduce the heat, and simmer the vegetables, covered, for 20 minutes.

> **4 large ripe tomatoes, peeled, seeded, and chopped or 1 1-pound can tomatoes**

Add the tomatoes and continue to simmer the mixture for 10 minutes longer.

At this point you may stop and continue later.

> **Reserved clams**
> **Salt**
> **Grinding of pepper**

Reserved bacon
Fine-chopped parsley

Add the clams and bring the chowder to serving temperature; do not let it boil. Season it to taste with salt and pepper. Serve it garnished with the bacon and parsley.

Serve with casserole-baked bread, page 288.

MUSSEL SOUP

4 servings
PREPARATION: about 40 minutes
(time does not include readying the mussels, page 232)

> **2 medium cloves garlic, peeled and chopped**
> **1 large onion, peeled and chopped**
> **8 sprigs parsley**
> **1 bay leaf, crumbled**
> **½ teaspoon thyme**
> **8 peppercorns**
> **2 cups dry white wine**

In a soup kettle, combine these ingredients. Bring them to the boil, and over high heat cook them, covered, for a few minutes.

> **4 dozen mussels prepared for cooking**

Add the mussels and steam them, tightly covered, for 5 to 8 minutes, or until they open; discard any that do not open. With a slotted spoon, remove them. Detach them from their shells, reserving any liquid; return the liquid to the kettle and reserve the mussels. Reduce the contents of the kettle to 1½ cups; strain it and transfer it to a large saucepan.

> **3 cups boiling milk**
> **4 tablespoons soft butter**
> **4 tablespoons flour**

Add the milk to the contents of the saucepan. In a small mixing bowl, combine the butter and flour; with a fork, blend the mixture until it is smooth. Add this *beurre manié* to the contents of the saucepan, stirring constantly until the mixture is thickened and smooth.

> **½ cup heavy cream**
> **Salt**
> **Grinding of white pepper**

Stir in the cream. Season the soup to taste with salt and pepper.
At this point you may stop and continue later.

> **Reserved mussels**
> **Fine-chopped parsley**

Bring the soup to serving temperature. Add the mussels and heat them through; do not allow them to cook. Serve the soup garnished with parsley.

Serve with muffins, page 289.

CHILLED CREAM OF MUSSEL SOUP

6 servings
PREPARATION: about 45 minutes
(time does not include readying the mussels, page 232)
CHILLING TIME: 3 hours

"Billi Bi," the name given by Maxim's in Paris to the favorite soup of William B. Leeds, a wealthy American tin magnate, is a deservedly popular first course, smooth, flavorful, and elegant. It may also be served hot.

> *3 pounds mussels prepared for cooking*
> *3 medium onions, peeled and quartered*
> *3 sprigs parsley*
> *3 tablespoons butter*
> *1½ cups dry white wine*
> *1 bay leaf*
> *Pinch of cayenne pepper*
> *¾ teaspoon thyme*

In a soup kettle, combine these ingredients. Bring the liquid to the boil, reduce the heat, and simmer the mussels, tightly covered, for about 6 minutes or until they open. Discard any that do not open. Into a saucepan, strain the liquid through two thicknesses of cheesecloth. Remove the mussels from their shells, remove the black rims, and reserve the mussels, covered, as garnish.

> *2 cups heavy cream*
> *1 egg yolk, beaten*
> *Salt*
> *Grinding of white pepper*

Bring the liquid in the saucepan to the boil. Stir in the cream and return the mixture to the boil. Away from the heat, whisk in the egg yolk and return the soup to the heat, stirring constantly, until it is somewhat thickened; do not allow it to boil. Season the soup to taste with salt and pepper. If you wish to serve the soup chilled, add the reserved mussels and refrigerate the mixture for 3 hours. If you wish to serve it hot, add the mussels to the soup only long enough to heat them through.

MUSSEL SOUP WITH SAFFRON

4 to 6 servings
PREPARATION: about 45 minutes
(time does not include readying the mussels, page 232)

> **3** *pounds mussels prepared for cooking*
> **2** *medium onions, peeled and chopped*
> **3** *parsley sprigs*
> **1** *bay leaf*
> **¼** *teaspoon thyme*
> **½** *teaspoon white pepper*
> **2** *cups Fish Stock, page 94, or clam juice (2 8-ounce bottles)*
> **½** *cup water*
> **½** *cup dry white wine*

In a soup kettle, combine these ingredients. Bring the liquid to the boil, reduce the heat, and simmer the mussels, tightly covered, for about 5 or 6 minutes or until they open. With a slotted spoon, remove them from the kettle. Over a bowl (to collect their liquid), remove the mussels from their shells (discard any that do not open); discard the shells. Strain the mussel liquid through two thicknesses of cheesecloth and return the mussels to it; reserve the mixture. Continue simmering the contents of the soup kettle for 15 minutes longer. Into a large saucepan, strain the broth; discard the residue.

> **4** *tablespoons soft butter*
> **5** *tablespoons flour*
> **2** *large pinches saffron, crumbled in ¼ cup dry white wine*
> **½** *cup heavy cream*

In a mixing bowl, combine the butter and flour; using a fork, blend the mixture until it is smooth. To the simmering broth, add this *beurre manié*, stirring until the mixture is thickened and smooth. Stir in the saffron and cream.

At this point you may stop and continue later.

> **Reserved mussels**
> **Fine-chopped parsley**

Bring the soup to serving temperature, add the mussels and heat them through; do not cook them. Serve the soup garnished with parsley.

CLAM OR MUSSEL PURÉE

6 to 8 servings
PREPARATION: about 40 minutes
(time does not include readying the clams or mussels, page 232)

**18 large cherrystone clams or mussels
prepared for cooking**

In a large saucepan, combine the clams and ¼ cup water. Over high heat, bring the liquid to the boil, reduce the heat, and cook the clams, covered, only until they begin to open. Over a bowl (to collect their liquid) remove the clams from their shells. Strain and reserve the liquid; reserve the clams.

**½ cup raw natural rice
Reserved clam liquid
3 cups clam juice (3 8-ounce bottles)
1 cup dry white wine**

In a saucepan, combine the rice, reserved clam liquid, bottled clam juice, and white wine. Bring the liquid to the boil, reduce the heat, and simmer the rice, covered, for 25 minutes or until it is very tender. Allow the mixture to cool somewhat.

**4 tablespoons butter
3 scallions, trimmed and sliced thin (the
white part only)**

In a saucepan, heat the butter and in it cook the scallions until they are limp. Add them and the butter to the rice. In the container of a food processor or blender, whirl the mixture, about 2 cupfuls at a time, until it is reduced to a smooth purée; transfer it to a large saucepan.

Reserved clams

In the container of the processor, whirl the clams until they are reduced to a smooth purée; add it to the contents of the saucepan.

**1 cup heavy cream, scalded
Few drops of Tabasco sauce
Salt**

Add the cream and season the purée to taste with Tabasco sauce and salt.

Fine-chopped parsley

When serving the purée, reheat it over gentle heat or in the top of a double boiler. Garnish each serving with a sprinkling of parsley.

CLAM AND MUSSEL STEW, SPANISH STYLE

4 servings
PREPARATION: about 40 minutes
(time does not include readying the clams and mussels, page 232)
COOKING: 5 minutes in a 400 ° oven

It seems somehow fitting to conclude this section on clam and mussel soups with a recipe from Spain that combines both shellfish.

> *24 cherrystone clams prepared for cooking*
> *24 mussels prepared for cooking*
> *½ cup dry white wine*

In a soup kettle, combine the clams, mussels, and wine. Over high heat, bring the wine to the boil and steam the shellfish, tightly covered, for 5 to 8 minutes or until they open; discard any that do not open. Transfer them to an ovenproof casserole. Strain the broth through a sieve lined with cheesecloth; reserve it.

> *4 tablespoons olive oil*
> *2 cloves garlic, peeled and chopped fine*
> *1 medium onion, peeled and chopped fine*
> *2 ripe tomatoes, peeled, seeded, and chopped*
> *¼ cup chopped parsley*
> *Reserved liquid*
> *Salt*
> *Grinding of pepper*

In a saucepan, heat the olive oil and in it cook the garlic and onion until barely golden. Add the tomato and cook the mixture, stirring often, for 5 minutes. Stir in the parsley. Add the reserved liquid. Bring the mixture to the boil, reduce the heat, and simmer it, covered, for 5 minutes.

At this point you may stop and continue later.

Return the broth to the boil, pour it over the clams and mussels, and bake the casserole, uncovered, at 400 ° for 5 minutes. Serve the shellfish and broth from the casserole.

Serve with casserole-baked bread, page 288.

If desired, the clams and mussels may be removed from their shells at the end of step one, kept covered to retain their moistness, and added to the hot broth at the time of serving.

They are easy, unusual, and festive. I enjoyed experimenting with them, and discovered that clams and eggplant have an affinity for each other — in much the same way that fresh basil complements tomatoes — and take pleasure in offering two clam-and-eggplant dishes. There is clam quiche and there is mussel quiche, both attractive main dishes for a light meal (or appetizing first courses, if you wish). There are various sauces to be used with pasta. And there are mussels in various creams. No section of the book made me feel more self-indulgent in the developing process. Enjoy yourselves equally!

CLAM AND EGGPLANT CASSEROLE

6 servings
PREPARATION: about 30 minutes
COOKING: 30 minutes in a 350° oven

2 medium eggplants, peeled and cut in 1-inch cubes

In boiling salted water to cover, cook the eggplant, uncovered, for 8 minutes. Drain it in a colander.

2 6½-ounce cans minced clams
Heavy cream

Drain the clams, reserving the liquid; set aside the clams. To the liquid, add heavy cream to equal 2½ cups.

3 tablespoons butter
1 large onion, peeled and chopped fine
1 small green pepper, seeded and diced
3 tablespoons flour
Reserved liquid
Reserved eggplant
Reserved clams
¼ cup fine-chopped parsley

In a flameproof casserole, heat the butter and in it cook the onion and green pepper until the onion is golden. Stir in the flour, and over gentle heat cook the mixture for a few minutes. Gradually add the reserved liquid, stirring constantly until the mixture is thickened and smooth. Fold in the reserved eggplant, clams, and parsley.

At this point you may stop and continue later.

Fine-chopped parsley

Bake the casserole, uncovered, at 350° for 30 minutes. Garnish it with a sprinkling of fresh parsley.

Serve with curried bulgur, page 291.

CLAM AND EGGPLANT SOUFFLÉ

4 servings
PREPARATION: about 1 hour
COOKING: 30 minutes in a 350° oven

Thoroughly butter a 2-quart soufflé dish.

1 medium eggplant

With the tines of a fork, pierce the eggplant in several places; arrange it on a baking sheet and cook it in a 400° oven for 40 minutes. Quarter it lengthwise, scoop out the pulp, and discard the skins. Transfer the pulp to the container of a food processor.

> **2 tablespoons soft butter**
> **4 tablespoons flour**
> **1 6½-ounce can minced clams, with their liquid**
> **1 tablespoon strained lemon juice**
> **2 tablespoons grated Parmesan cheese**
> **½ teaspoon nutmeg**
> **Salt**
> **Pepper**

To the contents of the processor, add these ingredients except the salt and pepper. Whirl the mixture until it is blended. Season it to taste with salt and pepper.

> **4 egg yolks**
> **¼ cup chopped parsley**

Add the egg yolks and parsley and whirl the mixture to blend it well. Transfer it to a mixing bowl.

At this point you may stop and continue later.

> **5 egg whites, beaten until stiff but not dry**

Into the mixture, beat one-fifth of the egg white; fold in the remainder. Using a rubber spatula, transfer the batter to the prepared dish. Bake the soufflé at 350° for 30 minutes, or until it is well puffed and golden.

Serve with broccoli, page 292.

CLAM-FILLED CRÊPES

4 servings as a main course;
6 servings as a first course
PREPARATION: about 30 minutes
(time does not include readying the crêpes, page 118,
which may be made well in advance and frozen)
COOKING: about 12 minutes in a 400° oven

> 2 *eggs*
> ½ *cup grated Parmesan cheese*
> 1 *cup ricotta cheese*
> 1 *10-ounce package frozen chopped spinach, fully thawed to room temperature and pressed dry in a colander*
> 1 *small onion, peeled and grated*
> ¼ *cup fine-chopped parsley*
> 2 *6½-ounce cans chopped clams, drained*
> *Salt*
> *Grinding of white pepper*

In a mixing bowl, beat the eggs lightly. Add the Parmesan and ricotta cheeses and the spinach; blend the mixture well. When it is smooth, stir in the onion, parsley, and clams. Season the mixture to taste with salt and pepper.

> **12 *prepared crêpes***

Spread the filling in equal amounts on each of the crêpes. Roll and arrange them, seam side down, in a lightly buttered ovenproof serving dish.

> **2 *cups Clam Dip, page 238,* or *Mornay Sauce, page 281***

Prepare the dip or sauce and spread it evenly over the crêpes.

At this point you may stop and continue later.

(If you plan to continue later, cover the dish well with plastic wrap.)

Bake the crêpes, uncovered, at 400° for 12 minutes, or until the sauce is bubbly.

Serve with green peas, page 294.

CLAM QUICHE

6 to 8 servings as a first course
4 to 6 servings as a main dish
PREPARATION: about 30 minutes
(time does not include readying the pastry)
COOKING: 30 minutes starting in a 450° oven

1 unbaked 9-inch pastry shell*
Melted butter

Brush the pastry shell with the melted butter. Chill the shell while you prepare the recipe.

4 strips bacon, diced
4 scallions, trimmed and chopped fine,
 with as much green as is crisp

In a skillet, render the bacon; with a slotted spoon, remove it to absorbent paper and reserve it. In the remaining fat, cook the scallions until translucent.

4 eggs
 Liquid from 2 6½-ounce cans minced
 clams (reserve the clams)
 Light cream
½ cup fine-chopped parsley
 Nutmeg
 Salt
 Pepper

In a mixing bowl, beat the eggs lightly. To the clam liquid, add cream to equal 1½ cups; blend the mixture with the eggs. Stir in the clams and parsley. Season the custard to taste with a grating of nutmeg and salt and pepper.

 At this point you may stop and continue later.
Over the bottom of the pastry shell, distribute the bacon and scallions. Pour in the clam mixture. Bake the quiche for 10 minutes at 450°; reduce the heat to 350° and continue to bake it for 20 minutes longer, or until a sharp knife inserted at the center comes out clean. Allow the quiche to stand for 5 minutes before serving it.

 As a main dish for a light meal, offer the quiche with mixed green salad garnished with sliced tomatoes and red onion rings.

---

* Using your favorite recipe for a 9-inch quiche crust.

FRIED CLAMS

4 servings
PREPARATION: about 45 minutes
COOKING: about 4 minutes in deep fryer preheated to 375°

3 dozen soft-shell clams, scrubbed

Shuck the clams and rinse them well under cold water in a colander. Dry them on absorbent paper. Cut away and discard the black skin of the neck.

1 egg
2 tablespoons water
Seasoned bread crumbs

In a small mixing bowl, beat together the egg and water. Insert a fork in the tough muscle of the clams, dip them in the egg, and then dredge them in the bread crumbs. Repeat the process and then allow the clams to dry for about 30 minutes on a rack. Fry them, a few at a time, in the preheated fat for about 4 minutes, or until they are golden.

Tartare Sauce, page 286

Drain the clams briefly on absorbent paper, arrange them in a heated dish, and offer the tartare sauce separately.

Serve with casserole-baked bread, page 288.

CLAM AND MACARONI CASSEROLE

4 to 6 servings
PREPARATION: about 35 minutes
COOKING: 30 minuters in a 375° oven

2 tablespoons butter
1 medium onion, peeled and chopped
2 tablespoons flour
1 teaspoon salt
Grinding of white pepper
1 cup milk

In a saucepan, heat the butter and in it cook the onion until translucent. Stir in the flour, and over gentle heat cook the mixture for a few minutes. Stir in the salt and pepper. Gradually add the milk, stirring constantly until the *béchamel* is thickened and smooth.

> **2 cups uncooked elbow macaroni**
> **2 6½-ounce cans minced clams, with their liquid**
> **2 cups (½ pound) shredded mild Cheddar cheese**
> **⅓ cup fine-chopped parsley**

Cook the macaroni according to the directions on the package; it should be *al dente* (do not overcook it). In a large mixing bowl combine the *béchamel,* macaroni, clams and their liquid, the cheese, and parsley. Using two forks, gently toss the ingredients to blend them well. Into a lightly buttered 2-quart casserole, spoon the mixture.

At this point you may stop and continue later.

> **Soft butter**
> **Paprika**

Dot the top with butter and sprinkle it with paprika. Bake the casserole, uncovered, at 375° for 30 minutes, or until the top is slightly crusty.

Serve with green bean salad, page 297.

MUSSELS À LA NEWBURG

4 servings
PREPARATION: about 40 minutes
(time does not include readying the mussels, page 232)

> **3 dozen mussels, steamed open, removed from their shells, the black rims removed, and their liquid reserved**

Strain the liquid through two thicknesses of cheesecloth, and over high heat reduce it to 1 cup. Reserve the mussels.

> **Newburg Sauce, page 282 (double the recipe)**

Follow the recipe for Newburg sauce, substituting for the light cream 1 cup heavy cream, scalded, combined with the 1 cup reduced mussel liquid. Into the hot sauce, stir the mussels.

Serve with rice, page 290.

MUSSEL QUICHE

6 to 8 servings as a first course
4 to 6 servings as a main dish
PREPARATION: about 40 minutes
(time does not include readying the
mussels, page 232, or the pastry)
COOKING: 30 minutes, starting in a 450° oven

1 unbaked 9-inch pastry shell*
Melted butter

Brush the pastry shell with the melted butter. Chill the shell while you prepare the recipe.

3 dozen mussels prepared for cooking
⅓ cup dry white wine
1 bay leaf, crumbled

In a soup kettle, combine the mussels, wine, and bay leaf. Over high heat, steam the mussels, tightly covered, for about 5 to 8 minutes, or until they open. Over a bowl *(*to catch their liquid*)* remove them from their shells; discard any that have not opened. Into a saucepan, strain the liquid, together with that in the soup kettle; over high heat, reduce it to ¼ cup. Reserve the mussels.

4 eggs
1 cup light cream
Reserved liquid
1 small onion, peeled and grated
¼ cup fine-chopped parsley
Nutmeg
Salt
Pepper

In a mixing bowl, beat the eggs lightly. Stir in the cream and mussel liquid. Add the onion and parsley. Season the custard to taste with a grating of nutmeg and salt and pepper.

At this point you may stop and continue later.

Over the bottom of the pastry shell, distribute the mussels. Pour in the custard. Bake the quiche for 10 minutes at 450°; reduce the heat to 350°

---

* Using your favorite recipe for a 9-inch quiche crust.

---

and continue to bake it for 20 minutes longer, or until a sharp knife inserted at the center comes out clean. Allow the quiche to stand for 5 minutes before serving it.

As a main dish for a light meal, offer the quiche with mixed green salad garnished with sliced tomatoes and red onion rings.

MUSSELS PROVENÇALE
(STEAMED MUSSELS WITH TOMATOES)

4 servings
PREPARATION: about 35 minutes
(time does not include readying the mussels, page 232)
COOKING: about 5 minutes

> *4 tablespoons olive oil*
> *2 cloves garlic, peeled and chopped fine*
> *1 medium onion, peeled and chopped*
> *¼ cup fine-chopped parsley*
> *3 large ripe tomatoes, peeled, seeded, and chopped*
> *1 cup dry white wine*
> *1 teaspoon basil*

In a soup kettle, heat the oil and in it cook the garlic and onion until translucent. Add the parsley, tomatoes, wine, and basil. Over high heat, bring the liquid to the boil and cook the mixture, uncovered, for 5 minutes.

> *4 dozen mussels prepared for cooking*

Add the mussels and steam them, tightly covered, for about 5 minutes, or until they open; discard any that do not open. Spoon the mussels into heated bowls and pour the broth over them.

Serve with casserole-baked bread, page 288.

MUSSELS IN CREAM

4 servings
PREPARATION: about 45 minutes
(time does not include readying the mussels, page 232)

This recipe yields a large quantity of sauce, which may be used as the basis for soup.

> 3 *cups dry white wine*
> 1 *medium rib celery with its leaves*
> 1 *large clove garlic, peeled and chop-*
>   *ped fine*
> 1 *large onion, peeled and chopped*
>   *fine*
> 1 *bay leaf*
> ¾ *teaspoon salt*
> ¼ *teaspoon white pepper*

In a soup kettle, combine these ingredients. Bring the liquid to the boil, reduce the heat, and simmer the mixture, covered, for 15 minutes. Discard the celery and bay leaf.

> 5 *dozen mussels prepared for cook-*
>   *ing*

To the contents of the soup kettle, add the mussels, and over high heat steam them, tightly covered, until they open; discard any that do not open.

> 1½ *cups cream (heavy or light)*
> 5   *tablespoons soft butter*
> 6   *tablespoons flour*
> 1   *cup fine-chopped parsley*

In a small mixing bowl, combine the butter and flour; using a fork, blend the mixture until it is smooth. Add this *beurre manié* to the kettle, and over medium heat cook the sauce, stirring gently, until it is thickened and smooth. Sprinkle with parsley and agitate the kettle to blend the ingredients. With a slotted spoon, arrange the mussels in heated soup plates and over them pour some of the sauce.

Serve with casserole-baked bread, page 288.

For *Mussels in Curried Cream:* add to the *beurre manié* 2 to 3 teaspoons sweet (Madras) curry powder, and complete the recipe. For *Mussels in Mustard Cream:* stir into the contents of the kettle, before the addition of the *beurre manié*, 2 tablespoons Dijon mustard; complete the recipe.

MUSSEL RISOTTO, ITALIAN STYLE

4 servings
PREPARATION: about 40 minutes
(time does not include readying the mussels, page 232)
COOKING: about 15 minutes

> **4 dozen mussels, steamed open, removed from their shells, their liquid reserved**

Strain the mussel liquid and to it add, if necesary, water to equal 2 cups. Reserve the mussels.

> **3 tablespoons olive oil**
> **2 large cloves garlic, peeled and sliced lengthwise**
> **4 large ripe tomatoes, peeled, seeded, and chopped**
> **Salt**
> **Grinding of pepper**

In a large saucepan, heat the olive oil and in it cook the garlic until it is brown; discard it. Add the tomatoes, and over medium heat cook them, stirring often, for 15 minutes. Season the sauce to taste with salt and pepper.

> **1 cup raw natural rice (preferably Italian)**
> **Reserved mussel liquid**

While the sauce is cooking, prepare the rice: in a saucepan, combine the rice and liquid. Bring the liquid to the boil, stir the rice once with a fork, reduce the heat, and simmer it, covered, for 15 minutes, or until it is tender and the liquid is absorbed.

> **Reserved mussels**
> **½ cup fine-chopped parsley**
> **Grated Parmesan cheese**

Add the cooked rice and mussels to the tomato sauce; or, if you prefer, combine them in a large heated bowl. Sprinkle over the parsley. Using two forks, lightly toss the mixture to blend the ingredients. Offer the grated cheese separately.

Serve with mixed green salad, page 295.

CLAMS OR MUSSELS FLORENTINE

6 servings
PREPARATION: about 45 minutes
(time does not include readying the clams or mussels, page 232)
COOKING: 35 minutes; preheat oven to 350°

> *2 10-ounce packages fresh spinach with the woody stems removed, rinsed, wilted for 20 seconds in lightly salted boiling water to cover, pressed dry in a colander, and chopped or 2 10-ounce packages frozen chopped spinach, fully thawed to room temperature and pressed dry in a colander*

Prepare and reserve the spinach.

> *24 cherrystone clams or mussels, steamed open, removed from their shells, their liquid reserved or 2 6½-ounce cans chopped clams, drained, their liquid reserved*

If you are using fresh clams or mussels, chop them coarse. Strain the broth and reduce it to ½ cup.

> *1½ cups heavy cream*
> *Reserved liquid*
> *2 tablespoons soft butter*
> *2 tablespoons flour*

In a saucepan, scald the cream and to it add the reserved liquid. In a small mixing bowl, combine the butter and flour; using a fork, blend the mixture until it is smooth. Add this *beurre manié* to the contents of the saucepan, and over medium heat cook the sauce, stirring constantly, until it is thickened and smooth. Combine half the sauce with the clams.

> *¾ cup fine-chopped Muenster cheese*
> *Grating of nutmeg*
> *Salt*
> *Grinding of white pepper*

To the remaining sauce, add the Muenster cheese, stirring until it is melted. Season the mixture to taste with nutmeg, salt, and pepper.
At this point you may stop and continue later.

> *¼ cup grated Parmesan cheese*

Over the bottom of a lightly buttered baking dish, arrange half the spinach; over it, spread the clam mixture; add the remaining spinach and then the cheese sauce. Over the top, sprinkle the grated cheese.

Place the dish in a baking pan with hot water halfway up its sides. Bake the clams Florentine for 30 minutes at 350°; increase the heat to 425° and continue baking for 5 minutes longer, or until the top is lightly browned.

Serve with saffron rice, page 291.

CLAMS OR MUSSELS MARINIÈRE

4 servings
PREPARATION: about 30 minutes
(time does not include readying the clams or mussels, page 232)
COOKING: about 5 minutes

The classic French dish for mussels, which I find very good made with littleneck clams.

3 tablespoons butter
¼ cup celery leaves
½ cup parsley leaves or 8 sprigs
3 scallions, trimmed and chopped
1 bay leaf, crumbled
¼ teaspoon oregano
¼ teaspoon thyme
1 cup dry white wine

In a saucepan, heat the butter and in it cook the celery leaves, parsley, and scallions until the scallions are limp. Add the herbs and wine. Bring the liquid to the boil, reduce the heat, and simmer the mixture, tightly covered, for 10 minutes. Into a soup kettle, strain the broth.

4 dozen littleneck clams or mussels pre-
pared for cooking
2 tablespoons soft butter

Add the clams to the soup kettle, and over high heat steam them, tightly covered, for about 5 minutes, or until they open; discard any that do not open. Remove them to a serving dish. Strain the liquid through two thicknesses of cheesecloth; swirl the butter into the broth and serve it separately. If desired, you may measure the broth and thicken it with *beurre manié,* page 17.

Serve with casserole-baked bread, page 288.

MUSSELS IN SAFFRON CREAM

4 servings

PREPARATION: about 40 minutes

(time does not include readying the mussels, page 232)

COOKING: 2 minutes (excluding the rice or pasta)

4 dozen mussels prepared for cooking

In a soup kettle, arrange the mussels; add ½ cup water. Over high heat, bring the liquid to the boil; reduce the heat and cook the mussels, covered, only until they begin to open. Over a bowl (to collect their liquid), remove the mussels from their shells. Discard any that have not opened. Strain the liquid and add the mussels to it; reserve the mixture.

3 tablespoons butter
1 clove garlic, peeled and chopped fine
1 medium leek, chopped fine (the white part only) or 1 large onion, peeled and chopped fine

In a large saucepan, heat the butter and in it cook the garlic and leek until they are translucent.

1 teaspoon loose saffron, crumbled

Add the saffron and cook the mixture for 2 minutes.

At this point you may stop and continue later.

2 tablespoons wine vinegar
Reserved mussels and their liquid
Salt
Grinding of white pepper

To the contents of the saucepan, add the vinegar, mussels, and their liquid; cook the mussels for 1 minute. Season the mixture to taste with salt and pepper.

½ cup heavy cream
¼ cup fine-chopped parsley

Add the cream and parsley. Continue cooking the dish only until it reaches serving temperature.

Cooked rice, page 290, or pasta

Serve the mussels in heated deep dishes over cooked rice or pasta.

CLAM OR MUSSEL RISOTTO, SPANISH STYLE

4 servings
PREPARATION: about 40 minutes
COOKING: 25 minutes in a 350° oven

> 2 *large cloves garlic, peeled and chopped fine*
> 1 *medium onion, peeled and chopped*
> 1 *small green pepper, seeded and chopped*
> 3 *ripe tomatoes, peeled, seeded, and chopped*
> 2 *cups clam juice (2 8-ounce bottles)*
> ¼ *teaspoon crumbled saffron*
> *Salt*
> *Grinding of pepper*

In a saucepan, combine the first five ingredients. Bring the liquid to the boil, reduce the heat, and simmer the mixture for 15 minutes. Season the sauce with the saffron and to taste with salt and pepper

> 24 *littleneck clams* or *mussels, thoroughly scrubbed*
> 1 *cup raw natural rice (preferably Italian)*
> ½ *cup fine-chopped parsley*

In a casserole, combine and blend the clams, rice, and parsley. Over them, pour the sauce. Bake the casserole at 350° for 25 minutes, or until the rice is tender and most of the liquid is absorbed.

Serve with mixed green salad, page 295.

CLAM OR MUSSEL SOUFFLÉ

4 servings
PREPARATION: about 25 minutes
COOKING: 30 minutes in a 350° oven

Thoroughly butter a 2-quart soufflé dish.

> **4 tablespoons butter**
> **4 tablespoons flour**
> **1 small onion, peeled and grated**

In a saucepan, heat the butter and in it, over gentle heat, cook the flour for a few minutes. Stir in the onion.

> **2 6½-ounce cans minced clams or mussels (you will have to chop the mussels), drained, their liquid reserved**
> **Heavy cream**

To the reserved clam liquid, add cream to equal 1 cup. Gradually add it to the contents of the saucepan and cook the mixture, stirring constantly, until it is thickened and smooth.

> **Reserved clams**
> **¼ cup fine-chopped parsley**
> **4 egg yolks**
> **Salt**
> **Grinding of white pepper**

Into the contents of the saucepan, stir first the clams and parsley and then beat in the egg yolks. Season the mixture to taste with salt and pepper.
At this point you may stop and continue later.

> **5 egg whites, beaten until stiff but not dry**

Into the soufflé batter, beat one-fifth of the egg white; fold in the remainder. Using a rubber spatula, transfer the mixture to the prepared dish. Bake the soufflé at 350° for 30 minutes, or until it is well puffed and golden.

Serve with green peas, page 294.

Clam or Mussel Sauces for Pasta

There are many clam sauces for pasta; I am being arbitrary in offering three that I enjoy. Happily, I found in culinary experimentation that the sauces are equally good made with mussels. Each of these recipes will dress one pound of pasta (my favorite is spinach linguine number 8). The preparation time of about 45 minutes does not include readying the clams or mussels, page 232.

SAUCE I

> 4 *dozen littleneck clams or mussels, steamed open, removed from their shells, chopped coarse, their liquid reserved or 3 6½-ounce cans chopped clams, drained, their liquid reserved*
> ½ *cup olive oil*
> 2 *large cloves garlic, peeled and chopped fine*
> 1 *medium onion, peeled and chopped fine*
> 1 *small green pepper, seeded and diced*

In a saucepan, heat the olive oil and in it cook the garlic, onion, and pepper until the onion is translucent.

> *Reserved liquid*
> ½ *cup dry white wine*
> ½ *cup fine-chopped parsley*
> 1 *bay leaf*
> ¼ *teaspoon thyme*
> ½ *teaspoon salt*
> *Grinding of pepper*

To the contents of the saucepan, add these ingredients. Bring the liquid to the boil, reduce the heat, and simmer the mixture, covered, for 15 minutes.

> *Reserved clams or mussels*

Add the clams or mussels and heat them through. In a large heated bowl, combine the cooked pasta and sauce; using two forks, toss the pasta so that it is well covered with the sauce.

Serve with mixed green salad, page 295.

Prepare the clams or mussels as suggested above.

> 1 *clove garlic, peeled and put through a press*
> ⅓ *cup olive oil*
> 1 *medium onion, peeled and chopped*
> 1 *6-ounce can tomato paste*
> ¾ *teaspoon basil*
> ½ *teaspoon oregano*
> 1 *teaspoon sugar*
> *Reserved liquid*
> ½ *cup dry white wine*
> *Salt*
> *Grinding of pepper*

In a saucepan, combine and blend the first nine ingredients; season the mixture to taste with salt and pepper. Bring it to the boil, reduce the heat, and simmer it, covered, for 15 minutes.

> 12 *large mushrooms, sliced thin*
> *Reserved clams or mussels*

To the contents of the saucepan, add the mushrooms; continue to simmer the mixture, covered, for 5 minutes longer, or until the mushrooms are wilted. Stir in the clams or mussels and heat them through. In a large heated bowl combine the cooked pasta and sauce; using two forks, toss the pasta so that it is well covered with the sauce.

Serve with mixed green salad, page 295.

SAUCE III

> 6 *tablespoons butter*
> 3 *large cloves garlic, peeled and chopped fine*
> ½ *cup fine-chopped parsley*
> 8 *scallions, trimmed and cut in ¼-inch rounds, with as much green as is crisp*

Prepare the clams or mussels as suggested above. In a saucepan, heat the butter and in it cook the garlic, parsley, and scallions until the scallions are limp.

Reserved clams or mussels and their liquid

Add the clams or mussels and their liquid. Heat the mixture to serving temperature. In a large heated bowl, combine the cooked pasta and sauce; using two forks, toss the pasta so that it is well covered with the sauce.

Serve with mixed green salad, page 295.

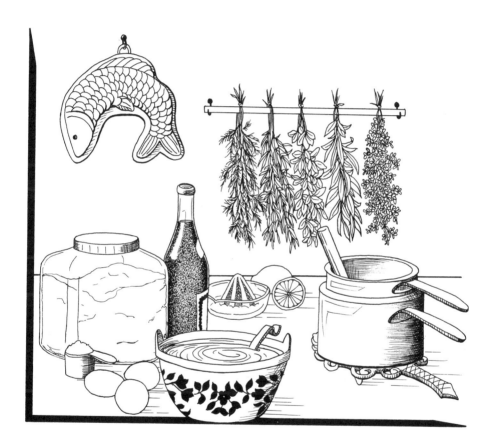

Clams and mussels are delectable raw and chilled or cooked and hot. Cooked and chilled, they are perhaps a little tricky, having a tendency to become rubbery in texture and flat in flavor. For this reason, I have limited the number of recipes in this section of the book to three which I make with pleasure and serve with assurance, readily admitting meanwhile that three dishes do not a section make!

CLAM ASPIC

6 servings
PREPARATION: about 25 minutes
CHILLING TIME: 6 hours

Lightly oil and chill a 5-cup ring or other mold.

> 1½ *envelopes unflavored gelatin soft-*
> *ened for 5 minutes in ¼ cup cold*
> *water and dissolved over simmering*
> *water*
> 2 *6½-ounce cans minced clams with*
> *their liquid*
> 2 *tablespoons strained lemon juice*
> 2 *cups tomato juice*
> ½ *teaspoon salt*

In a mixing bowl, combine and blend these ingredients. Chill the mixture until it is syrupy.

> 1 *medium rib celery, diced*
> 3 *tablespoons fine-chopped gherkins*
> 3 *scallions, chopped fine (the white part*
> *only)*

Into the contents of the mixing bowl, stir the celery, gherkins, and scallions. Transfer the mixture to a lightly oiled ring mold and chill the aspic for 6 hours, or until it is thoroughly set. Unmold it onto a chilled serving dish. Fill the center with Mixed Vegetable Salad, page 298.

CLAM OR MUSSEL MOUSSE

6 to 8 servings
PREPARATION: about 35 minutes
CHILLING TIME: 6 hours

Lightly oil and chill a 6-cup ring or other mold.

> **2 envelopes unflavored gelatin, soft-
> ened for 5 minutes in ½ cup cold
> water**

Over simmering water, dissolve the gelatin; reserve it.

> **2 6½-ounce cans minced clams or
> mussels (you may have to chop the
> mussels), with their liquid**
> **1½ cups cream-style cottage cheese**
> **Strained juice of 1 small lemon**
> **A few drops of Tabasco sauce**
> **1 teaspoon Worcestershire sauce**
> **1 teaspoon salt**
> **Reserved gelatin**

In the container of a food processor or blender, combine these ingredients. Whirl the mixture until it is smooth. Transfer it to a mixing bowl
and chill it until it just begins to set.

> **⅓ cup fine-chopped parsley**
> **1 cup small frozen peas, fully thawed
> to room temperature**
> **4 scallions, trimmed and chopped, with
> as much green as is crisp**

With a spoon, beat the gelatin mixture briefly so that it is smooth. Fold in
the parsley, peas, and scallions.

> **1 cup heavy cream, whipped**

Fold in the whipped cream. Using a rubber spatula, transfer the mixture
to the prepared mold. Chill the mousse for 6 hours, or until it is
thoroughly set.

> **1 bunch watercress with the woody
> stems removed, rinsed and thoroughly
> drained**

Onto a chilled serving plate, unmold the mousse; garnish it with watercress.

Serve with muffins, page 289.

MUSSEL SALAD

4 servings
PREPARATION: about 25 minutes
(time does not include readying the mussels, page 232)
CHILLING TIME: 2 hours

> *4 dozen mussels, steamed opened, re-*
> *moved from their shells (their liquid*
> *reserved for another recipe)*
> *Vinaigrette Sauce, page 287*
> *Fine-chopped parsley*
> *Fine-chopped scallions*

In a mixing bowl, toss the mussels with vinaigrette sauce; add parsley and scallions to taste. Chill the mussels for 2 hours.

> *Mayonnaise, page 281 (optional)*
> *Salad greens of your choice*
> *Avocado halves (optional)*

If desired, drain the mussels, discarding the vinaigrette sauce, and toss them with a little mayonnaise; arrange them on salad greens or in the cavity of seeded avocado halves.

Serve with muffins, page 289.

For *Mussels Rémoulade:* prepare the mussels as indicated above, toss them with Rémoulade Sauce, page 285, chill them as directed, and offer them on salad greens or in avocado halves.

EIGHT

The Sauce That Enhances

Some foods are especially compatible with sauces. Fish is a particularly good example of this gustatory consonance. Baked, broiled, fried, poached, or steamed, fish is made even more delectable by the addition of a complementary sauce. Is this true because fish, having its own particular flavor, is not overcome by sauces? Perhaps; I think this fact does contribute measurably to the happy marriage of fish and sauce. The following thirty-odd sauces, by no means an exhaustive list, comprise those that I find useful, tasty, and easily made. All of them may be used with hot fish and many are good with chilled fish; that is to say, a sauce made to be served cold or at room temperature is often a pleasant addition to hot fish — *pesto genovese,* for example, or mayonnaise — whereas a sauce designed to be served hot will not go well with a dish intended to be eaten chilled. Sauce-making is a very creative kitchen activity. Use these recipes as a point of departure for your own variations.

SAUCE ALLEMANDE
(*for hot fish*)

YIELD: about 1½ cups

In a saucepan, heat 2 tablespoons butter and in it, over gentle heat, cook 2 tablespoons flour for a few minutes. Gradually add 1 cup chicken broth *or* half chicken broth and half fish stock, stirring constantly until the mixture is thickened and smooth. Season it to taste with salt and white pepper. Blend in ⅓ cup light cream. To 1 beaten egg yolk, add half the hot sauce. Then transfer all of the egg yolk–sauce mixture to the contents of the saucepan. Blend the sauce and cook it over the lowest possible heat for a few minutes; do not allow it to boil.

BÉARNAISE
(*for hot fish*)

In a small saucepan, combine 3 tablespoons tarragon vinegar, 1 teaspoon chervil, 4 crushed peppercorns, 1 teaspoon fine-chopped scallion, and 1 tablespoon crushed tarragon. Bring the mixture to the boil, reduce the heat, and simmer it until the liquid is reduced by half. Strain it into the container of a food processor or blender. Add 1 tablespoon water and 4 egg yolks, at room temperature. In another saucepan, melt and bring to the boil 8 tablespoons butter. With the motor running, add the butter in a thin, steady stream. Add ¼ teaspoon crushed tarragon and salt to taste. Transfer the sauce to a serving dish, or if you wish to reheat it later, to the top of a double boiler, in which it may be brought to serving temperature over simmering water.

FLAVORED BUTTERS
(*for hot fish*)

Beurre Maître d'Hôtel (to garnish 4 servings): in a small mixing bowl, blend 4 tablespoons butter, 2 tablespoons strained lemon juice, 1 tablespoon fine-chopped parsley, a few grains of cayenne pepper, and ½ teaspoon salt. Shape the butter in 4 portions and refrigerate it for about 30 minutes.

Almond Butter (to garnish 4 servings): in a small saucepan, combine 4 tablespoons butter, ½ cup fine-chopped toasted almonds, ¼ cup fine-chopped parsley, and ¼ cup dry white wine. Over high heat, cook the mixture, stirring, until it is well blended. Add 1 tablespoon strained lemon juice.

Anchovy Butter (to garnish 4 servings): in a small mixing bowl, blend 5 tablespoons butter and 2 tablespoons anchovy paste. Stir in 2 anchovy fillets, drained on absorbent paper and chopped fine, 1½ tablespoons strained lemon juice, and 2 tablespoons fine-chopped parsley. Shape the butter in 4 portions and refrigerate it for about 30 minutes.

Brown Butter (to garnish 4 servings): in a small saucepan, combine 4 tablespoons butter and 1 tablespoon dry bread crumbs; over medium heat, cook the mixture until the butter is golden and the crumbs are brown. Off heat, stir in 1 teaspoon strained lemon juice and a little salt and white pepper to taste.

Parsley Butter (to garnish 4 servings): in a small saucepan, combine 4 tablespoons butter and ¼ cup fine-chopped parsley; heat the mixture until it bubbles. Off heat, stir in 1 teaspoon strained lemon juice and a little salt and white pepper to taste.

Tarragon Butter (to garnish 4 servings): in a small mixing bowl, blend 4 tablespoons butter and 1 teaspoon tarragon, crushed in a mortar with pestle. Stir in a few drops of lemon juice. Allow the butter to stand at room temperature for about 1 hour, in order that the flavors meld. Shape the butter in 4 portions and refrigerate it for about 30 minutes.

CHEESE SAUCE
(*for hot fish*)

YIELD: about 2¼ cups

In the top of a double boiler, heat 2 tablespoons butter and in it cook for a few minutes 1 small onion, peeled and grated; add 2 tablespoons flour, and over gentle heat cook the mixture, stirring, for 1 minute. Stir in ½ teaspoon salt and ¼ teaspoon white pepper. Gradually add 1½ cups milk, stirring constantly until the mixture is thickened and smooth. Off heat, stir in 1 cup grated American or Cheddar cheese and 1 tablespoon strained lemon juice. Cover the sauce closely so that it will not crust and heat it at the time of serving over simmering water.

CUCUMBER SAUCE
(*for chilled fish*)

YIELD: about 1½ cups

In the container of a food processor or blender, combine 1 medium unpeeled cucumber, seeded and chopped coarse, ¼ cup Mayonnaise, page 281, 3 gratings onion, 2 tablespoons fine-chopped parsley, ½ cup sour cream, 2 teaspoons vinegar, ¼ teaspoon salt, and a grinding of white pepper. Whirl the ingredients until the sauce is smooth. Transfer it to a serving dish and chill it.

CURRY SAUCE
(*for hot fish*)

YIELD: about 1¼ cups

In a saucepan, heat 3 tablespoons butter and into it stir 3 or 4 gratings of onion. Stir in 1 to 2 teaspoons curry powder, depending upon your taste (sweet Madras curry is recommended) and 2 tablespoons flour. Over gentle heat, cook the mixture for a few minutes. Gradually add 1 cup milk, stirring constantly until the mixture is thickened and smooth. Adjust the seasoning to taste with salt.

If desired, ⅓ cup white raisins may be added to the sauce.

DILL SAUCE I
(*for hot fish*)

YIELD: 1½ cups

In a saucepan, heat 3 tablespoons butter and in it, over gentle heat, cook 2½ tablespoons flour for a few minutes. Gradually add ½ cup bottled clam juice *or* liquid from poaching fish and 1 cup light cream *or* milk, stirring constantly until the mixture is thickened and smooth. Stir in 2 teaspoons dill. Season the sauce to taste with a grating of nutmeg, salt, and white pepper.

DILL SAUCE II
(*for chilled fish*)

YIELD: about 1½ cups

In a mixing bowl, blend 1 tablespoon fresh *or* 2 teaspoons dried dill, 1 teaspoon Dijon mustard, 3 gratings onion, and 1½ cups sour cream. Season the sauce to taste with a few drops of Tabasco sauce and salt. Transfer the sauce to a serving dish and chill it.

DILL PICKLE SAUCE
(for hot or chilled fish)

YIELD: about 1½ cups

In a mixing bowl, blend 1 tablespoon capers, drained and chopped fine, 1½ teaspoons Dijon mustard, ¼ cup fine-chopped dill pickle, 1 cup Mayonnaise, page 281, and 3 tablespoons fine-chopped parsley. Allow the sauce to sit for 1 hour at room temperature so that the flavors meld. Transfer it to a serving dish and offer it at room temperature for hot fish or refrigerated for chilled fish.

EGG SAUCE
(for hot fish)

YIELD: about 1½ cups

In a saucepan, cook together 2 tablespoons butter and 1 scallion, trimmed and chopped fine (with as much green as is crisp). Stir in 2 tablespoons flour, and over gentle heat cook the mixture for a few minutes. Stir in ½ teaspoon salt and a grinding of white pepper. Gradually add 1¼ cups milk, stirring constantly until the mixture is thickened and smooth. Add ½ teaspoon Dijon mustard and 1 teaspoon Worcestershire sauce. Just before serving the sauce, stir in 1 hard-cooked egg that has been forced through a coarse sieve.

HERB SAUCE
(for hot fish)

YIELD: about 1½ cups

In a saucepan, heat 2 tablespoons butter and in it cook 1 small clove garlic, peeled and chopped fine, and 2 scallions, trimmed and chopped fine (the white part only), until the scallions are translucent. Stir in 2 tablespoons flour, and over gentle heat cook the mixture for a few minutes. Add ¼ teaspoon each of marjoram, oregano, and thyme, which you have ground together in a mortar with a pestle. Gradually add 1½ cups milk, stirring constantly until the mixture is thickened and smooth. Over the lowest possible heat, cook the sauce, stirring often, for 10 minutes. Season it to taste with salt and a grinding of white pepper.

HOLLANDAISE SAUCE
(*for hot or chilled fish*)

YIELD: about 1 cup

Have all ingredients at room temperature.

In the container of a food processor or blender, combine 3 egg yolks, 2 tablespoons strained lemon juice, 2 tablespoons water, ¼ teaspoon salt, and 2 drops Tabasco sauce. In a small saucepan, heat to the boiling point 8 tablespoons butter. With the motor running, add the bubbling butter in a thin, steady stream. Turn off the motor when the sauce has thickened. If you wish to hold the sauce, transfer it to the top of a double boiler to be heated over simmering water.

HORSERADISH SAUCE
(*for hot or chilled fish*)

YIELD: about 1¼ cups

In a mixing bowl, blend ½ teaspoon Dijon mustard, 1 tablespoon prepared horseradish (or more to taste), 1 teaspoon lemon juice, 1 cup sour cream, 1 teaspoon sugar, and ½ teaspoon salt. Transfer the sauce to a serving dish and offer it at room temperature for hot fish or refrigerated for chilled fish.

MARINARA SAUCE
(*for hot fish*)

YIELD: about 3 cups

You may cook the fish in the sauce, if desired.

In the container of a blender, reduce to a smooth purée half the contents of 1 29-ounce can Italian tomatoes. Transfer it to a large saucepan. In the container of the blender, reduce to a smooth purée the remaining tomatoes, 1 large clove garlic, peeled and chopped coarse, 1 large onion, peeled and chopped coarse, and ½ cup dry white wine. Transfer the mixture to the saucepan. Add 2 bay leaves, ½ teaspoon oregano, 2 teaspoons sugar, 1 teaspoon salt, and a generous grinding of pepper. Bring the mixture to the boil, reduce the heat, and simmer it, uncovered, for about 20 minutes, or until it is somewhat thickened. Remove and discard the bay leaves.

If desired, you may add ½ cup pitted black olives, sliced thin.

MAYONNAISE

YIELD: about 1¼ cups

Have all ingredients at room temperature.

In the container of a food processor or blender, combine 1 egg, ¼ cup fine olive or vegetable oil, 3 tablespoons strained lemon juice, ¾ teaspoon Dijon mustard, and ½ teaspoon salt. Turn on the motor and whirl the ingredients for 5 seconds. With the motor running, add in a thin, steady stream ¾ cup fine olive or vegetable oil. As soon as the oil is added, turn off the motor.

For *Aioli* (garlic mayonnaise): add with the initial ingredients 2 or 3 large cloves garlic, peeled and chopped. Complete the recipe.

For *Curried Mayonnaise:* add with the initial ingredients 1 or 2 teaspoons curry powder to taste (I find 1½ teaspoons is right — sweet Madras curry is recommended, by the way). Complete the recipe.

For *Green Mayonnaise:* add with the initial ingredients ½ cup parsley leaves, rinsed and dried on absorbent paper, 1 cup chopped spinach leaves, rinsed and dried on absorbent paper, 3 scallions, trimmed and chopped (the white part only), and ½ teaspoon sugar. Complete the recipe.

MORNAY SAUCE
(*for hot fish*)

YIELD: about 2½ cups

You may cook the fish in the sauce, if desired.

In a saucepan, heat 4 tablespoons butter and in it, over gentle heat, cook 4 tablespoons flour for a few minutes. Gradually add 2 cups milk *or* light cream, stirring constantly until the mixture is thickened and smooth. Off heat, add and stir until melted 2 tablespoons grated Parmesan cheese and 4 tablespoons grated Swiss cheese. Stir in ½ teaspoon Dijon mustard. Season the sauce to taste with salt and a grinding of white pepper. (For a very rich sauce, beat into the completed recipe 1 egg yolk and ¼ cup heavy cream. This variation cannot be used as a cooking sauce.)

The Sauce That Enhances / 281

MOUSSELINE SAUCE
(for hot fish)

YIELD: about 2 cups

In the top of a double boiler set over hot — not boiling — water, cook 4 egg yolks with 2½ tablespoons soft butter until the butter is melted; stir constantly. Add 2½ tablespoons soft butter and repeat. When the second addition of butter is melted, add 2½ tablespoons soft butter and repeat. Remove the pan from the heat and stir rapidly for 2 minutes. Stir in singly 3 teaspoons strained lemon juice. Add ¼ teaspoon each salt and white pepper. Return the pan to simmering water and stir until the mixture is thickened. At once remove it from the heat and allow it to cool. (If by chance it curdles, beat in 1 or 2 tablespoons boiling water.) When the mixture has reached room temperature, fold in ½ cup heavy cream, whipped.

Spoon the sauce over cooked serving pieces of fish arranged in a single layer in a baking dish. Set the dish 2 inches under a preheated broiler for about 2 minutes, or until the sauce is golden.

NEWBURG SAUCE I
(for hot fish)

YIELD: about 1¼ cups

In the plush mid-nineteenth century, a habitué of Delmonico's Restaurant in New York City was a newly rich Mr. Wenburg, who enjoyed displaying his affluence and position. When his display became too much for the proprietors of the establishment, Mr. Wenburg was asked not to return. A sauce made especially for him, however, had become so popular that Delmonico's could not banish it, too. Sauce Wenburg became overnight the Newburg sauce we enjoy today.

In a saucepan, heat 1 tablespoon butter and in it, over gentle heat, cook 1 tablespoon flour for a few minutes. Gradually add 1 cup light cream, stirring constantly until the mixture is thickened and smooth. Away from the heat, whip in 2 beaten egg yolks. Stir in 2 tablespoons dry sherry. Season the sauce to taste with salt and white pepper. Over the lowest possible heat, cook the sauce, stirring, for a few minutes; do not allow it to boil.

If desired, for the customary pinkish hue of Newburg sauce, you may add in step one, 1 to 1½ teaspoons paprika (preferably sweet Hungarian) before you stir in the cream.

NEWBURG SAUCE II
(for hot fish)

YIELD: about 2¼ cups

As there are always variations in cooking, I offer this second recipe for Newburg sauce as one that may also appeal to you.

In the top of a double boiler over direct heat, melt 2 tablespoons butter and in it cook 2 tablespoons flour for a few minutes. Stir in ½ teaspoon each dry mustard, paprika (preferably sweet Hungarian), and a few grains of cayenne pepper. Blend the mixture well. Gradually add 2 cups light cream, stirring constantly until the mixture is thickened and smooth. Adjust the seasoning to taste with salt. Off heat, beat in 2 egg yolks, 1 tablespoon dry sherry, and 1 tablespoon cognac. Transfer the sauce to a serving dish, or, if you wish to reheat it later, do so over simmering, not boiling, water.

ORANGE SAUCE
(for hot fish)

YIELD: about 2 cups

In a saucepan, heat 3 tablespoons butter and in it, over gentle heat, cook 3 tablespoons flour for a few minutes. Stir in ¼ teaspoon nutmeg, ½ teaspoon salt, and ¼ teaspoon white pepper. Gradually add 1½ cups milk or light cream, scalded, stirring constantly until the mixture is thickened and smooth. Add 2 tablespoons bitter orange marmalade and the grated rind and strained juice of 1 large orange. Stir the sauce until it is well blended.

PAPRIKA SAUCE
(for hot fish)

YIELD: about 1½ cups

In a saucepan, heat 2 tablespoons butter and in it, over gentle heat, cook 1 medium onion, peeled and grated, for a few minutes. Stir in 1 tablespoon paprika (preferably sweet Hungarian) and 1 tablespoon flour. Gradually add 1 cup chicken broth, stirring constantly until the mixture is thickened and smooth. Stir in 2 tablespoons tomato paste and 2 tablespoons heavy cream. Season the sauce to taste with salt and white pepper.

PESTO GENOVESE (BASIL AND GARLIC SAUCE)
(for hot fish)

YIELD: about 1½ cups

Truly a triumph of Italian cuisine, *pesto* sauce was originally made by grinding the basil leaves and garlic in a mortar with a pestle (*pesto,* indeed, is the Italian word for "pestle"). Thanks to the food processor, making this delicious accompaniment to hot fish — or clear soups or boiled pasta — is considerably facilitated. You must, however, use fresh basil leaves; dried basil simply will not work. The sauce refrigerates and freezes well.

In the container of a food processor equipped with the steel knife, combine 2 tablespoons soft butter, 2 large cloves garlic, peeled and chopped coarse, ½ cup olive oil, 4 tablespoons grated Parmesan cheese (*or* 2 tablespoons grated Parmesan cheese and 2 tablespoons grated Romano cheese), 2 tablespoons pine nuts, 2 tablespoons water, and a pinch of salt. Whirl the ingredients until the mixture is smooth. With the motor running add, a few at a time, 1 (packed) cup fresh basil leaves, rinsed and dried on absorbent paper. Whirl each addition until the mixture is smooth. Transfer the sauce to a serving dish or storing utensil and cover it with plastic wrap so that the wrap rests on the sauce (to prevent its discoloring). Refrigerate the *pesto* until it is firm and then add a spoonful or two to the top of cooked fish.

POTATO AND GARLIC SAUCE
(for hot fish)

YIELD: about 1½ cups

A delicious confection from the south of France.

In the container of a food processor equipped with the steel blade, combine 2 egg yolks, 4 large cloves garlic, peeled and chopped coarse, and 1 medium potato, boiled for 25 minutes or until very tender, peeled and chopped coarse. Whirl the ingredients until the mixture is smooth. With the motor running, add ¾ cup olive oil in a thin steady stream. Add the strained juice of 1 medium lemon, ½ teaspoon salt, and ¼ teaspoon white pepper. Transfer the sauce to a serving dish, or if you wish to heat it later, to the top of a double boiler, in which it may be brought to serving temperature over simmering water.

For *Rouille* (also a garlic-based sauce from the south of France): add to the initial ingredients 2 slices pimiento, ½ teaspoon thyme, and a few drops of Tabasco sauce. This sauce may be used with hot fish or with fish soups.

RAVIGOTE SAUCE
(*for hot or chilled fish*)

YIELD: about 1 cup

In a mixing bowl, combine 1 hard-cooked egg, chopped fine, 1 teaspoon Dijon mustard, 1 small onion, peeled and chopped fine, 2 teaspoons fine-chopped parsley, and 2 tablespoons white wine vinegar. Add ½ teaspoon tarragon, ½ teaspoon salt, and ¼ teaspoon white pepper. Blend the ingredients and then, while adding gradually ⅓ cup olive oil, beat the mixture well. For added zest, 1 tablespoon capers, crushed, may be added to the sauce.

RÉMOULADE SAUCE
(*for chilled fish*)

YIELD: about 1½ cups

In a mixing bowl, blend 1 cup Mayonnaise, page 281, ¾ teaspoon anchovy paste, 2 teaspoons capers, 1 hard-cooked egg forced through a sieve, 1 clove garlic, peeled and put through a press, 1 teaspoon Dijon mustard, 1 tablespoon fine-chopped parsley, and 2 teaspoons fine-chopped *fresh* tarragon. Allow the sauce to stand for 1 hour at room temperature so that the flavors meld. Transfer it to a serving dish and refrigerate it.

SAUTERNE SAUCE
(*for hot fish*)

YIELD: about 1½ cups

In the top of a double boiler, combine and blend 1 cup dry sauterne, 4 egg yolks, 2 teaspoons sugar, 1 teaspoon vinegar, and a few grains of salt. Over simmering water, cook the mixture, stirring constantly, until it thickens. Do not allow it to boil. Transfer the sauce to a serving dish and offer it at once.

SHERRY SAUCE
(*for hot fish*)

YIELD: about 1¼ cups

In a saucepan, heat 4 tablespoons butter and in it, over gentle heat, cook 2 tablespoons flour for a few minutes. Gradually add ½ cup of liquid from poaching fish *or* bottled clam juice, and ½ cup milk *or* light cream, scalded, stirring constantly until the mixture is thickened and smooth. Stir in ¼ cup dry sherry. Adjust the seasoning to taste with salt and white pepper.

SWEET-AND-PUNGENT SAUCE
(*for hot fish*)

YIELD: about 3 cups

You may cook the fish in the sauce, if desired.

In a saucepan, blend 3 tablespoons sugar, 3 tablespoons cornstarch, and ½ teaspoon ginger. Add 1 cup chicken broth *or* liquid from poaching fish, 1 20-ounce can pineapple chunks and their liquid, 3 tablespoons soy sauce, and ¼ cup cider vinegar. Over high heat, bring the mixture to the boil, stirring constantly until it is thickened and smooth.

If desired, you may add to the ingredients before cooking the sauce: 1 clove garlic, peeled and through a press, and/or the fine-grated rind and strained juice of 1 medium orange.

TARTARE SAUCE
(*for hot or chilled fish*)

YIELD: about 1¼ cups

In a mixing bowl, blend 1 tablespoon capers, drained and chopped fine, 1 teaspoon Dijon mustard, 2 tablespoons fine-chopped gherkins, 2 teaspoons lemon juice, 1 cup Mayonnaise, page 281, 2 gratings onion, and 2½ tablespoons fine-chopped parsley. Allow the sauce to stand at room temperature for 1 hour so that the flavors meld. Transfer it to a serving dish and offer it at room temperature for hot fish or refrigerated for chilled fish.

VELOUTÉ SAUCE
(*for hot fish*)

YIELD: 1½ cups

In a saucepan, heat 2 tablespoons butter and in it, over gentle heat, cook 2 tablespoons flour for a few minutes. Stir in ¼ teaspoon salt and a grinding of white pepper. Gradually add 1 cup *Fumet,* page 94, stirring constantly until the mixture is thickened and smooth. Over very low heat, cook the sauce, stirring often, for 10 minutes. Stir in ¼ cup heavy cream.

For *White Wine Sauce:* to the completed recipe, add ¼ cup dry white wine and then whisk in 1 tablespoon soft butter.

VINAIGRETTE SAUCE
(*for hot or chilled fish*)

YIELD: about 1 cup

In a jar with a tight-fitting lid, combine 1 teaspoon Dijon mustard, 1 teaspoon sugar, 1 teaspoon salt, ½ teaspoon white pepper, 2 tablespoons very hot water. Close the jar and shake it vigorously. Add 4 tablespoons wine vinegar. Again close the jar and shake it vigorously. Add ¾ cup fine olive oil. Close the jar and shake it vigorously once more. Store the sauce in the refrigerator. Offer it at room temperature for hot fish or refrigerated for chilled fish.

NINE

Compatible Companions to the Frugal Fish

The following recipes have been thoroughly screened and carefully selected in order to keep their number few. Within their categories — farinaceous foods, vegetables, and salads — they are virtually interchangeable as menu-makers. They are foods to which I continually return as pleasant complements to fish dishes. They are easily prepared, and while I prefer to use fresh produce whenever available or time permits, it is reassuring to know that these recipes may be prepared with frozen foods.

CASSEROLE-BAKED BREAD

YIELD: 2 loaves
PREPARATION: about 15 minutes
RISING TIME: about 2¼ hours
BAKING: 50 minutes in a 375° oven

A homemade bread which requires no kneading, which offers several possibilities for different flavors, and which, when baked in a casserole, gives an original look to your dining table — although, as you will see, you may also bake the recipe in loaf form.

In a warm bowl, dissolve 2 packets dry yeast in 2 cups warm (not hot) water *or* milk *or* skimmed milk. Add 4 tablespoons melted butter, 2½ tablespoons sugar, and 2 teaspoons salt; stir the mixture to dissolve the sugar and salt. Add singly 4 to 4½ cups unbleached flour *or* whole wheat flour *or* a combination of the two. Beat each addition until the mixture is well blended; the dough should be soft and sticky. Cover the bowl with a damp cloth and allow the dough to rise in a warm place until it is double in bulk (about 1 hour). Butter 2 1-quart straight-sided round casseroles *or* 2 8-inch loaf pans. Stir down the risen dough and divide it equally between the casseroles or loaf pans. Cover the dough with a damp cloth and allow it to rise until it reaches the top of the utensil. Put the bread in a 375° oven and bake it for 50 minutes, or until it is crusty and golden and sounds hollow when tapped on top. Remove the loaves from the pans and allow them to cool on a rack.

You may vary the flavor by adding to the flour, before combining it with the liquid, one of the following:

> **2 teaspoons dried dill weed**
> **½ cup grated Parmesan cheese**
> **½ teaspoon each: basil, marjoram, tarragon, and thyme**
> **The grated rind of 1 large orange**
> **2 teaspoons rubbed leaf sage**

You may vary the texture by adding to the flour one of the following:

> **1 cup bran**
> **1 cup cornmeal**
> **1 cup oatmeal**
> **1 cup wheat germ**

(Decrease the amount of flour suggested in the basic recipe by 1 cup.)

MUFFINS

YIELD: 12 muffins
PREPARATION: about 10 minutes
COOKING: about 12 minutes in a 400° oven

There is something jolly and welcoming about hot, golden muffins. They are easily made, and like homemade bread, make a special occasion of the meal.

In a mixing bowl, combine and blend 2 cups flour, 1 tablespoon baking powder, 2 tablespoons sugar, ½ teaspoon salt. In a second mixing bowl, using a rotary beater, blend 1 egg, 1 cup milk, and 4 tablespoons melted butter. Into the dry ingredients, stir the liquid — only sufficiently to moisten the flour. With the dough, fill buttered muffin cups two-thirds full. Bake the muffins at 400° for 12 minutes, or until they are golden.

If desired, in place of the milk you may use 1 cup plain yogurt. For variations in flavor and texture, see those in the preceding recipe, Casserole-baked Bread.

NEW POTATOES

4 servings

With the exception of green peas, page 294, I am acquainted with no accompaniment more compatible to fish than new potatoes. This discovery is hardly mine — I wish that it were — for you will notice that the most reputable restaurants offer them as an almost standard complement to fish dishes.

Scrub well but do not peel 12 to 16 (depending upon their size) new potatoes. In boiling salted water to cover, boil them, covered, for 10 to 12 minutes, or until they are fork-tender but still firm; do not overcook them. Drain them in a colander and allow them to dry a moment. You may leave the potatoes unpeeled (I do, as I find the young skin flavorful); or you may peel them, or peel the midsection, leaving the ends unpeeled. In a heated serving dish, arrange the potatoes and dress them with soft butter and season them to taste with salt and pepper.

You may garnish buttered new potatoes with fine-chopped dill, fresh mint, or parsley.

For *Steamed New Potatoes:* place the potatoes prepared for cooking in the upper part of a steamer over briskly boiling water. Cover and cook them for 12 minutes, or until they are fork-tender but still firm.

RICE AND BULGUR

6 servings
PREPARATION: about 25 minutes

Rice and bulgur are interchangeable as accompaniments to the dishes for which they are suggested. Both grains add substance to a meal without making the diner feel too full. Because they absorb the liquid in which they are cooked, there is no last-minute draining. They are prepared identically, and their preparation is of the simplest order. In short, two estimable grains!

In a saucepan, heat 1½ tablespoons butter and in it, over gentle heat, cook 1½ cups raw natural rice *or* bulgur for a few minutes, stirring the grain with a fork to coat it well. Add 3 cups liquid (water, clam juice, chicken broth) and salt to taste. Bring the liquid to the boil, stir the grain once with a fork, reduce the heat, and simmer it, covered, for 15 minutes, or until the grain is tender and the liquid is absorbed. (As the cooking liquid, you may also use water flavored with 3 or 4 bouillon cubes.)

Rice and bulgur may also be cooked in a casserole. In a flameproof casserole, mix the butter and grain as indicated above (if your casserole is not flameproof, prepare the rice for cooking as directed and transfer it to a casserole). Bring the cooking liquid to the boil and add it, with salt to taste, to the contents of the casserole. Bake the casserole, covered, at 350° for 20 minutes, or until the grain is tender and the liquid is absorbed.

You may vary the flavor of rice and bulgur by adding herbs or spices to the grain when coating it with butter. Specifically called for are:

Curried Rice: use 1 to 1½ teaspoons curry powder (preferably Madras curry) and

Saffron Rice: use ¼ to ½ teaspoon crumbled saffron.

And there are other possibilities open to you; for example, you may use one of the following:

> *1 teaspoon ground allspice*
> *1 or 2 bay leaves (remove them after*
> *the cooking)*
> *¼ cup currants*
> *1 teaspoon dried dill weed*
> *2 or 3 tablespoons fine-chopped onion*
> *Grated rind 1 medium orange*
> *½ teaspoon crumbled rosemary*
> *½ teaspoon crumbled sage*
> *½ teaspoon thyme*

The prepared rice or bulgur may be garnished with:

> *Toasted slivered almonds*
> *Dots of soft butter*
> *Sprinkling of fresh dill weed*
> *Small mushrooms, sliced and sautéed*
> *Fine-chopped parsley*
> *Chopped pimientos*
> *Pine nuts*
> *Raisins, plumped in hot water for 5*
> *minutes and drained*
> *Fine-chopped scallions, with as much*
> *green as is crisp*

GREEN BEANS

4 servings

Available in the market virtually year-round and one of the most successfully frozen vegetables, green beans are a colorful and flavorful complement to fish dishes.

From 1 pound fresh green beans, remove the stem ends. Rinse and drain the beans. If they are very young, leave them whole; if not, halve them *or* cut them in 1-inch pieces *or,* with a bean cutter, cut them lengthwise. Cook them in boiling salted water to cover for 10 to 12 minutes, or until they are tender-crisp; do not overcook them. Drain them at once, dress them with soft butter, and season them to taste with salt and pepper.
You may garnish buttered green beans with:

> *Toasted slivered almonds*
> *Small mushrooms, sliced and sautéed*
> *Fine-chopped parsley*
> *A sprinkling of grated Parmesan cheese*
> *Thin-sliced scallions* or *fine-chopped red onion*
> *Thin-sliced water chestnuts*

You may use, in place of the butter, heavy cream (very good with a sprinkling of nutmeg).
In the recipe for Mixed Green Salad, page 295, you will find other garnishes and herbs that go well with green beans.
Frozen green beans are available whole, cut, and "French style" (cut lengthwise). Two 10-ounce packages yield 4 generous servings. To cook them, follow the directions on the package; do not overcook.

BROCCOLI

4 servings

Broccoli *en branche* is decorative on a dinner plate; served whole or chopped, it provides a pleasant flavor contrast to fish.

In cold salted water, soak 1½ pounds fresh broccoli for 30 minutes; drain it. Cut off and discard the tough base of the stalk and coarse outer leaves. Separate the broccoli so that two or three pieces will yield a serving. Peel the stalks and slit larger ones lengthwise for an inch or two to facilitate their cooking evenly. In about 1 inch of boiling water, cook the broccoli, tightly covered, for 15 minutes, or until the stalks are tender-crisp; do not overcook it. Transfer it to a heated serving dish, dress it with melted butter, and season it to taste with salt and pepper.

The garnishes suggested in the preceding recipe for green beans also go well with broccoli; in addition, buttered bread crumbs are a frequent garnish for broccoli.

Several sauces complement broccoli; I recommend *Beurre Maître d'Hôtel*, Almond Butter, Cheese Sauce, Curry Sauce, Egg Sauce, Hollandaise Sauce, any of the Mayonnaise Sauces, Mornay Sauce, or Vinaigrette Sauce (all will be found in the chapter on sauces).

Fresh broccoli may also be served chopped or puréed: after cooking the broccoli, chop it to your desired consistency or purée it in the container of a food processor; add butter, salt and pepper, and perhaps a little heavy cream; over gentle heat bring the vegetable to serving temperature.

Broccoli spears and chopped broccoli are available frozen; 2 10-ounce packages yield 4 servings. Cook the vegetable according to the directions on the package; do not overcook it. Dress and garnish it as you would fresh broccoli.

BRUSSELS SPROUTS

4 servings

These "little cabbages," fresh looking and so neatly self-contained, are appetizing to look at; their piquant flavor adds interest to a main dish.

Cut off the stems and discard the wilted leaves from 1¼ pounds fresh Brussels sprouts. In cold salted water to cover soak them for 15 minutes; drain them. In boiling salted water to cover, cook them, covered, for 10 minutes, or until they are just tender; do not overcook. Drain them at once, dress them with soft butter, and season to taste with salt and pepper.

The garnishes suggested for green beans, page 292, also go well with Brussels sprouts; in addition, buttered bread crumbs are a frequent garnish for them.

The sauces suggested for the preceding recipe for broccoli may also be used with Brussels sprouts.

Frozen Brussels sprouts allow us to enjoy this vegetable year-round; 2 10-ounce packages yield 4 generous servings (one package is a bit skimpy). To cook them, follow the directions on the package; do not overcook.

GREEN PEAS

Green peas, like new potatoes, seem to have an affinity for fish and fish dishes; their delicate sweet flavor does not compete with the taste of the fish and their bright color enlivens the appearance of the plate.

In ½ inch boiling water, cook 2 pounds fresh-shelled peas, covered, for 10 to 12 minutes, or until they are just tender; do not overcook them. Drain them at once and transfer them to a heated serving dish. Dress them with soft butter and season them to taste with salt and pepper.

The garnishes suggested for green beans, page 292, also go well with green peas.

You may use, in place of the butter, heavy cream and a sprinkling of nutmeg.

Three or four fresh mint leaves, chopped fine, lightly tossed with buttered green peas, are especially tasty.

For *Green Peas à la Française:* rinse the leaves of 1 medium head Boston lettuce; stack and shred them. In a saucepan, combine and toss together the lettuce, 1 small onion, peeled and chopped fine, 2 pounds fresh-shelled young green peas, 3 tablespoons butter, 1 teaspoon sugar, ¼ cup water, and a grinding of white pepper. Bring the ingredients to the boil, reduce the heat, and simmer them, covered, for 8 minutes, or until the peas are tender.

Two kinds of frozen peas are available: regular peas and small or tiny peas (sometimes labeled "petits pois"). I prepare the regular peas according to the directions on the package, taking care not to overcook them. The small or tiny peas are so tender that, if you thaw them fully to room temperature, you need only heat them with soft butter and salt and pepper; they really require no cooking.

CHOPPED SPINACH

Lending itself to several variations, chopped spinach is nutritionally a worthy complement to fish; but perhaps even more important is the fact that it tastes good with fish.

Remove the woody stems from 2 10-ounce packages fresh spinach. Rinse the leaves well. In a large soup kettle, bring to the boil several quarts of lightly salted water. Into it, plunge the spinach; allow it to wilt for 20 seconds. In a colander, drain it immediately, pressing the vegetable against the sides of the utensil to rid it of any excess water. Chop it fine. Transfer it to a saucepan and stir in soft butter and salt and pepper to taste. If desired, add a sprinkling of nutmeg.

One or two tablespoons prepared horseradish added with the butter is very tasty.

The garnishes suggested for green beans, page 292, also go well with chopped spinach.

If desired, you may omit the butter and combine the undressed chopped spinach with sufficient Cheese, Curry, or Mornay Sauce, pages 277, 278, and 281, to bind the vegetable.

For *Creamed Spinach:* in a saucepan, melt 3 tablespoons butter and to it add the prepared chopped spinach; over medium heat, cook the vegetable, stirring, for 3 minutes. Sprinkle the spinach with 1 tablespoon flour, stirring. Add ½ cup cream (heavy or light, depending upon your taste); cook the mixture, stirring constantly, until the cream thickens. Season the creamed spinach to taste with salt, pepper, and nutmeg; garnish it, if desired, with toasted slivered almonds.

A simpler *Cream-Style Spinach* may be made by adding sufficient sour cream to the prepared chopped spinach to bind the vegetable; season it to taste with salt, pepper, and nutmeg.

Creamed spinach may be transferred to a baking dish, sprinkled with ½ cup grated Parmesan cheese, and heated in a 350° oven for 12 minutes, or until the cheese crusts.

Frozen chopped spinach is a notable time-saver; 2 10-ounce packages yield 4 servings. If desired, you may cook it as directed on the package; I do not, allowing it instead to come fully to room temperature and then pressing it as dry as possible in a colander.

MIXED GREEN SALAD

Although salads should only be dressed just before they are to be served, the greens may be prepared ahead and kept chilled in plastic bags. Greens may be stored together, but any flavor-accent accompaniment (cucumber, scallions) should be kept separate in order that each component retains its own taste.

Basic salad greens, which may be used in almost any combination, are:

> **Lettuce (*every kind*)**
> **Endive**
> **Escarole**
> **Spinach**
> **Watercress**

Arugola (roquette) and celery cabbage are pleasant flavor-accent greens.

A sprinkling of snipped fresh herbs (or dried herbs, but use these more sparingly) will enhance mixed green salad. I suggest:

Basil
Chervil
Chives
Dill weed
Marjoram
Oregano
Parsley
Summer savory
Tarragon

For color, you may add mimosa egg (hard-cooked egg forced through a sieve); and for texture, sprinkle the dressed salad with croutons.

To prepare: Rinse and dry (either in a salad drier or on absorbent paper) your chosen combination of greens. Tear them into pieces of uniform size (I cut my salad with kitchen shears, admittedly heretical). Refrigerate them as suggested above. Toss them with Vinaigrette Sauce, page 287, at serving time.

Mixed Green Salad becomes *the* vegetable of the meal when embellished with other ingredients:

Artichoke hearts
Bamboo shoots
*Broccoli stalk, raw, peeled, and cut in
julienne strips*
Carrot, grated
Celery, diced
Cherry tomatoes, halved or whole
Cucumber, sliced
Mushrooms, sliced
Hearts of palm
*Green or red sweet pepper, seeded and
cut in julienne strips*
Radishes, sliced
Red onion, peeled and chopped or *cut
in rings*
Scallions, trimmed and chopped
Tomatoes, preferably peeled, sliced or
cut in wedges
Water chestnuts, sliced

GREEN BEAN SALAD

6 servings
PREPARATION: about 30 minutes

Trim, halve, and rinse in cold water 1½ pounds fresh green beans; drain them in a colander. To boiling salted water to cover, add the beans and cook them, uncovered, for 12 minutes, or until they are tender-crisp (young beans may require less time, older ones, more). Refresh them in cold water; drain and dry them on absorbent paper. Refrigerate them, covered, until you are ready to serve them.

When ready to offer the salad, turn the beans into a large bowl and toss them with Vinaigrette Sauce, page 287. Garnish the salad with fine-chopped red onion or fine-chopped parsley.

For other ways to embellish Green Bean Salad, see the preceding recipe for Mixed Green Salad. One admonition, however: if the beans are young and cooked *al dente,* you will want no other garnish than those suggested here.

One final note: very young beans, while requiring stemming, need not be cut in half (indeed, *should* not!).

BULGUR SALAD

6 servings
PREPARATION: about 20 minutes
STANDING TIME: about 1 hour
CHILLING TIME: 3 hours

In a mixing bowl, combine 3 cups coarse bulgur with 6 cups boiling salted water. Allow the bulgur to stand until the water is at room temperature. In a sieve, drain the bulgur, pressing it with the back of a spoon to rid it of excess moisture. Return it to the mixing bowl. While the bulgur is soaking, trim and chop in ½-inch segments 12 scallions, with as much green as is crisp; rinse and drain 1 large bunch parsley, remove the leaves and chop them fine; peel, seed, and chop 3 ripe tomatoes; grate the rind and strain the juice of 1 medium lemon; prepare ½ cup chopped fresh mint leaves (optional, but a delectable addition), and measure ½ cup finest olive oil *or* vegetable oil. To the readied bulgur, add these ingredients, tossing the mixture with two forks to blend it well. Transfer the salad to a serving dish and chill it, covered, for 3 hours. (If fresh mint is unavailable, use 2 teaspoons dried mint ground in a mortar with a pestle — not the same, but an acceptable substitute.)

SPINACH AND MUSHROOM SALAD

6 servings
PREPARATION: about 20 minutes

Remove the woody stems from 2 10-ounce packages fresh spinach; rinse the leaves in cold water and dry them in a salad spinner or on absorbent paper. Refrigerate them. In a container with tight-fitting lid, combine ½ pound thin-sliced mushrooms and the strained juice of 1 medium lemon. Cover the container and rotate the mushrooms to cover them with the lemon juice; this step will prevent their discoloring and lend them added flavor. Drain off any excess lemon juice. Refrigerate the mushrooms.

When ready to serve the salad, combine the spinach and mushrooms in a large bowl and toss them with Vinaigrette Sauce, page 287. Croutons sautéed in garlic-flavored olive oil are a pleasant addition — and a good salad stretcher.

MIXED VEGETABLE SALAD

6 servings
PREPARATION: about 20 minutes

Mixed vegetable salad provides an attractive and appetizing filling for cold mousse prepared in a ring mold; it may also be served as a chilled side dish. There are various brands of canned mixed vegetables available, and a few are quite acceptable; most of them, however, suffer the complaint of the run of canned vegetables — no distinctive texture and no distinctive taste. For this reason, I use frozen mixed vegetables, which I subject to the following (idiotically) simple treatment.

Cook, according to the directions on the package, 2 or 3 10-ounce packages frozen mixed vegetables; it is important *not* to overcook them. Refresh them in cold water and drain them in a colander. In a mixing bowl, toss them with Mayonnaise, page 281, and season the mixture to taste with salt and white pepper. Use only sufficient mayonnaise to bind the vegetables. (The salad may be made with any of the mayonnaise-based sauces, but if you use *aioli* — garlic mayonnaise — I recommend that, when making the sauce, you use no more than 1 large or 2 small cloves of garlic.)

MINIATURE PUFFS FOR HORS D'OEUVRE

36 puffs
PREPARATION: about 15 minutes
COOKING: 35 minutes in a 400° oven

The recipe doubles for a large cocktail party; the unstuffed puffs may be refrigerated or frozen.

½ cup water
4 tablespoons butter
¼ teaspoon salt
½ cup flour

In a saucepan, combine the water and butter. Over high heat, bring the water to the boil. When the butter is melted, stir in the salt and then, all at one time, the flour. Reduce the heat and cook the mixture, stirring constantly, until it draws away from the sides of the pan and forms a ball.

2 eggs

Beat in the eggs singly. Drop the dough by the teaspoonful onto a lightly buttered baking sheet. Bake the puffs at 400° for 35 minutes, or until they are well raised and golden. Allow them to cool on a wire rack.

To fill the puffs, cut them in horizontal halves, add to the bottom half a teaspoonful or so of the filling of your choice, and replace the top half. Serve the puffs at room temperature, or if desired, heated briefly in a 350° oven.

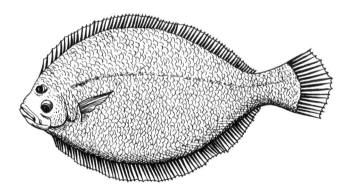

Index

The index is arranged not only in the customary alphabetical order, but also to facilitate menu-making for the cook, according to the headings in the table of contents.

Index / 303

304 / Index

Index / 305

Index / 307